THE CHARTIST LAND COMPANY

THE
CHARTIST LAND
COMPANY

Alice Mary Hadfield

DAVID & CHARLES: NEWTON ABBOT

Set in eleven point Bembo two points leaded
and printed in Great Britain
by Latimer Trend & Company Limited Plymouth
for David & Charles (Publishers) Limited
South Devon House   Newton Abbot   Devon

CONTENTS

PART ONE
THE HISTORY OF THE COMPANY

PART TWO
THE ESTATES—1846 ONWARDS

APPENDICES

ILLUSTRATIONS

PLATES

PART ONE

THE HISTORY OF THE COMPANY

CHAPTER 1

ORIGINS

AS you drive along the country roads in certain parts of Gloucestershire, Worcestershire or Oxfordshire, you will pass small houses which do not look like council houses or a housing estate, and yet are all of a similar and distinct pattern. Nearly all have large holdings of land. They are not architecturally interesting, but arouse your curiosity. What are they? Who built them here in this out-of-the-way district? Who lives in them now? There is another estate, that you will not notice even if you drive past it down Long Lane from Chorley Wood in Hertfordshire, so enclosed is it in its hedges and hidden under its trees. These are the five estates of the Land Company, a venture of a hundred and twenty-five years ago, which was the product of the Chartist movement and of Feargus O'Connor. In turn, its title was the Chartist Land Company, the Chartist Co-operative Land Company, and the National Land Company. It was founded in 1845 and was closed by Act of Parliament in 1851. Its estates were administered by Chancery and slowly dispersed in ownership over another seventy years. The buildings were of such good structure that cared-for ones are in occupation, sound and strong, today.

There are very few Chartist remains. The movement passed into the general reforming activity of the nineteenth century in England, and all its objects (except annual Parliaments) were achieved without specific reference to the People's Charter of 1838: vote by secret ballot, correction of the sizes of constituencies, no property qualification for members of Parliament, payment of members of Parliament, and, eventually, universal adult male suffrage. Its leaders mostly led busy but obscure lives. Chartist colours and Chartist hymns are forgotten, and I know of no pub called The Chartist. But the estates remain, some 200 attractive little houses with good acres belonging to them, which stand as a memorial to the Chartist movement.

They were not approved at the time by the movement's leaders, but were regarded as a distraction of energy and attention from the main political drive at a crucial stage. The early upsurge of reforming energy, inexperienced, ardent, incoherent, was a demonstration of enormous, unordered strength, and as such it drew to itself many restless spirits trying to ride the storm. Of these, the most daemonic was Feargus O'Connor.

His biographers, Donald Read and Eric Glasgow, have dug up the fossil of his erratic, uncomfortable life.[1] He was born about 1796 in County Cork, of a family that claimed to be a royal line in Ireland. His uncle Arthur was exiled to France for revolutionary plotting with the French during the French wars, and was always Feargus's model. His father, Roger, brought up a big family on very little means but with values that means cannot buy, extreme radical ideas and tribal aristo-cratic aims. The family was Protestant.

Feargus had a sketchy education at small Irish schools. He was a great lad for sport and escapades, and was allowed to remain a big fish in small pools for too long. He had love affairs, and wanted to marry his schoolmaster's daughter, but his father wrote to him that the marriage would exclude him from the royal rank of the O'Connors, and that a liaison would be dishonourable. We do not know if the decision was a struggle, but Feargus gave up the girl and returned to the ramshackle hearth of the O'Connors. His father's principles would not allow him to take employment, and he knocked about the little townships of Cork and Meath—a tall, strong, ginger-haired fellow, marked by a bulging forehead that made his eyes look sunken and emphasised his turned-up nose. He was an expert with horses, cards, a crowd of fellows and a scene. By 1817 his father Roger was distinctly non-sane, and was on trial for the attempted hold-up of a mail coach.

In 1820 Feargus's uncle Robert died, and left Feargus money and a mansion called Fort Robert, on long lease. He now had some hope of a life, and was probably happier than at any other time. He liked seeing to his farms, got to know the labourers and their outlook. He studied at King's Inn, Dublin, and was called to the Irish bar in 1830. Daniel O'Connell was building up his Irish party, aiming at achieving a separate

Home Rule parliament in Dublin and a reform of land tenure throughout the island. Feargus joined the local Whigs and became a forceful,
popular speaker. In the first election after the passing of the great Reform Act of 1832 he stood as candidate for County Cork, and with
O'Connell's backing he was elected, a Protestant landlord representing
Roman Catholic peasantry. His local paper called him 'the recognised
champion of popular rights, and the object of popular favour'.[2]

He was now thirty-six, unmarried, not too old for a career but with
not a year to lose. But he would work with no one. He clashed with
O'Connell in public meetings and in committees, challenged him for
leadership of the Irish Parliamentary party, and was twice rejected by
it. He soon became a lone wolf in politics, and no use as a House of
Commons man. Close work and reasoned speaking did not suit him,
and his vehement orations and highly-coloured fancies did not suit the
Commons, nor his inconsistency and swiftness to slide out of a statement or position.

He found different company outside Parliament. Here were the
London working classes, the bulk of uneducated but thinking and self-
taught radicals, eager for help and for direction. William Lovett, their
leader, welcomed Feargus at first, invited him to speak at meetings, and
let him in on audiences more easily impressed and less informed than
the House of Commons. His energy and liveliness appealed to them,
and his gift for comic anecdote and personal barb. There was always a
good evening if Feargus was speaking. But the same results followed
from the same causes, and Feargus would not work with radical
leaders any more than with Irish.

At the end of 1834 Parliament was dissolved. Now Feargus found
that, having played his own hand alone, he was left to it. In the general
election he was voted in, but another candidate for Co Cork petitioned
against him on the ground of his property qualification being unsound,
and the enquiry disqualified him. Fort Robert was not his own freehold property. He was not prepared to stay in Ireland, and was soon
busy on the edge of the political world in England, living in Hammersmith, London. A by-election in Oldham drew him for the first time
up to the north, to the crowds, the industrial poor, and the hungry. He
spoke to big audiences and had a big success.

From then on, for eleven years he bedevilled the Chartist movement. Lovett and the literate and serious artisan radicals worked with him while they could, but became more and more suspicious of him. He spoke always in inflammatory style and always against easy targets unemployment, rents, the Poor Law, the Church, the franchise. He used a powerful line of sarcasm and abuse and could always win laughs. His attack on the Whigs annoyed O'Connell, who preferred the Whigs in any form for Ireland to the Tories. O'Connell tried to persuade him to lay off the Whigs, but Feargus only ballooned higher on the heat of his fancy. In the summer of 1836 O'Connell openly denounced him as a Tory radical, and discarded him from the Irish party. At the same time Lovett and his colleagues ceased to tolerate Feargus's alliance. These were laboriously self-educated and thinking men, heirs to an English intellectual tradition that went back to the religious and social radicalism of the eighteenth and seventeenth centuries. Above everything, they desired the working classes to emerge from the fascination of leadership, and they saw that O'Connor could easily distract them from doing so.

Newspapers became the rage when the Stamp Act was repealed in 1836 and they could be sold cheaply. Next year, Feargus and a Leeds printer, Joshua Hobson, raised a subscription from the big Yorkshire towns and founded a newspaper. Feargus's uncle, Arthur, had worked for a paper called the *Northern Star*, so Feargus gave his paper the same name. Subscribers got 10 per cent of the profits but no share in control, and Feargus was solely responsible. It proved to be easily his most successful venture. By February 1838 he was selling 10,000 copies a week, far ahead of any provincial paper. In that May the London Working Men's Association, under Lovett, published the People's Charter, and by September the *Northern Star* had become the Chartist organ, whatever the steadier leaders wanted.

Over the next four years Feargus developed the style of speaking which made his enemies call him a malignant demagogue. The struggle for the Charter was on all over England. Its leaders were trying to build up a public opinion, to free the movement from the taint of violence with which France, Austria, Italy, had infected all efforts of the people, and to present the working class as fit for responsibility and voting power. They wanted to ally with other reform movements, get Chartists elected to Parliament, and show the good sense of English working people. This found support in Birmingham and London, but in the northern cities Chartism was slipping from the control of the moderate men who started it. Pressure from masses of hungry people, willing to believe in any marvellous change, swayed the movement and affected its character. Meetings became too big to be housed indoors, and moved out to the moors behind the narrow streets, where darkness, torchlight and the night sky strengthened all wild feelings. Feargus became a leading speaker. His emotional projection of an image of the working man inflated and supported his audiences, while to Feargus himself those crowded halls, and twilit moors, dense with rough faces and dark, awkward bodies, flaring torchlights, growling of thousands of voices breaking into yells at the sight of him, shock of sensation at every crude climax in the speech, wave on wave of cheering at the end, became a stimulus that he had to have.

In his speaking he made no rational approach. Extremes of abuse, threats, fantasies, expectation and praise thundered from him in his striking voice. Reasonable men had no surface chance against him. Soon they hated him for intoxicating the people instead of raising them, for using them as an experience of power instead of bringing them to develop and control it in themselves.

The moderates lost. The petition for the Charter was presented to the House of Commons in 1839 and was rejected by 235 votes to 46. Strikes and agitation followed, and the *Northern Star* roared abuse. Feargus was prosecuted for publishing seditious libels and, before his trial, went over to Ireland. While he was there the only attempt at armed rebellion was made, in the Newport rising under Frost, Williams and others. Feargus always said that he knew nothing about it. The leaders were sentenced to transportation. Meantime Feargus failed to rally the Irish; they would cheer him but would not put themselves out for him. Daniel O'Connell had totally displaced him even in County Cork.

At his trial, he was given a light sentence of eighteen months' imprisonment in York Castle. He made good use of his time. His weekly letter in the *Northern Star* was an Epistle to the Chartist Churches. When he came out in August 1841 he was the acknowledged leader of left-wing Chartism, though this cut very little ice with ordinary people. His release was celebrated by a procession in which Feargus, wearing a working man's fustian clothes, rode in a coach shaped as a sea shell, green and pink for Chartist colours. The *Northern Star* published a poem about him called 'The Lion of Freedom', with the refrain,

We'll rally around him again and again.[3]

Set to music, it spread rapidly as a Chartist song, and Feargus regularly used the image of a lion for himself.

The winter of 1841–2 was one of desperate unemployment, poverty and hunger. Once again a petition for the Charter was presented to Parliament, in May 1842. It was rejected, largely because opinion associated it with the 'cowardly malignant demagogue' Feargus O'Connor. Feargus saw that the movement must gain much more political power before it could succeed. A big proportion of its members had no vote and therefore were of little danger or promise. In the *Northern Star* of 7 May 1842 Feargus wrote of two ways to get this political power; either to ally with the middle classes who had it, or to think of a plan for settlement of large numbers on the land, each man holding freehold property of the minimum annual value of 40s required to qualify for a county vote.

The idea of allying with the middle classes failed to prove practicable, and Feargus's mind turned away from politics to his other notion, settlement on the land. Donald Read and Eric Glasgow outline this new development in Chapter XI of their biography. Feargus began in February 1843, with articles in the *Northern Star* attacking machinery. He moved on to the idea of gaining independence from employer and landlord. A series of letters appeared in the *Northern Star* from 15 April to 27 May 1843, addressed *To the Producers of Wealth, and all those who live by Industry on the Land*. One said

> You are, in a word, a poor, beggarly, lousy set of devils. . . . Without house or home, or bread, or clothes, or fuel; begging the means of subsistence, and thankful to him who will coin your sweat into gold!

Life on the land, in your own cottage and smallholding, was presented as the life of freedom, where a man need ask no employer for wages and no landlord for a roof. It would be a way out of the ills of the new industrial society. Feargus, now forty-seven, without domestic life, church life or real friends, with every sphere of work mined by enemies and his own past behaviour, his nerve weakened by excesses of excitement and emotion, probably looked back to his early life and dreamed of settling hundreds of his devoted followers in that Irish, secure, sylvan existence—but without the burden of shiftlessness and poverty. Ownership of land could bring a vote and mark a step towards universal suffrage.

Letters to the Producers of Wealth, which appeared in the *Northern Star* in April and May 1843, moved on to suggest plans. 20,000 acres could support 5,000 heads of families, with 4 acres per family, in roughly forty estates, each with its community centre, school, library and hospital. Success would make the people demand action by the government to plant more estates, though no socialism or partnership with the state was meant. Ownership and control were always to be individual. The government would not do this until universal suffrage compelled them to obey the will of the people. The achievement of such a land plan and of the Charter therefore went together. They were 'Siamese twins'.

Sir Robert Peel's government paid no attention. As its owner drew more and more out of the main stream of events into the Land Company channel, the circulation of the *Northern Star* fell steadily. The Chartist conference in Birmingham in September 1843 declined to be sidetracked by land schemes from the pursuit of the six points of the Charter, though they agreed in principle with the glowing landscape painted by O'Connor. Feargus pressed on. He wrote a book called *A Practical Work on the Management of Small Farms*, which went into details on crops and management, and drew upon recollections of his estate farms in Ireland. He continued his travelling and speaking, and at every meeting developed his views on the land. Reception was always good. Where the audience was weak on the political ideas of the Charter, it was strong on the benefit of not sweating in the factory but standing at the door of your cottage and growing your own dinner.

Interest in Chartism was low, so low indeed that falling circulation of the *Northern Star* caused O'Connor to move the production of the paper in November 1844 from Leeds to London, at 340 Strand, with the printing machines at 16 Great Windmill Street. He had quarrelled with Hobson, and M'Gowan was now printer. Chartist conference programmes were not clear, so that Feargus was better able to push his convictions. Leading Chartists said the conference in London in April

B

1845 was notably thin. Feargus was there, hot with zeal, and persuaded the meeting to agree to the founding of a Chartist Co-operative Land Society. There was no clear directive as to the organisation, and Feargus came out of the meeting in full effective control.

Briefly, the plan was this. A capital sum of £5,000 should be raised from 2,000 shares costing £2 10s (£2·50) each. Out of this, 120 acres of good arable land should be bought at the current price of £18 15s (£18·75) an acre. This would provide 60 cultivators with 2 acres each, and £2,250 would be left to build cottages and buy stock. These allotments would be let by the company to the members in perpetuity for £5 per year, bringing in £300 per year as estate rent. This sum, sold at 20 years' purchase, would raise £6,000, which would buy land for 72 cultivators. Their rent would bring in enough to buy land for 86, and so on. All the surplus industrial population could be removed from the slums and planted on the land by a process which only needed the energy and initiative of one man to start it, and he was there. In fact he was ready to receive subscriptions for shares at the office of the *Northern Star*. A set of rules was published containing the above outline of the plan.

A howl arose from all the leading Chartists—and a hum, one might say, from every business man, banker, and farmer. Many of them seized their pens and wrote to the newspapers. The best were angered by the flight from serious political reform. O'Connor had formerly said that social happiness was to proceed from political equality, a proposition of reason and effort, whereas now he wrote that political equality could only spring from social happiness, a recipe of emotion and magic. The economics of the plan were easily torn to pieces, but Feargus was totally unmoved by criticism. His staff were Chartist followers: Philip M'Grath, a journeyman dyer and briefly a master dyer, and a member of the executive of the National Chartist Association for three years;[4] Thomas Wheeler, a Chartist delegate, and Christopher Doyle, a power-loom weaver of waterproofs from Manchester.[5] Thomas Allsop, Feargus' London broker, advised on cash.

He spent the rest of 1845 in continuous travel and activity to study the management of land in smallholdings. He visited France and Belgium, and met socialist and communist leaders, among them Friedrich Engels and Karl Marx. These two had declared absolutely against private holding of land, in large or small units, as they considered it the main stronghold of opposition to change in society. O'Connor had no thought of anything but private ownership of land. Indeed his conviction of the restoration of personality which would be effected by owning a cottage and a piece of land depended on a private, personal relationship between man and property. 'My plan has no more to do with Socialism than it has with the comet,' he wrote in the *Northern Star*.

In December 1845 the first Chartist conference devoted only to the Land Plan was held at Manchester. Here the split between O'Connor and the Chartist leaders broke wide open. He wanted them to come in with him in full support of the Land Plan, but they had decided that it was impracticable, and a red herring to distract Chartists to follow the cult of O'Connor. He quarrelled with them all, one by one and all together, without any second thoughts. As he fell out with each he wrote fiery sentences denouncing him in the *Northern Star*. By the end of the conference he was entirely and happily on his own, with his newspaper and his following among the masses. He set up his Land Plan office at 83 Dean Street, Soho.

The propounding of the plan was one thing, the organisation of the company was another. To hold public money the directors had to have legal standing, and the conduct of the company had to be in accordance with law. Feargus knew a handy lawyer in Manchester, William Prowting Roberts, of 59 Princess Street. Roberts had an office also in London, and his chief clerk, George Chinnery, could act as agent. In January 1846 Roberts sent Chinnery to chew over legal rules and safeguards, or obstacles.

As Feargus considered reality over his brandy and cigar by the fire in his rooms, there were four kinds of law to choose from as a base. One concerned the various Friendly Societies, which represented a form of savings; one was the new Joint Stock Companies Act of 1844, which laid down basic business conduct and account-keeping; one was a royal charter, available for some kinds of non-profit-making or benevolent activity; and one was the private Act of Parliament, most commonly used for such single purposes as the building of canals or railways.

To Feargus, what were the snags? Friendly Societies did not buy property; they provided regular benefits, and invited strict financial scrutiny. The cost of registering under the Joint Stock Companies Act was fixed by the duty of 1s (5p) per £1,000 of capital, or, for the Land Company, per 400 holders of £2 10s (£2·50) shares. Stamp duty would amount to £3 15s (£3·75) for every 100 names.[6] If that were paid, nobody's consent need be asked to the registering of the company, or could be withheld. The cost of getting a royal charter was anyone's guess, but a number of scrutinies and permissions would be necessary. The cost of a private Act of Parliament, if uncontested, was about £2,500, but many landowner MPs would refuse to contemplate the immigration of colonies of Chartists, on a scale proposed to aim at being nation-wide, among their home acres. This was the crucial moment for the Land Company. An elementary grasp of reality, of accepting the common need to work with the law, might have saved it. Feargus had always refused to serve, or even to be equal, and now he had his will. He was absolute boss. The Land Company depended solely on him—and he would have no one above him, not even the law.

Subscriptions began to come in. Each week the amounts were published in the *Northern Star*, with names of the Chartist branches from which the money came, and often names of the persons themselves. In January 1846 nearly £200 a week was recorded. Meetings for enrolling members of the 'Chartist Co-operative Land Company' were advertised each week on regular days at different places. Chartist branches all over the country collected 3d and 6d a head towards shares.

The clerk Chinnery found himself in charge of the legal moves from his London office in Robert Street, Adelphi. In December 1845 or January 1846, he and a lawyer named Macnamara drew up a set of rules for the company aimed at getting it registered under the Friendly Societies Acts, probably chosen as the cheapest. Tid Pratt, the registrar of Friendly Societies and known as a wise counsellor to small groups, examined them and said no, the rules and objects of the society were not suited to Friendly Societies. Feargus accepted that if he was to do it legally he might never do it at all. He believed that the start without sanction of the law was a gamble that he could bring off. The age was one of growth and experiment. Personal fortunes were being built up everywhere from risky beginnings in railways and mines. To him, the gamble on starting the Land Company was not an unreasonable one.

But it was essential not to let people know the gamble was intentional. He continued a series of negotiations and press-announcements about registration which must seem now to be deceptions, as at no time during them did he alter those basic foundations of the company in a lottery and in his own private ownership of the property, which prevented the registration he claimed to be seeking.

Every week the paper carried news of small-farm management, discussion of crops and manure, whether a man could keep a family on the produce of 4 acres. Feargus's book on small farms was reviewed and recommended because 'the reader will find that Mr. O'Connor has avoided all those hard names, and suited the language to the toiling labourer, whose college is generally the workshop, or at best, the Sunday School'. On 11 January 1846 the first of many leaders appeared addressed to 'the Fustian Jackets, Blistered Hands and Unshorn Chins'. This was the touch that made the people trust him. Although he used them as a weapon for his own activities, and would drop them in a week if something better offered, he did see the life of the people as something in itself and not only something to be changed.

His organisation looked simple. W. P. Roberts was treasurer, Thomas Wheeler secretary (sometimes called financial secretary); directors were himself, Philip M'Grath, Christopher Doyle and Thomas Clark. Two East London tailors were auditors, James Knight and William Cuffey. (Names are never enlarged on in O'Connor's records. They simply appear in the *Northern Star* as his oldest friend or the people's most trusted servant, of a week's standing.) There was no fuss about red tape, directors' meetings or minutes. All the money came in as small cheques, postal orders and stamps. M'Grath listed it for the weekly printing, and passed it to M'Gowan the printer, who saw that the money and the list tallied and then deposited the money in O'Connor's account at the London Joint Stock Bank. He received a bank voucher for it and made a memo. As numbers rose, the directors decided to work the company in sections of 6,000, using the capital subscribed by each section exclusively for the benefit of that section.

The circulation of the *Northern Star* began to rise again. In January, February and March of 1846, every week it recorded items such as

Warwick, per J. A. Donaldson, £2 14s 6d; Georgie Mills, per R. Burkett, £5 2s 6d; Hamilton per W. Weir, £1 16s 2d. Or, Note. The sum acknowledged from Boulogne on the 3rd Jan. should have been £4 17s not £3 17s.

Boulogne had written in during the week. Letters were answered:

To correspondent from Montgomeryshire. Any person who joins the Chartist Cooperative Land Society previous to the close of the 1st section, will of course be one of that section whether he has paid up his share or not. I thank those persons who have sent me notices of estates to be sold, and I wish them from all districts to continue sending such information, as we shall very speedily be in a situation to make a large purchase.

Work fell on the directors in all this correspondence, and, as payment, a levy was started, called a voluntary contribution, of 3d per share held throughout the company once a year.

Feargus pressed two main advantages of the Land Plan on his particular public. It was to provide for the surplus industrial labour, and so keep up the level of wages of those remaining in industry; and secondly, to give a cultivator the whole result of his work instead of the quarter or less that wages represented of industrial output. Machinery stood between employer and labourer.

Nor would we wish to destroy it if it could be made MAN'S HOLIDAY instead of MAN'S CURSE; but it must be destroyed, or its injustice and inequality must be curbed by the possession of THE LAND.[7]

The traditional radical theme of the working men's loss of the land had force here. O'Connor was right that English agriculture could be carried on a great deal more vigorously than was the common practice, and could support many more people. Response came from countrymen who also realised it, but who had no hope of being able to buy a bit of land, and from people in decayed country towns, where old wool spinning and weaving industries had moved north without replacements, as well as from the man in the slums. Branches were formed in Bath, Devizes, Trowbridge, Yeovil, Bradford-on-Avon and other south-country towns. On 21 February 1846 the *Northern Star* reported receipts for the Land Company from Tunbridge Wells, Cheltenham and Devizes, and from 'Two Old Farmers' at Birkenhead, and in April from Tiverton and Newton Abbot. By April 1846, 1,487 people had paid up in full.

The Chartist leaders paid no more attention to O'Connor and suspected the plan was a device to restore the failing finances of the *Northern Star*. The Press in general thought the same, and Members of Parliament and local administrations thought it a device to exalt O'Connor by the hopes and savings of the poor. However, they left him alone and waited to see if it worked.

CHAPTER 2

BEGINNINGS AND THEIR
SIGNIFICANCE, 1845–6

IN March 1846 Feargus bought the first piece of land for a Chartist estate, at Heronsgate, or Herringsgate, near Rickmansworth, Hertfordshire, for £1,860. Instantly the touch of reality set people aflame and money began to pour in. Branches were named in the paper at Alva, Ashton-under-Lyne, Blackburn, Bolton, Bradford, Bury, Brighton (at the Artichoke), Camper Mill, Cheltenham, Colne, Georgie Mills, Glasgow, Great Glen (Leicestershire), Halifax, Huddersfield, Hyde, Kidderminster, Leeds, Leicester, Lye Waste, Manchester, Mauchline, Newark, Newcastle-on-Tyne, Newton Abbot, Nottingham, Norwich, Oldham, Plymouth, Preston, Radcliffe, Rochdale, Salford, Skegby, Sheffield, Stockport, Stoke Subhandhome, Sutton, Tiverton, Tunbridge Wells, Warwick, Wigan, Wotton-under-Edge, and Worcester.* The list was not complete, as is shown by the places of origin of the first allottees, which included Bilston, Macclesfield, Keighley, Pershore, Reading and Rouen. In a speech at Limehouse in May, O'Connor said that many men had given up the pub to find the money for the Land Plan. While no one man could buy land retail, by co-operation many could get it. The act of co-operation raised them from the helplessness of single economic units, and restored hope of dignity and independence. On 19 May their cash balance was £8,081.

When the moment of payment for the land at Heronsgate arrived, in May, the little group of organisers were in a fix. The company was not registered, had no legal existence, could not hold property. It was the last moment of warning. Roberts signed the cheque on the London

---

* This list is reproduced as printed; obscure names may be mills or factories.

Joint Stock Bank, and O'Connor signed the contract and became the owner of the property.

He and Christopher Doyle were deep in plans for houses, roads and allotments, and at the same time were going off at an hour's notice to examine farms and estates offered for sale elsewhere. Their expeditions were thrillingly hinted at in the *Northern Star*. The boom was on. Another purchase in Hertfordshire was made: Carpender's Park, 130 acres within a mile of Pinner Station, but was resold in a month at a profit.

Good friends were joining O'Connor now. Ernest Jones, a leading Chartist, a serious, idealistic young man, came to help on the staff of the company, and became its poet. Henry Cullingham, a London builder and skilled worker, was to prove a heart of oak. He became Feargus's foreman, and also a speaker at local meetings, explaining the Land Plan and Chartism, defending Feargus against public suspicions. Daily life on the Heronsgate site was absorbing and satisfying. Up the bricklayer's ladder, measuring the line for the fence, leading the horse and sand cart up the difficult slope, digging to test the soil, cutting out old timber, ordering slates, bricks, pipes, arbitrating for Doyle and Cullingham in wage arguments, Feargus was chieftain at last.

In July Tid Pratt again refused to register the company under the Friendly Societies Acts.[8] The Land Society or Company offered no friendly benefit, no interest on share money, no time point when a member would either get an allotment of land or interest or his money back, nor any scheme of sickness, unemployment or funeral benefit. It was in fact simply a lottery, with prizes for a few paid for by all and nothing for anyone else. An enemy newspaper, *The Manchester Examiner*, said the refusal was because the company was 'a huge mass of absurdities in its mere business rules and calculations'.

The first section of the company now held £10,998. The second section was on the way with £811. No one, visiting Heronsgate and seeing Feargus on fire with his work, doubted his seriousness. But he had his other, external life; he dressed well, he ate and drank well, he gave himself fantastic airs, he ran a newspaper which might pay for itself and might not. Many people, more concerned for the numbers of poor shareholders than impressed by the progress of the Land Company, were watching and writing letters and articles in local papers and in *The Times*. Feargus hated them all, and ignored the letters. He described himself inspecting another estate near Ipswich in August, umbrella in one hand and a spade in the other, testing the soil. On Heronsgate estate he was up at 4.30, at work outside at 8, in bed at midnight.

In September 1846 he made a journey into 'the out of the way county of Devon, the land of Parsons, sour cyder, and low wages', as he wrote on 12 September—one of the original comments on Devon. He added that the county was totally parson-ridden and landlord-ridden; the serfs of the land luxuriated in a genial climate, on sour cyder and 7–9s (35–45p) a week. Devonians were certainly interested in this curious man. The organisers of the tour were Mr Elms and Mr Crews of the Newton Abbot branch of the Chartist Association. O'Connor was met at Exeter Station by Mr Wilkinson, former Mayor of Exeter, and taken to his house for a meeting of '40–50 honest men and women'. At 8 am he and Wilkinson left by train for Teignmouth, along that wonderful sea-coast line. They were met by Mr Garratt, railway contractor, teetotaller and Chartist, and taken to his house. At 12 o'clock, the seaside crowds on a fine September morning heard distant music, and saw a beautiful open van approach, occupied by a teetotal band in military uniforms, playing Chartist airs, followed by a handsome open carriage drawn by four blood-tits with postboys. A mile from Newton they were joined by a procession from Torquay.

The band and carriage drove to the Globe Inn, where they temporarily disappeared from view. At 2.30 the public meeting began in the market place at Newton Abbot, with Mr Wilkinson in the chair. M'Grath spoke first. He spoke of England, the love and duty they all felt towards their country, and the need to cultivate the land more fully and to belong to it more closely.

Feargus rose to speak. 'At last my mangled fame has burst like a radiant light through that murky halo by which faction hoped to obscure it,' he said. 'Can any man in Devonshire point out to me any ten acres in Devonshire, lying together, and cultivated to one fourth part of their highest power of bearing?' Of course not, because agricultural serfs could only work at the landlord's bidding. But the Chartist Co-operative Land Company would give everyone a chance to work for himself. It would 'solve the problem of criminal law, dispense with government sanatory improvement, educational aid, and a standing army'. Its members found they could be loyal without being servile, could honour without fear, and love without coercion. He was calling them to work, and work harder—for themselves and their security in their old age. 'There is no home and no refuge in old age for the toil worn slave, upon whose industry all have lived . . . but the bastille (the new Union workhouse), and the dead house, and the pauper's cold grave'. Rightly, this evoked a 'great sensation'. It was the fear of the day.

Feargus carried them on. He said he left in Hertfordshire '35 dumb but eloquent propounders of the principles of the People's Charter', the smallholdings of Heronsgate. With these solid proofs, 'I may proudly lay head upon my pillow, and dying, exclaim, "Thank God I have left the world better than I found it!"'

There was a tea-party for 250 in the large ballroom of the Globe. The band played throughout. So many people arrived, some after walking thirty miles, that tea had to be in two relays. Wilkinson spoke. He talked of their anxiety to raise the labourer's standing, improve the social order, and live as honest cultivators of their own country's soil, as the Creator meant. There were 160 members of the Land Company in Newton Abbot, and they would welcome more.

The Devonshire visit did not result in a Land Company estate. The countryside seemed to frighten off the organisers. In the following October, when Feargus was describing the needs of a Chartist estate, he wrote of an estate in Devon he went to see. It was three miles up a rugged mountain, the cost of transport of bricks from the nearest point was £2 a thousand, or more than the cost of the bricks, and the land was unreclaimed. What would a set of Lancashire operatives say of his judgment while they were dragging their furniture up this mountainside, to a wilderness ten miles from a town?

Enthusiasm for the Land Society was not now sustained only by pressure from O'Connor. Working-class people had seen with their own eyes the enchanting houses and plots of land being prepared at Heronsgate. A demonstration on 17 August had been one of Feargus's sparks of brilliance.

The better-off public remained unconvinced. Smallholdings were not, after all, unknown. People looked on O'Connor as a dangerous man, blown up with his own conceit and now dallying with communism. They saw the Land Company still unable to comply with basic legal requirements. Countrymen doubted the ability of any man to make a living off 2, 3 or even 4 acres of land. Many foresaw the allottees failing to do so and having to 'come on the rates'.

It had always been urgent to legalise the company. Roberts, Allsop, M'Gowan, and all the directors, saw that any day someone would find a foothold to sue O'Connor, and they would all be caught with him. But he took little interest in their urging. Instead, he proposed in August 1846 to go a step further, and found a land bank. In this, members could deposit money at 4 per cent interest, and save towards the £250 purchase money of their allotments. Deposits would progressively reduce an allottee's 'rent'. There was no clarification of whether 'rent' meant instalments on the purchase price, or the ground-rent to the company.

Starting a bank would invite legal investigation at once. Alarm increased among the directors, but O'Connor was ready for them. Borne along on his floodtide of success, he was prepared to plunge on his gamble with only provisional registration under the Joint Stock Companies Act. He betted that success would bring public acceptance, and the registration would be completed. On 26 September he announced in the *Northern Star* that the directors were going to register the company under the Joint Stock Companies Act.

Accordingly, Feargus sent Chinnery to approach the Registrar of Joint Stock Companies, Whitmarsh. The position was made clear. To be registered provisionally, directors of a company need only produce a statement of the company's business, principles and purposes, and the names and addresses of the promoters and officers. No examination was made of the soundness of the business part of the project, as under provisional registration a company could not conduct any business but could make all preparations to do so. It was allowed to carry a name with the words 'registered provisionally', open subscription lists, allot shares and receive deposits on them. The company was forbidden to buy or contract for or hold land, or to contract for services, works or supply of stores. Promoters were forbidden to buy land for the company. Provisional registration lasted for twelve months, and could be renewed for another twelve. During that time the conditions for full registration must be carried out: a return of capital and number of shares, and a list of at least a quarter of the shareholders and their addresses.

It was as much as O'Connor, and probably Roberts, had hoped for. He signed and paid the 1s (5p) fee on 24 October. When the announcement was made on 31 October in the *Star* a surge of relief went through all the 10,000 members. The word 'provisional' was just red tape to them.

A prospectus soon followed, with details for the public: the Land Company had been fifteen months in existence; section 1 was complete, with 6,000 members holding 10,000 shares at £2 10s (£2·50) each, on which they had paid £13,000 (£12,000 to be paid); section 2 was nearly complete, with 4,000 members and £2,000 subscribed; the benefits were—for one share, a house, 2 acres and £15 aid money to start with; for one-and-a-half shares, a house, 3 acres and £22 10s (£22·50); for two shares, a house, 4 acres, £30. Leases for ever would be given to occupants. Facilities would be arranged for buying one's allotment and so becoming a freeholder. Rent was to be regulated at 5 per cent on the capital spent on each allotment. Shares might be bought in weekly instalments of 3d. There was no indication in the prospectus that the method of gaining a house and land was by lottery.

The draft deed of registration gave the name of Roberts as treasurer. This was a lie, and almost certainly deliberate, to appear to spread the load of financial control from O'Connor sole.[9] Roberts had proved a poor hand at being treasurer, for he found the mass of business of receiving small sums in postal orders or stamps, listing and receipting them, keeping track of expenditure, far too time-consuming and laborious. His dilatory methods enforced no central account-keeping. No one knew anyone else's accounts, and only Feargus knew his spending on the estates. O'Connor kept Roberts's name on the deed, but had the work transferred to his own name. Henceforth, he signed the cheques and chose his own assistants. Among them was his nephew Roger, who worked for eighteen months without salary and complained very loudly, according to later reports.

October 1846 was a time of triumph for Feargus. The company was provisionally registered, one estate was building, a second was bought. The *Northern Star* of 31 October spread his success before the public. Already the company was starting on the requirements of full registration. Every shareholder must send his name in to be entered in the deed book. Registration gave shareholders power over the officers, and gave the officers power to compel shareholders to pay up. O'Connor said there were a lot of beggars in the company who only paid a trifle of their share money in order to have the right to make trouble.

There must have been criticisms, perhaps of too fancy standards at Heronsgate, for he said he had travelled 5,000 miles in search of estates, and had sleepless nights, wet feet, hungry belly and abuse as his wages. He looked for some rest now until December when he got possession of Lowbands, in Worcestershire.* The ballot for allottees from the second section for 30 acres of the new estate would take place on Friday, 11 December, at Birmingham. 30 acres would be kept over after locating those already balloted for. On the same day, a ballot would take place for the next thirty of the first section to be located. On 18 January the ballot would take place for the next thirty of the second section to be located. These directions promise multiple confusion, and I would think they brought it. I have not been able to sort out the story of the sections, nor how many of the ballots were genuine locations or runners-up in case of default, nor if a defaulter were compelled to sell only to a runner-up.[10]

From the point of view of a successful man, the name of Chartist had now become a liability. Chartism, inferring an old-fashioned, unsophisticated group, was slipping out of date as its points were taken over by the general movement of English opinion. Feargus decided to drop the name. Only one other would suit him, and his publicity campaign had it ready: The National Co-operative Land Company. The change of name certificate is dated 17 December 1846, and carries the dashing signature of Feargus O'Connor. The 'business' entry on the certificate was extended to 'purchase Lands—to erect Houses—to allot same to shareholders in manner provided by deed of settlement—to make advances of money to allottees and to raise money for the purposes aforesaid'.[11]

The first Land Conference held in a climate of success now gathered in Birmingham in December 1846. Provisional registration lightened everyone's spirits. Feargus wrote in the *Northern Star*, 'when I have a

* By realignment of county boundaries, Lowbands later became part of Gloucestershire.

Change in the * *Name and Business* ____ of the

PROVISIONAL } *Chartist Cooperative Land* Company. { Dated *17*
REGISTRATION. } { *Dec'r* 18..

* *Name*	* *Name*
As originally registered.	As altered.
Chartist Cooperative Land Company	*National Cooperative Land Company*
Business as Originally Registered	*Business as Altered*
For the purpose of purchasing Land and erecting Dwellings and Schools	*To purchase Lands — to erect Houses to allot same to Shareholders in manner provided by deed of settlement — to make advances of money to Allottees and to raise money for the purposes aforesaid*
	Signature

* Insert "Name," "Business," or "Place of Business," as the case may be.

1   Certificate of alteration of name and business of the Land Company,
17 December 1846, with a signature of Feargus O'Connor

pig and a cow everybody bids me good morrow'. The company had a new office at 144 High Holborn, London, but 83 Dean Street was kept on, and part of it let.

The conference named trustees: T. S. Duncombe, MP, John Sewell, auctioneer, and Ernest Jones, all of London. An audit committee of five was elected to examine the Heronsgate accounts.[12] The size of cottage to be built was keenly argued. Big, roomy cottages were a waste of money and of land space. A man was not going to be staying in the house, he was going to be out working on the land, and a big house was a tax on him. It also took longer and cost more to build. Members of the company were solidly for numbers of houses against size. The conference resolved that no cottage should be bigger than four rooms of 12 ft square. For any additional size, the man must pay extra. The incentive behind this was not entirely mean-minded. Chartists knew their own world.

> Poor woolcombers in Bradford huddled together in one room, ventilated with a charcoal stove, would think themselves in a palace in a three-roomed cottage, and would consider it a hardship to have their release from those hells postponed for the gratification of those who wished for large homes.

The conference ruled that fathers were not to put infants' names down, or one man might acquire sixteen acres of land, and let cottages decay, or begin to sub-let. The conference ended by voting 35s a week as pay for directors, and deciding to hold a conference every year. A Grand Soirée in the People's Hall was attended by 500 people, and was reported in the *Gloucester Chronicle* on 26 December 1846.

The land bank was eagerly awaited. All members unquestioningly thought that the huge sums coming in every week should be deposited in their own bank, rather than be used, perhaps risked, by some other bank. The promulgation came on 26 December 1846, in the *Northern Star*. The Land and Labour Bank was to consist of three departments, deposit, redemption, and sinking fund. The deposit branch offered $3\frac{1}{2}$ per cent interest, the redemption branch 4 per cent and the sinking fund $2\frac{1}{2}$. Deposits could be from 3d. The general public, as well as members of the Land Company, were invited to support the bank.

Instead of the old 3d levy, a comprehensive levy of 6d per share per annum was to be made to cover expenses of the bank, management of the company, directors' wages and lecturers' expenses.[13] All profits were to go to the benefit of the shareholders. O'Connor pointed out that occupiers were safe from increases of rent, and that by co-operation the plan would make a small proprietary class which could establish a fair price for its labour, render poor rate and workhouse unnecessary, develop the national resources fully, and accomplish many other public benefits.

Socialists were enraged. A rival paper, *The National Reformer*, declared that land societies were agents of property against the working class and nationalisation of land. Others agreed with O'Connor. Letters came in from many Chartist branches praising the bank. Carlisle, Hull and Leicester wrote at once. Leicester called it the Archimedes lever that would evade the difficulties of sale or mortgage of land at reduced price, and give security for small savings.

A third set of rules was now issued, which included all the alterations supposedly aimed at qualifying for the Joint Stock Companies' Act,[14] though none of them touched the lottery principle. The third set of rules continued in force until the Lowbands Land Conference of 1847.

The land bank went into operation in January 1847, at 493 Oxford Street, London, which was a side entrance to 144 High Holborn, the office of the Land Company. A balance sheet dated 29 September to 25 December 1846 was issued, saying that 'the little shrub has grown up a strong and stately tree', with over 60,000 members holding 180,000 shares, and £90,000 worth of capital.[15] The staff of the bank were—chief clerk Mr Wheeler, O'Connor's secretary Hewitt helping in the office, and for short periods each Gathard and Jones. McCarthy, Doyle and Clark dropped in to lend a hand when called on.

Criticism, which had been fairly mild so far when there was little information to go on, now began to strengthen, feeding on the details provided. Alexander Somerville, who was to be a continuing gadfly to Feargus, began to write in the *Manchester Examiner*, under the name of 'The Whistler at the Plough', dissecting Feargus's figures, logic and aspirations. A rhyme of his maddened Feargus:

> In the middle of the day, when the sun doth shine,
> What the devil shall I do with this loom of mine?
> In the middle of the day when the sun shines hot
> What the devil shall I do with my two acre spot?

C

In winter, he wrote, the allottees will shiver for want of roads to go out after dark, and in summer they'll melt for want of water. Supposing men who guide machines in Manchester should not earn a fourth part of what was written in O'Connor's book?

CHAPTER 3

THE GOOD YEAR, 1847

1847 was the happiest year for the Land Company. It achieved 600 branches in England, Scotland and Wales, a national coverage.

The fire of faith caught hold of the working classes. Suddenly the chance of getting a house, land, a share in these thousands of pounds they read of in the *Star*, became real. Crowds came to hear O'Connor speak, intense and less wild than at Chartist meetings. The word of salvation was heard in Bradford, Todmorden, Leicester.

> He speaks;—and, list'ning to his voice,
> New life the dead receive,
> The mournful broken hearts rejoice,
> The humble poor believe.[16]

Who were these people? Or rather, since their names can mean little, what did they do? To what place in society did they belong? One of the lists collected for the deed of full registration, and dated 1 May 1847[17] included the following 56 professions: coalminer, weaver, labourer, calico printer, shoemaker, limeburner, block printer, stockinger, baker, woolcomber, innkeeper, smith, tailor, stonecutter, cabinetmaker, joiner, potter, cordwainer, mason, grocer, piecer, moulder, nailor, victualler, postman, skinner, butcher, embroiderer, farmer, hatter, spinner, milkman, servant, gardener, lacemaker, overlooker, warehouseman, tinman, clerk, thatcher, plumber, painter, plasterer, mechanic, clothier, fustian cutter, grinder, bricklayer, trunkmaker, seamstress, warper, turner, carpenter, slater, schoolmistress, cotton band maker. Two English names are entered from Calais as lacemakers. In the list there are at least two women, and three skilled craftsmen—cabinetmaker, potter, embroiderer—one clerk and four countrymen—farmer, milkman, gardener and thatcher. Not all came from industrial towns. In 1848 between two and three hundred came from Brighton.

To link up with the discussion and thought animating the branches, a group of lecturers was formed to travel round, give talks, keep people in line with the aims of the directors, explain points and lead discussions. Dr McDouall, Ernest Jones, Samuel Kidd, John West, M'Grath, and Clark were among the number. Regular lecturers received £2 a week and travelling expenses. McDouall, in Preston in January weather, spoke of the low rent of a Chartist cottage and land compared with rent paid in Preston for no land and a cottage 'where even the back accommodation was miserable in the extreme'. He said the man unskilled in agriculture was more likely to learn modern methods than the regular farmer.[18] To publicise the Land Company further, O'Connor and Ernest Jones started a monthly paper, *The Labourer*, which lasted from the beginning of 1847 to the end of 1848.

The second section of the Land Company closed on 21 January 1847, and the third section opened. Numbers were increasing through the rush of Irish immigrants arriving at Liverpool to escape the potato failure at home. A thousand a day landed in January, and on one Sunday 2,120.[19] Inmates of Preston Union workhouse rose from 536 in the December quarter of 1844 to 862 in the March quarter of 1847.[20] The ballot for location of the second section was announced for Monday, 22 February.

The design of the three-roomed cottage was printed in the *Northern Star* of 13 February, with commentary. Feargus designed it himself, as far as any evidence goes. On all the estates today the shape is instantly recognisable, the centre brought forward under a flattened gable, a little ornament cut under the peak, a chimney at each end of the roof-tree, and the roof steeply sloping down at the back to the working rooms behind the living quarters. Two-storeyed and semi-detached cottages are only found at Heronsgate. All other estates have separate bungalows. O'Connor said the maximum rent for four acres and aid money of £30 would be £12 a year.

Criticism drove him to work out details of how a man could support a family on three acres. He produced calculations full of figures, but quite unreal. He spoke of cows and milk, when the amount of land needed to raise hay to keep a cow in milk was nearer 6 acres than 3; of honey and flax, which required special skills unknown to most people. Above all, he spoke of selling produce, when neither Heronsgate nor Lowbands were within reach of any worthwhile market. He added attractive little tips, which would win over any newcomer; keep ducks 'because a wall a foot high will keep them in, and because hens are very bad farmers and ducks are very good ones, they will follow you out to the field and will gobble up the slugs and worms and never require more'. Horses were wasteful, compared with all other farm creatures. 'Sundays included . . . my ducks never made any difference, and my cows gave milk, but my horses *didn't work and ate.*'

The deed for complete registration was laid before the Registrar in January, and was returned to Chinnery with amendments. He discussed with the directors how to bend the facts to the requirements of the law. On 25 March a circular and a handbill[21] were issued, signed by John Gathard, and stamped at the Joint Stock Company Registry Office on 1 April 1847. The objects, benefits and progress of the company were laid out, including the fact that an allottee would get a vote. This promise quietly disappeared from all the estates during the life of the company, owing to the difficulty of conveying land to an allottee when the title of the conveyor was in doubt. Conveyances were not attempted until the Court of Chancery took over the tangled affairs left by the closing down of the company. Votes reappeared then.

In February O'Connor inspected an estate at Mathon, near Malvern and paid £1,505 deposit on it. Eighty-five allotments there were balloted for in March and May, with Cirencester, Brighton, Newton Abbot, and Peterborough among the winners. Sections one, two and three took part, provided the members had paid up on their shares. It was announced by the directors that the number of locations balloted for from each section would be proportioned to the amount of capital paid by each.

On 1 May the allottees were installed at Heronsgate estate, and the Land Company was in full operation. No rent was yet fixed. Daniel O'Connell died in May, but Feargus was beyond the reach of any rational career now. In June the company had four sections. A week's receipts were £795 odd, made up of items like 'Todmorden 2s od— Redmarley 1s od—Patience Masters 1s 4d—Elizabeth Masters 1s 4d— Cinderford Iron Works—Torquay £3 9s 10d—Swindon £10—

NATIONAL LAND COMPANY.

PROVISIONALLY REGISTERED.

SHARES £1. 6s. EACH.

The object of this Company is to enable Working Men, for a trifling sum, to obtain possession of Land and Dwellings, upon such terms, that, by honourable and independent labour, they may maintain themselves and families in comfort and respectability.

BENEFITS ASSURED.

The following are the benefits which the Company guarantees to its members :

HOLDERS OF TWO SHARES—A COMFORTABLE HOUSE, TWO ACRES OF GOOD LAND, AND £15.

HOLDERS OF THREE SHARES—A HOUSE, THREE ACRES, AND £22. 10s.

HOLDERS OF FOUR SHARES—A HOUSE, FOUR ACRES, AND £30.

LEASES FOR EVER WILL BE GRANTED TO THE OCCUPANTS.

Thus ensuring to them the value of every improvement they may make upon their allotments. The Company affords great facilities to those members who have the means of purchasing their allotments. The rent will be moderate, as it will be regulated by a charge of 5 per cent. upon the capital expended.

The Company having been called into existence for the benefit of the WORKING CLASSES, the Rules enable the poorest to avail themselves of its advantages, as the Shares may be paid by instalments as low as

THREE PENCE PER WEEK.

THE RULES OF THE COMPANY (PRICE 4s.)

can be obtained of MR. WHEELER, the Secretary,

AT THE OFFICE, 83, DEAN STREET, SOHO, LONDON,

where members may be enrolled, and every information obtained ;

Or of

2   A handbill issued by the company early in 1847

Worcester 2s 6d'. O'Connor announced that when section four was full he would close the company. Four sections of 6,000 would embrace 120,000 (*sic*) people, a family, he reckoned, sufficiently large for one man to take care of. Others could take on the work after that.

Advertisements began to come out in the *Northern Star* from people offering to buy allotments on the estates. A scheme was floated to help Frost, Williams and Jones, the Chartists who had been transported after the rising in Newport. For this, an O'Connorville tea-tray was designed, and a ballot for it advertised in June with the object of buying a 4-acre share in the Land Company for each man's family. I have been unable to find any result of the project.

In this June O'Connor bought Snigs End near Lowbands, and an estate in Minster Lovell parish. The Land Company, or rather O'Connor, now owned roughly 846 acres. Financial procedure of handling little weekly sums, remained very much the same as in the early days. M'Gowan, printer and publisher of the *Northern Star*, was still O'Connor's financial agent and confidential man. Lists of the week's receipts were sent down to the *Star* office on Thursday, and printed. On Saturday, one or two directors brought the week's subscription money to M'Gowan, who checked it against the column in the *Star*. M'Gowan also handled the receipts for the *Northern Star*, and sent in his own bills as printer and publisher. Directors gave O'Connor a note that these were correct, and O'Connor authorised M'Gowan to pay them.

M'Gowan paid the subscription money each Saturday and Tuesday into whatever bank O'Connor named. Feargus used a large number of banking businesses as well as his own Land and Labour Bank. He was a man who liked to be able to lay his hand quickly on cash in various places. At Lowbands and Snigs End he used the Gloucestershire Banking Company, and M'Gowan had to send cash in registered envelopes to be deposited there or else deposit it with the London agents, Jones, Lloyd & Co. At Minster Lovell he used Clinch & Co of Witney. Roberts held deposits for him up in Manchester. In London he used the London Joint Stock Bank, the Land and Labour Bank, and Mr Allsop the stockbroker, as well, maybe, as other uncovenanted hideouts. Yet he was not a swindler or embezzler. On his travels, branch secretaries gave him their local subscriptions to carry to London. Once he brought £400 in a portmanteau to Price, the Land Bank manager. In the end he financed the Land Company for over £3,000. But he was incapable of simple business activity, and his least transaction worked up into a conspiracy. He never gave M'Gowan or anyone else a receipt, yet he never allowed M'Gowan to juggle the accounts for the *Northern Star* and the Land Company. He insisted on M'Gowan's buying the paper for the week's print on credit at £4 more than he need have paid if he had given cash for it out of the receipts of the Land Company.

In July Thomas Wheeler, the financial secretary, gave up the job to Philip M'Grath, probably thankfully. He retired to an allotment at O'Connorville, with his son. M'Grath kept no better minutes of meetings than Wheeler had done. By now it may have been thought wiser not to do so.

Finally, on 7 July, George Sweet gave counsel's opinion: the Land Bank could not be operated as auxiliary to the Land Company, nor could directors of the company be also proprietors of the bank; the property of the company did not belong to it until complete registration and could not be made directly available as security to depositors in the bank; and whereas the private property of each partner was the usual security, in the Land Company the sums involved would be too big for this; half-shares could not be held by members of a joint-stock company; finally, before the company could start any business it must be completely registered.

There was one solution, and Sweet named it. Mr O'Connor could open a private bank and lend to the company on mortgages of its property, authorised by two extraordinary meetings. This was a solution the directors were used to accepting.

Feargus himself had no misgivings. He advertised for a bank manager. All this argy-bargy about legal technicalities irritated him feverishly. His success was bound to bring public recognition and establishment, whatever the petty critics and fainthearts might say.

There were plenty of these, from inside the company and from outside. Thomas Aclam, the Barnsley allottee, harassed Feargus for details of how the property was to be conveyed, and on other practical points which enraged Feargus. He gave Aclam a sharp rap for all to read in the *Northern Star*, saying that the property was owned by himself until twenty minutes after complete registration, when it would be con-

veyed to trustees for all members. But if people criticised the organisa-
tion, there was general praise from those who examined the estates
themselves. Wales and Scotland sent scouts, George Morgans from
Merthyr Tydfil to look at Lowbands and staff from the *Glasgow
Saturday Post* to Heronsgate. Their good reports were published in the
Northern Star.

A by-election was announced for Nottingham, and Feargus decided
to stand as a Chartist and a Radical. He had always been popular there
as a speaker, and he saw the need of public status to back up the Land
Company. His supporters were enthusiastic for the same reason, and
the whole of July 1847 was spent in electioneering. At the same time
W. P. Roberts stood for election to Blackburn Borough Council. A
portrait of Feargus was drawn, and prints of it were put on sale. Gammage, a hostile Chartist, wrote in his history of the movement,
'O'Connor appeared to be rising in invincibility'.

Feargus astonished his enemies and achieved his highest level of
success by winning the second seat at Nottingham. Tory voters gave
him their second votes to keep the Whigs out. Joy overflowed at the
news. In Barnsley, candles were lit in every working-class window, and
the Chartist flag of green and pink hung out over the poor streets.
People gathered to toast the victory and sing Chartist songs. In spite of
poverty, collections were taken up for O'Connor's election expenses.
Twenty-eight Chartists stood for election to Parliament and ten were
elected. Roberts was rejected by Blackburn in the borough council
election, polling 68 votes against the winners' 649 and 602.

Enthusiasm was still rising. Chartists and members of the Land Company of the Leicester and Loughborough villages, where extreme
poverty and depression held hundreds in the decaying stocking-
knitting industry, organised a meeting. They gathered on the banks of
the Soar from 2 to 6 pm. The Chartist hymn was sung, there were
speeches, and the Land Plan was explained amid 'breathless attention'.
Catt's *Pictorial History of Manchester* contains an imagined discussion
between two workmen on the Land Plan, while on a picnic to Dur-
ham. On the Union farm of Chorlton-on-Medlock on Trafford Moss,
6 paupers in 1846 had increased to 85.[22]

Feargus was always the best persuader, both to keep up present zeal
and to inspire more. At a meeting he described the case of Charlie

Tawes, allottee from Radford to O'Connorville (Heronsgate). Charlie had been shut up in a Whig bastille (Union workhouse), separated from his wife and children.[23] Now he had been reunited with them and raised to independence. Now he had four pigs in his sty (tremendous cheering). Would he have ever got them by sticking in Radford workhouse? If the government would put half the money spent on building workhouses into buying land for poor men, it would destroy the new Poor Law system.

The 1847 Land Conference was held on Lowbands estate in August. It met in the Lowbands schoolroom looking out over fields to the horizon of the Malvern hills. The *Preston Guardian* reported that fifty Chartist delegates were present. Feargus arrived in the triumph of his election to Parliament. The first big item was the separation of the Land Bank from the company in accordance with counsel's opinion of 7 July. Newspapers and outside critics might denounce the finances of the *Northern Star*, the Land Company, the bank and the master juggler, but the members of the company had complete faith in their leader, their father. They felt much safer with him in charge than with a handful of themselves messing the money about. A unanimous decision appointed O'Connor as sole proprietor of the bank, wholly unconnected with the Land Company. No other appointments were made, no trustees, directors, or officers of the bank, and no deed of settlement to establish it.

Counsel had also said that half-shares could not be held by members of a joint-stock company. The conference settled this by reducing the price of a share to £1 6s (£1·30) and making 2 shares the qualification for balloting for 2 acres, 3 shares for 3 acres and 4 shares for 4. Difficulty in managing the sections was overwhelming now that members were joining so fast—Chinnery said thousands a week at this period—so the conference abolished sections. From now on all the company was to be managed as one.

The conference decided that the original company should close at the end of the year, but another one could be started to deal with the rush of members, with new officials to do the work. A fourth set of rules was issued, consisting roughly of an epitome of the necessary deed of registration, with little relation to the practice of the company.[24] The directors, Doyle, Clark, M'Grath and Wheeler, were voted salaries of £2 a week, a rise of 5s (25p). O'Connor refused to have any salary.

The conference dispersed from Lowbands, where the delegates had been most uncomfortably lodged, as they complained later. Two stage-coaches, each drawn by four horses, took them to the railway at Gloucester. O'Connor, with relief, returned to building the estate at Minster Lovell (Charterville). He had to appoint Doyle as overseer, since he himself was now occupied for long stretches at Westminster. The outside world and talk of registration and shares meant less and less to him. He could still speak and work with his wonted intensity, but for shorter periods. He had always drunk a good deal, and now he relied on it.

Being unmarried, and living as he did in lodgings, with no real cronies, in his times of collapse he could manage to be alone. If his appearance of exhaustion was noticed, or patches of confusion came into his speaking, these were attributed to overwork and wearing himself out in the cause of the company. There is no evidence at this time that anyone noticed he was going mad. It began to be suspected in the House of Commons during the coming year.

There was no alteration in the financial side. M'Grath, the financial secretary, was responsible for collecting the weekly money and preparing the list for the *Northern Star*, paying small expenses and handing the balance to M'Gowan. He admitted later that the rule that other directors should countersign cheques on the company's account had not been kept. Cullingham, King and Doyle all kept painstaking receipt and expenditure accounts on the different working sites. Cash books recorded the money Cullingham or King received from O'Connor, and how it was paid out on Saturday night to carpenters and workmen working either for wage or by contract. Day books showed the number of houses each carpenter etc contracted for and the amount of cash he had received up to date on those contracts. Sale books showed the receipts for sale of old material off the estates. But no central account was kept. Bank vouchers showed deposits, and cheques showed O'Connor's drawings, but no account showed what his cheques were spent on.

The drive for signatures to the deed of registration went on. Thomas Clark brought it to Blackburn and argued the case for the Land Company there. People said £9 million would be needed to locate 40,000 members. He replied that the working class spent £30 million every year on gin and beer. He said that 18,000 had signed, and, as soon as a quarter of the membership had signed, the registration would be completed.[25] Chinnery told a different story. He took the deed to Manchester, where he talked with Roberts, who had himself been directly warned by Whitmarsh that the company was still illegal. For a week Chinnery took the deed and lists of names round to the branches in Manchester, Stockport and Macclesfield, and induced Roberts to send his chief clerk out from Manchester to all the local centres on a seven-weeks' tour. There was no mention of 18,000 signatures.

It was a wearisome and distasteful job, waiting about in taverns and chapel halls in the evenings for working men to come in, dirty, often stinking, slow, argumentative, writing their names with difficulty. The lists for signing still lay at the Land Company's office in Holborn, with two clerks attending. But in the absence of any central organisation and secretarial staff, the effort to collect signatures dwindled. Neither Chinnery nor Roberts appeared to note that only a quarter of the number of shareholders needed to be registered. They failed also to see that, as every member had to have two shares to qualify, and very few had more than four, a calculation could be made of the number of signatures required. In fact, by the time of the enquiry in 1848, 6,000 signatures were required, holding 25,393 shares and £33,000 of capital, and Chinnery and the directors had collected 7,566, so that anyone with business ability could have seen that this obstacle to complete registration was already overcome. As it was, Chinnery said that after February 1848 he gave up all efforts to collect and count signatures, and never presented the deed and documents for registration.

CHAPTER 4

CRACKS APPEARING

THE result of the conference decision to close the company was a rush to join. Between August 1847 and January 1848, 42,000 members were added. Receipts rose in these five months to between £5,000 and £6,000 a week. At Stourbridge numbers rose from 7 in February to 240 in September.

On 4 September 1847 the first bank manager was named, James Knight. He lasted one week. O'Connor said he was experienced, with good testimonials. The *Manchester Examiner* agreed, and reported that he examined the Land Bank for a week, and

> said that to be engaged on such an affair would be destruction to the fair fame his former honourable services had earned for him. He fled as from a pest house, leaving £600 a year to get his freedom.

A notice appeared in the *Star* that letters were to go to the manager, with no name given, until a few weeks later T. Price took the job.

Price showed up at the Parliamentary enquiry as sensible. When he took over, the redemption fund stood at £611, in 1700 accounts, all of private people, and rose to £683 by 31 December. Deposits were £5,948 on 1 January 1848. Price, with Allsop the broker, bought exchequer bills with the bank's money, and no other securities. They were good value and yielded 7 or 8 per cent, which helped to pay interest and expenses. He drew attention to the fact that, although allottees were as yet paying the company no rent, they could all sublet and take rent for themselves.[26]

In October 1847 Thomas Wheeler withdrew from the list of directors, and William Dixon took his place. Wheeler was happier on his 2-acre allotment at O'Connorville. On 23 October Dixon applied for a 'renewed certificate of provisional registration in lieu of the certificate of 24th October 1846'.

But from this point the rickety organisation of the company broke down altogether under the rush of success. It was no longer a domestic matter of a working-class group who all understood one another. Country-wide interest and examination were turned on it, and its lack of organisation produced disastrous confusion. Success, too, involved costs for registration altogether beyond the cash resources of the company. At 1s (5p) per £1,000 of capital and stamp duty of £3 15s (£3·75) per 100 names, this five months' increase meant a bill for £1,580 in fees. Inability even to pay the fees was an indication of capital being totally inadequate to do the company's job.

The muddles made easy targets for the newspapers, among whom by now O'Connor had formed a battalion of enemies. He said that only the *Economist* treated the Land Plan with respect. He wrote a leader in the *Northern Star* in October, 'To Editors', beginning 'You Ruffians', and another to 'The Fricassee of Editors'. He addressed the editor of the *Dispatch* as 'You unmitigated ass! You sainted fowl! You canonised ape!' *The Times* was sympathetic to the company's aims and effort, but as crushing as the rest on its methods and prospects. The *Manchester Examiner* said in October 1847 that deliberate deception of the shareholders was being practised by O'Connor. If this were true, it was treatment they had often welcomed. But his control of the power he had called into being was gone. Country papers reprinted from the national press, and suspicions spread.

The crisis in confidence came at the end of October. On 28 October. the company's receipts for the week were £3,063. On 4 November, £2,750; on 11 November, £1,500; on 18 November, £893.[27] They never recovered. The crisis was not recognised at the time. O'Connor announced the buying of another estate by the company's 'bailiff, contractor, architect, engineer, surveyor, farmer, dung-maker, cow and pig jobber, milkman, horse jobber and Member of Parliament'. It was probably Snigs End. He had now spent £33,982 on buying land, apart from any building. In November he had a glorious evening in Manchester—from his own report. A public meeting was held for him to dispute with newspaper men. The hall and approaches to it were crammed. Three reporters and O'Connor's book of accounts were hoisted up through a window. People stood till midnight. Cries of 'water!' went up as the females fainted. Cabbages 2½ ft wide, called the Whistler's nosegays, were suspended from the galleries. A tremendous argy-bargy went on about the Land Company rules, the *Northern Star* office and circulation, and Feargus's debts. A letter was read from his sister-in-law denying that he had ever been summonsed for debt in Ireland. Feargus roared away, defending his honesty, challenging everybody to take back the money they had paid in to the company or the bank. He was answered by cries of 'No, we have bags more for you,' and storms of applause—and £250 was paid in that evening.

Clark and Dixon were still taking the deed of registration round parts of the north, Yorkshire and Derbyshire, then Leicester and Nottingham, although many people now believed that O'Connor, as a Member of Parliament, would introduce a special bill to legalise the company as it stood, and so defeat its enemies. The sheer numbers and success of it seemed to make it secure. The signing at Nottingham was made into an O'Connor festival at the opening of Parliament. Two halls were hired, and 400 ladies attended the tea. A ballot was held in November, still drawn in sections in spite of the ban. Six women succeeded out of 96 allocations. An O'Connor tartan was advertised for dresses, vestings and shawls.

Autumn withered the acres of O'Connorville, and the first winter closed on the Land Company settlers. Yet each man had his cottage, his stove, bed and table, his fuel store, sacks of potatoes, turnips and flour. Outside, he had his fowls, pigs, rows of cabbages in the frost, wood to pick up for his fire. Winter closed in all over England, with unemployment and bitter cold. In Blackburn the unemployed tramped the streets, knocking at shops and big houses begging for food. In Glasgow 16 mills were closed and 36 were working short time. Public responsibility for relief was undeveloped, outstripped by the problem. Some millowners paid their year's instalments of poor rate in one, in an effort to keep the overseers in funds.[28] In Preston relief was given at 1s per head per week, and none to any family where one member was still at work. Private charity organised itself to save the children and stay the extreme of despair. The *Preston Guardian* said a committee gave 1,280 quarts of soup a day, at ½d a quart with bread, and was going to double the quantity with another boiler.[29] Rickmansworth parish watched the O'Connorville families with dread.

On 18 December 1847 the *Star* announced that O'Connor would petition the House of Commons for a bill to legalise the company, as soon as Parliament assembled. Meantime the company would be closed on 31 December. A new Land Company was to be started, in response to public demand, with improvements. The money would be entrusted to Mr O'Connor.

This break in the movement of the company seemed to release all the uneasiness in members' bosoms. Objections to a new company and arguments about the old one broke out furiously, intensified by the pro- or anti-O'Connor issue. Hammersmith branch started a clothes and hat club to encourage the wearing of the O'Connor tartan. On 8 January Feargus announced that he had bought another estate, Great Dodford in Worcestershire. A ballot was held at the Chartist Assembly Rooms, Dean Street, Soho, on 27 January.

Volume of business overwhelmed the directors. In February they wrote in the *Star* that the four of them, Dixon, Doyle, M'Grath and Clark had 100 letters a day, 80 of which had to be answered. After the last ballot, 18,000 tickets had to be selected and distributed to branches for the next one. Daily remittances of cash had to be entered. Shareholders on the office list numbered 2,500, some of whom continually called and made enquiries.

Regular accounts of the 60,000 members' quarterly payments had to be kept. The register of shareholders had to be completed to comply with the Joint Stock Companies Act. They reckoned seven clerks, as well as the four directors, were needed.

A more serious breach opened. Ernest Jones, speaking at Middleton, was asked if a man could buy land on an estate not yet balloted for, and answered that a shareholder could have it for what it cost and title-deeds would be made out without the ballot.[30] Buying-power was admitted—death to the hopes of the poor who clung to the equality of chance.

Money, food, work—these were crushing cares this winter. In Europe revolutionaries were stirring; Louis Philippe fled from Paris in February and the French set up a republic. All over England the old feeling for the Charter was up again. O'Connor was involved in plotting and planning for a monster demonstration to present the petition for the Charter to Parliament, as well as in his own Land Company difficulties. The petition was lodged at the Land Company's office in five huge bales.

On 19 February notice of the new Land Company appeared in the *Star*. Shares were to be £5 for 2 acres, £7 10s for 3, £10 for 4. On the same day O'Connor presented his petition to introduce a bill to legalise the company to the House of Commons.

He was only just in time. Suspicion was stalking him, not only in men who felt socially responsible for his possible victims, but among the thousands who began to feel themselves victims. Ten days after his petition, the chairman and officers of the Salisbury branch presented a petition in support of O'Connor's.[31] Similar petitions followed from Bolton-le-Moors, George Adams a cabinet maker of Cheltenham, the Mayor of Northampton, the Horncastle branch, and Worksop. The inhabitants of Greenock petitioned the House to put the company under the Joint Stock Companies Acts. All these petitions were accepted by the House. At the same time a speaker, Tomlinson, from Halifax, in a public lecture on the Charter and the Land Plan, called O'Connor the captain of salvation of the working classes, like the British lion, and denounced the press as his persecutor. Six members of the Preston branch won an allotment in the ballot, and the Mayor granted the Exchange Rooms for a tea party and ball in honour of their location on the land.[32]

In the House of Commons were many men who had known O'Connor for a long time. They were determined that he should not jettison his poor, unopportunitied followers by some shady move. John Bright and Sir Benjamin Hall, an ironmaster from Wales, began the simple but deadly method of keeping Feargus publicly to what he had said. As in his younger days, the House of Commons was the worst place for Feargus. His self-praise and frothy speeches, especially long ones, froze the listeners, whether in the corridors and committee rooms or on the benches of the House. He tried to slip points over on a thin attendance in the House by quickness and assurance, and thereby aroused everyone's suspicions.

In the week of 13–18 March he published arrangements for the demonstration on Kennington Common to march with the Charter

D

petition to Parliament, and he also introduced his petition for a
Bill to amend the existing laws on Friendly Societies to afford sanction
for the National Land Company. The speech reads well. He did not
think the House would refuse its sanction simply because the plan was
novel. Railways had been new once. His estates converted neglected
farms; there was a school on each; farmers liked the allottees, and found
them neither Whig nor Tory but working men; a well-occupied
working class was better for the nation than paupers; the land was the
natural place to absorb unemployment created by machines; a neighbouring landowner, Lord Beauchamp, had refused to obstruct the
building of an estate, saying that if the plan was bad it would fail and
if it was good it ought to succeed; the working classes were intensely
concerned in the question; £180,000 had been subscribed, with no
protection for the subscribers against himself (laughter and 'hear!
hear!'). If the House would not extend the Benefit Societies Act, he
was entitled to ask them to pass a separate Act to cover the company.
(Hear! Hear!) He sought now to remove the impediments to enrol-
ment under the Benefit Societies Act. He proposed to give every
member an interest of 1 per cent as soon as his shares were paid up,
until he got a place in the ballot. Interest should accumulate, and be put
towards paying off the member's purchase price of the land. A separate
subscription should be raised for a joint stock fund for medical and
sick benefits, funeral expenses etc.

Philip M'Grath was chairman of the National Chartist Convention
which organised the great petition. The demonstration took place four
weeks later, on 10 April, and turned into a fiasco. The bales of the
petition were brought from the Land Company's office to Kennington
Common with great show, in a waggon drawn by four splendid horses
from the Land Company estate at Snigs End, trimmed with red, green
and white streamers. But from there the march to Westminster was
forbidden by the police, except for forty-nine people, according to a
law of which the Chartists said they had never heard. O'Connor
showed nervous panic, and hastily spoke to the people urging them to
disperse. The petition was taken in cabs to Westminster, where it was
examined and its signatures found to be far fewer than O'Connor had
claimed. Cripps, Member for Cirencester, one of the examiners, said
afterwards in the House that O'Connor was unworthy of belief and

was deluding poor people shamefully. Feargus, turning frantic, started threatening Cripps and throwing himself about. Disorder and shouting spread, the Speaker called them to order, and Feargus fled the Chamber.

The whole country was agitated by the Chartist threat and collapse. Chartism and the Land Company were both discredited by their association with O'Connor. A good deal of understanding of the aims of both movements was shown in Parliament and in the Press, discriminating between the movements and the leaders. Cobden said that 'by contriving to array the working classes against every man who was disposed to assist in carrying forward their objects' O'Connor had done more to retard their political progress than any other public man. The *Manchester Examiner* of 15 April said that noble hopes, sacrifices and deeds were not fairly represented by a strain of ranting and Irish braggadocio. On 18 April the paper wrote, 'The Chartists may rail . . . but their cause has been ruined by the Celts.'

O'Connor retreated to Snigs End estate in Gloucestershire. It was April, and very wet, but pear and plum were in blossom. The builders working on the little houses, carpenters sawing and hammering, carters and strong horses bringing loads of sand and lime, quietened him. He was able to write his leader to the Fustian Jackets, Blistered Hands and Unshorn Chins, although these indeed were fast separating from him. Receipts of the old Land Company were £169 and of the new, £12. Deposits in the bank were £84.

He had to leave Snigs End to make a public entry into his constituency city of Nottingham, and here his sickness was apparent to all. He was confused, exhausted, and at times hardly conscious. But he responded to the need for a speech. The *Star* of 29 April reported that an Irishman called from the hall, 'Mr O'Connor, you are Irish, you must come back to your own country.' An old man near him answered, 'Nay, he's our feyther, and we canna part wi' him. We'll lend him ye, but yo mun send him back agen.' Whether the story is true or not, Feargus saw himself as this figure in their thoughts. In many cases it was still true. Cirencester branch passed a resolution of confidence in him, aware of his trial at this time. To observers, this trust by the very poor, by those whom neither church nor government nor neighbour had reached, seemed to cry out for rescue. On 12 May Feargus brought in his Bill to legalise the company. Everyone could see that if the Bill failed, he would blame the House, and this would be the greatest let-out possible for him. The *Manchester Examiner* proposed: 'Would it not be well to have the thing fairly proved before a committee of the House of Commons?' The second reading of the Bill was fixed for 12 June, and Sir Benjamin Hall began to make enquiries.

He went to the Registration Office and examined all the documents. Meantime, in May, a row developed inside the company, but as reports are all from the *Northern Star*, the case is not clear. A party in the company was alarmed at the absolutism of O'Connor, at the expenditure, and at their own helplessness to check or influence him. They called a meeting of directors and dissident representatives but O'Connor was not invited. Resolutions were passed condemning some of his methods, which belong to the Snigs End and Minster Lovell chapters. This precipitated a crisis. Feargus began efforts at direct alliance with the mass who only read his newspaper against the upper rebels who knew something more. He tried to invoke that power which he had once discovered in the Lancashire and Yorkshire meetings. The columns of the *Star* were turgid with rage. Drunken sots come among the society, he wrote, and cheat and run off. He had to travel from Snigs End to Bromsgrove and be back at Snigs End at midnight to sit up writing his defence against parties who never spoke to his face. His health and temper would not stand snarlings and carpings and poisoned arrows. He only wanted to be allowed to go if he was not wanted.

With the company unprotected by law, this was the solution which must never happen, as Feargus owned all the estates and the bank. Sir Benjamin Hall's report caused the House to decide, on 24 May 1848, to appoint a Select Committee to enquire into the company, before the second reading of the Bill. On 31 May the committee was named: O'Connor, Viscount Ingestre, Viscount Drumlanrig, the Judge Advocate (Mr Hayter), Messrs Henley, Langston, George Thompson, Sharman Crawford, Monsell, Sullivan, Stuart Wortley, Scholefield, Captain Pechell, Sir George Strickland, Sir Benjamin Hall. Three weeks later Mr Wortley was discharged, and Mr Walpole appointed in his place. They were empowered to call witnesses and take evidence, and to publish minutes of their meeting in a printed report. Five reports were issued, on 9, 21 and 30 June and 14 and 28 July, and the final recommendation appeared on 1 August 1848. This five-part report is the chief source of knowledge about the company.

The news that Parliament was going to examine the company produced a wave of enthusiasm, optimism and support for Feargus. Letters poured in to the *Star*. Hull branch arranged a tea party and ball in the Assembly Rooms, which they begged Feargus to attend. Paddington Chartists, at a public meeting proposed a scheme that the government should give them 1,000 acres of Epping Forest, on which they would locate 300 families. A landowner in Lincolnshire had divided his estate, Red Hall, into allotments modelled on O'Connor's, and now invited Feargus to come and act as auctioneer at the sale. He enjoyed this, and the affair was a great boost for him and the Land Company. The fact that subscriptions were being asked for losses at O'Connorville in Hertfordshire, to buy manure and seed, passed less noticed.

In fact, the members of the company believed, with Feargus, that one only had to examine the company to see its excellence. Its enemies were those who knew nothing first-hand about it, but were jealous of its success, jealous of O'Connor, and 'against the people'. The directors and Price the bank manager were less confident, but they believed that the reproductive principle of the company would work to provide continuing capital and that therefore basically the company was sound, and its success and size would induce the government to legalise it. They looked forward to the company being reorganised and properly staffed. The *Manchester Examiner*, on the other hand, quoted from *The Economist* on 27 June that the Irish characteristics of the Land Plan were its guarantee of failure—absence of capital, absence of combined labour and of machines, demand at one season for much more labour than the owner could supply and at another season lack of employment, and, above all, the accumulation of rent arrears.

CHAPTER 5

THE ENQUIRY, 1848

THE Select Committee met, and chose William Hayter, the Judge Advocate, as chairman. The other members were not chosen for a specific interest in smallholdings or agriculture, but, as most members of parliamentary committees are appointed, from both Houses and both parties, men who could be relied on to attend the meetings and to consider matters fairly. Sir Benjamin Hall may have applied to serve on it, as he undoubtedly wished to protect 'the people' from being swindled by O'Connor. Feargus hated him, and at times wrote ferociously about the chairman, but could not sustain any serious complaint about the rest of the committee.

The enquiry began with an examination of the formation, constitution and operation of the company. Chief witnesses called were Chinnery, Whitmarsh and Tid Pratt, the two Registrars, and M'Grath the financial secretary to the company. Step by step the whole unwise progress was traced; the half-moves to get registered, the refusals to spend or do what was necessary, the advertisements and persuasions of people to give money for shares in a company which did not exist, buying of property in defiance of legal instructions, the consequent necessity of vesting it all in O'Connor absolutely, the bank which was also illegally constituted and owned absolutely by O'Connor. The doubtful part played by W. P. Roberts was displayed; his being appointed treasurer and not doing the work, and the fact that he personally, and as the result of private loans to O'Connor, held the title deeds of the company's property. Legal costs for the company's business had so far netted him £3,823.

The committee pointed out that, with one share costing £1 6s od (£1·30), the company's membership of over 60,000, holding 180,000

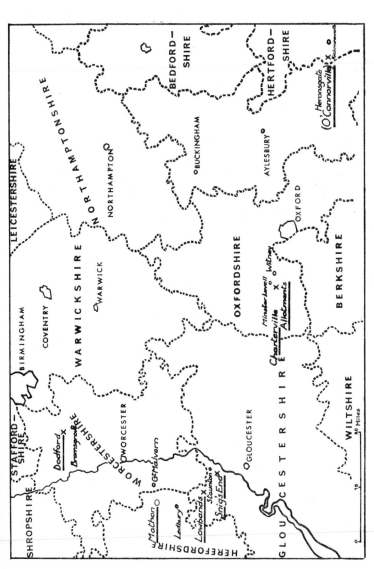

3 Map showing the position of all the Land Company estates

shares, meant a capital sum of £234,000, while the current set of rules stated that the capital was to be £130,000, with power to add £65,000, making a total of £195,000 as the limit. It was admitted that no allottee possessed a title in lease or a grant to his land, and no member got any interest on his share money. Chinnery said he was completely overwhelmed in the registration process by the vast number of names. 25,393 had signed. 'The proper and necessary regulations for the government of the company' had not been adhered to 'owing to the want of an expensive machinery in the way of a secretary and clerks'.

Philip M'Grath took a more robust line. He strongly supported Feargus on every point. He gave a lively account of the origins and growth of the company, of the working of the ballot, of the weekly receipts and transfer of money to the Land Bank or to M'Gowan for weekly payments of wages on the estates or expenses of building or farming materials. He alone passed on the receipts, and if he paid expenses before he passed them on, no one knew but his guardian angel and his little account book. Mr O'Connor, he said stoutly, was a very good man to work with. He averred that there was no dissatisfaction with the number of blanks in the ballot, no aggravation among the big landowner neighbours of the settled estates, no serious discontent among the allottees. They had not got titles or the vote, but everyone hoped these would come. Meantime they paid no rent. All irregularities he defended by saying that there was nothing else they could do at the time, but as soon as the company was legalised they would put all right.

At the second meeting, reported on 16 June, M'Grath continued his evidence, and O'Connor also spoke. M'Grath now defended the allottees, saying that only one had been before a magistrate, and that only for drunkenness. The schools were finished, and masters appointed to O'Connorville and to Lowbands. He and O'Connor spoke of the 250 houses built, the 16 miles of hedging planted at Lowbands, and the plantations of pear trees. Between them, they gave a convincing picture of sincerity and hard work. The committee did not doubt them. But other elements were needed to ensure the promised benefits for shareholders.

Price and M'Gowan spoke on the finances. Questioned about the finances of the *Northern Star*, M'Gowan said profits were a little up, and had averaged £90 a week over the last quarter. Price said O'Connor had instructed him to lend £6,391 from bank funds to the company before he took over the bank management. Bank officials' salaries were paid out of bank funds and not by the company. Capital, consisting of deposits, some held in Exchequer Bills and some on loan to the company, was £11,400. Price said the inexperienced staff of the company had done well, and kept honest, if rough, accounts. Nothing in their dealings was repugnant to the moral sense.

The third and fourth meetings were the crux of the enquiry. The first two had dealt with what had actually happened, good or bad. The next two dealt with prospects—whether the company had contrived a hopeless situation instead of a new life of opportunity for its allottees, and whether the form and operation of the company could ever produce the benefits it offered. Much fiercer wrestling developed in these two meetings.

The main witness was John Revans, a Poor Law specialist. He was now employed under the Poor Law Board to enquire into the operation of the present law of settlements which controlled workhouse and parish relief.

Revans told the committee that early in that year the board had asked him to visit the National Land Company estates, and see to what extent fresh settlements (roughly, rights to relief) would be obtained by allottees in the various parishes, and what might be the effect on poor rates of any sudden amount of population being thrown on the rates of poor agricultural parishes. He had gone round the estates at the end of March. The allotments were of a peculiar nature, different from anything existing in the country before. Large numbers of them could support men long enough to gain them a settlement in the parish, but there was no capital behind the allottees to carry them through bad years. He had learnt that the allottees were likely to remain tenants for some years before getting a title to their land. Even as tenants, they could obtain a settlement on the parish by renting a holding worth £10 a year in rent, occupying it for a year, residing there forty days, and paying poor rates. At Lowbands and Snigs End the 3- and 4-acre allotments would give a settlement; at Minster Lovell the 4-acre; at O'Connorville none would, as the biggest allotment only worked out at £8 17s (£8·85) a year rent, but most of the O'Connorville allottees attended parish meetings and were accepted as members of the parish, having resided there a year. It was therefore not too difficult to get a settlement, and uneasiness was on the side of the parishes rather than of the allottees. Their rural parishes were quite unable to raise a rate sufficient to support them. Rent was roughly 4 per cent of the total outlay on the allotment, but tenants could sub-let and get 5 or 6 per cent in rent, which would entitle the sub-tenants to a settlement. Rent of 30s (£1·50) an acre on the big Minster Lovell allotments would be 5 per cent, and this was not outrageous. Thus the conversion of a farm of 100 or 200 acres into fifty or sixty cottage allotments might suddenly reduce to nothing the value of every other property in the parish, by an enormous increase of poor rates. Revans quoted Cholesbury in Buckinghamshire as a place where this had happened.

The question for the Poor Law Board was—would the allottees fail? If they realised even moderately the expectations held out by Mr O'Connor, Revans said they would be no danger to the parish. Could a man make a living and pay rent on 4, 3 or 2 acres, with no capital? Revans was a believer in modern machine methods and an opponent of spade cultivation. He gave a blood-chilling account of Lowbands and O'Connorville, now in their second year of land-manuring and cultivation. Nine of O'Connorville's thirty-six settlers and six of Lowbands' forty had already fled. Manure had been provided for the land's first year, but now the dunghill by every gate had gone. One cow to ten allotments and a few pigs were the whole source of manure. By Mr O'Connor's forecasts there should have been eighty animals on each estate. No hay or straw was grown to mix with dung and make manure. One man even paid a neighbouring farmer 3s (15p) a week to graze his cow, and lost the manure thereby. Local farmers lent ploughs, seed drills, horses, even labour, to help the allottees, whom they described to Revans as poor things who could not bear the cold wind of March or a sudden hot spell in February. Many allottees sheltered indoors and hired a local man to dig for them, and paid 12s (60p) against the local 9s (45p) a week. How long could that last? Revans had asked other local men if they would be able to make a living on three acres, and pay the rent. They said they would like to try but would like to have Saturday night too, ie pay night.

Revans advanced to his conclusion. The advantage of the Land

Company allottees over most farmers was fixity of tenure. Most others were tenants-at-will and must keep their capital in a form in which they could take it away. This had ruined Irish agriculture. On the other hand, in Ireland all farmers were small farmers. The small man was not competing against the big skilled landowner as in England. On these National Land Company estates the allottees were as hopeless as hand-loom weavers against the power-loom, and knitting-needles against the stocking-frame. They even had to buy bread, because their wives could not bake. Revans had sent his conclusions to the Poor Law Board:

> That all those who occupy the Land Company's Allotments, with nothing more than the produce of their allotments to depend upon, will fail to obtain a living; that most who do occupy will continue in possession sufficiently long to acquire a settlement. And consequently that the operations of the Land Company are likely to lead to serious and sudden burthens upon the poor's rates of those parishes in which they acquire land.

Uproar broke out. An army of theories was ranged on either side, reinforced by men's hopes, convictions and needs. O'Connor was invited to answer Revans; he spoke for once without froth or malice. 'Well knowing that railways would only be a temporary speculation' he had sought a means to raise the lot of the working man. He was against both communism and socialism, and aimed at individuality of possession and co-operation of labour. 'I was determined to establish a settlement where the poor man could estimate the value of his own labour, below which he would not sell it in the market.' Passionately he relived the work he had done on the estates, his care for the allottees. He had provided 'a market, better than the gin-palace or the beer-shop, for those who had small savings to carry to the labour field'. While the country was agitating over the Ten Hours Bill his allottees worked from light to dark on their own land and went to their own beds instead of the workhouse. He had had no more notion of receiving £5,000 in subscriptions than of flying through the air. Out of bundles of papers he produced piles of unreadable accounts. The committee was convinced by his sincerity, and doubtful of his sanity.

His chief foreman, Henry Cullingham, the London builder who had been with him from the first plans for O'Connorville, was called. Like M'Grath, he spoke well for his master. Mr O'Connor attended to the

Land Company affairs from 5 am to 11 or 12 at night. Tradesmen and workmen were always paid, even if Mr O'Connor had sometimes to pay out of his own pocket. The men kept a sharp eye on the pay. Every halfpenny received from Mr O'Connor and paid out on Saturday night was receipted and noted. His cash book for small bills for smith's work, corn, turnpike charges etc, and his day book for daily work by contractors were produced, correct. Since Mr O'Connor entered Parliament, Cullingham advised him how much would be needed for wages each week, and he sent Cullingham the sum, say £250, and Cullingham and Mr King and other foremen paid what was due. Cullingham balanced the books and either gave Mr O'Connor the balance or held it over. This was always done on Sunday morning after paying out.

The committee ascertained that no allottee had yet paid the company any rent. It went on to the bitter question of whether any man could, and these allottees would, raise a family and pay rent on 2, 3 or 4 acres. Revans and Feargus fired off everything each one knew on his side. The committee listened, letting each man speak as he would. Feargus made wild estimates which irritated his listeners. When he said that one allottee got £50 for half an acre of cabbage, Revans said bluntly he did not believe him. They questioned an outside smallholder, John Sillett from Kelsale, near Saxmundham in Suffolk. He had been a grocer and draper, and then acquired a house and two acres. For seven years he had worked these acres with a three-pronged fork, and kept himself, wife and family as well as when he was a grocer.

Michael Sullivan, a committee member, visited Snigs End and Lowbands one weekend, travelling by train to Gloucester and by open carriage to the estates. He told the committee that he had examined crops, houses, bedrooms, kitchens, piggeries. He was very surprised at the high standard of building and cultivation on Lowbands. Wheat and potatoes were as good as any farmer's. There was only one cow, as everyone was changing over to pigs. He spoke to a cotton overseer, framework knitter, tallow chandler, stocking maker, cabinetmaker, shoemaker, cotton spinner. His visit is described in Chapter 9.

The committee pressed O'Connor on why the allottees had no title or security, and why he did not transfer the property to them or to trustees. He gave an answer of mixed anger, contempt and nonsense.

He demanded to have the public excluded from committee meetings, saying that garbled reports were reaching the papers. The committee allowed his request.

Feargus slipped out of London and went down to Herefordshire. The Mathon estate was offered for sale again, and he bought it for £15,000, and paid a further deposit.[33] He agreed to complete the purchase by 29 September. No matter what the committee said, he was carrying on the company.

The committee had heard the company's side at length. It now advanced to present the public's, or the Government's, side. First, the Government accountant, Mr W. H. Grey, stated that Mr O'Connor's accounts were unintelligible as presented. No original balance sheets audited by Messrs Cuffey and Knight, the auditors named in the company publicity, had been produced, but only copies or newspaper copies of ten or eleven balance sheets which were different from O'Connor's own unaudited accounts.

Feargus replied by offering to show Grey all necessary papers if he would come down into the country with him. Very co-operatively Grey agreed, and left London with O'Connor, whom he must have regarded as likely to go off his head or try some money swindle and certain to have uncomfortable notions of hospitality. They went to Great Dodford, and lodged, perhaps at some farmhouse where Feargus lived during his visits, or perhaps at the Dodford Inn. Grey came back an ally of Feargus, though not of the Land Company. He reported to the committee that Feargus had shown him a mass of papers, though not the audited originals which he had promised. Roughly £109,000 had passed through Feargus's hands, and Grey had traced the amount at the London Joint Stock Bank, the Witney Bank and the Gloucestershire Banking Co. Mr O'Connor's accounts were sadly confused, but

from the frank and open manner in which everything has been submitted to my inspection, and from the readiness with which every enquiry of mine has been met, I am thoroughly satisfied, not only that the whole of the money has been honourably appropriated and is fully accounted for, but also that several thousand pounds more of Mr O'Connor's own funds have been applied in furtherance of the views of the National Land Company.

In fact, ever since Feargus saw the threat of a parliamentary enquiry coming, the falling off of subscriptions, and the refusal of most of the allottees to pay rent, he had been financing the building of Great Dodford himself rather than draw on any of the Exchequer Bills which were all that was left of the company's capital in cash. The stock-broker held £6,000 worth, and the bank manager £8,000 worth, bought with members' deposits of £16,000, and therefore owing interest to the depositors. The company owed the bank £6,000, £320 interest on this sum, and £142 on current salaries for the year. The bank had available only £9,000.

The company was almost out of funds. Were its constitution and prospects worth backing by legalising it, offering shares in it to the public, or any other means? Edward Lawes, the barrister who drew up the Public Health Act, was called. He said that the company was established for the purpose of a lottery, where many paid for a few to gain, and the banking business was a fundamental part of it. O'Connor's offer to give interest of 1 per cent on members' subscriptions made no difference, since to pay interest as long as people subscribe to a lottery scheme does not make it cease to be a lottery. The bank was essential to the reproductive principle on which the finances of the company were founded, and a society established for a part purpose of banking was not one to which the Act for Friendly Societies could apply.

What then of the Joint Stock Companies Acts? Registration under them would not remove the bar of illegality of operating a business by lottery. To all the turnings and twistings and offers to abandon the lottery by O'Connor and the other directors, Lawes stolidly presented the fact that the subscriptions of 70,000 people had been needed to locate 250. No man's single subscription would locate him, for the cost of location moved between £200 for the smallest and £300 for the largest allotment.

An analysis of the company's finances was then presented by Lawes and by Finlaison, an actuary of the National Debt. Almost half the 70,000 membership had fully paid up. M'Grath's account showed total receipts of roughly £91,000: some £35,000 had been spent on buying land, and £50,000 on forming and building estates, making some £86,000 cash spent altogether. £4,000 odd was listed by M'Grath under expenses of management. Apart from £3,000 or £4,000 which might be owing to O'Connor, the cash assets were £7,093. This tallied with Price's statement earlier. The company owed the Land Bank £6,853, authorised by O'Connor, and made up of debt, interest on it and some unpaid salaries. The real surplus was £240. The O'Connorville estate had to pay two life annuities, the Charterville and Snigs End estates had each to pay interest on mortgages. Half the aid money was still to be paid. Whether the estate of Mathon, of which the purchase was never completed, was included, is not clear, but the point makes little difference to the bankrupt picture. Ground rents were calculated at 5 per cent on a value of £209 for 2-acre allotments, £254 for 3-acre, and £300 for 4-acre. If all allottees paid all their rent without costs to collect it, the total would be £2,841 a year.

The reproductive principle was to work by selling or mortgaging this £2,841 (increasing as new estates were built and worked) and mortgaging the land and cash property of the company. The number of subscribers was around 70,000. At £300 each for location, the sum needed was £21 million. Fully paid up at an average of £3 18s (£3·90) for 3 shares, 70,000 shareholders would bring in a capital of £273,000. The most optimistic mortgage rate at the time was two-thirds of the value. The first mortgage on £273,000 would yield £182,000; when mortgaged, that would yield £121,333, and so on in amounts diminishing by a third each time. At the fifteenth mortgage the gain would be £936, and vanishing point would be the eighteenth mortgage when the gain would be £210, or not enough to locate one man. £546,114 would then have been raised on the original capital, making a total of £819,114. This would locate 2,730 people at £300 each. 67,270 members, whose money had paid for the others, would remain unprovided for. On its own principle the company was shown to be able to locate only one thirty-fifth of its shareholders.

That result concerned money only. Concerning time, the result was as bad. If all the capital were mortgaged and a new estate bought and built within one year, the company would take 75 years to house its members. If mortgaging and building occupied two years, the company would house them in 150 years, and so on. Money and time; two realities Feargus had never faced.

He could not now bear reality. At his best, he answered confusedly, brokenly, turning over papers, searching for escape in some list he had never compiled, some figures he had never made out. More often he was frivolous, answering irrelevantly, making puns of the questions or the committee members' names, throwing papers in the air, loosing what he meant to be deadly darts of insolence at the chairman. None of the committee now thought him sane. More than ever, it was their concern to rescue the 70,000 poor men from his power. The last fact-finding report of the committee was dated 21 July.

On 30 July, at 5 pm, the verdict of the committee was read to the House of Commons. There were five points and an opinion. First and second, that O'Connor's bill was useless because the National Land Company was not consistent with the principles of Friendly Societies. Third, that the company as at present constituted was illegal and would not fulfil the expectations held out by the directors to the shareholders. Fourth, that the records and accounts had been most imperfectly kept, but that the irregularity had been against Mr O'Connor's interest and not in his favour, so that he was owed a sum of nearly £3,400. Fifth, that so many people were concerned in the company, and all had been conducted with such good faith, that the committee suggested that parties concerned might be permitted, if they so desired, to wind up the undertaking and relieve themselves from the penalties to which they had subjected themselves. At the end, the committee showed its comprehension of the human hopes and longings involved in the company's short career, by giving its opinion 'that it should be left entirely open to the parties concerned to propose to Parliament any new measure for the purpose of carrying out the expectations and objects of the promoters of the company'.

Feargus had time to get his presentation of the verdict into the *Northern Star* of 1 August. Poor man! The faithful bailiff and father of his children had never given them the smallest warning that any danger threatened the plan he was unfolding and sharing with them. Now he had to say at once that it was condemned. From his words, his unsophisticated readers would only dimly guess it. He was jubilant at the personal vindication of himself over the company's money. He assured everyone that although it looked bad that he owned all the property, he had made a will on the day before the April meeting on Kennington Common, leaving everything to two trustees for the National Land Company. He recalled that Finlaison had said that the plan of the com-

Page 65 O'Connorville: (*above*) original allottees: (left) Thomas Meyrick; (right) Philip Ford; (*below*) a pair of semi-detached two-storey cottages. Entrance is through kitchens at the side. The right-hand cottage is unaltered except for the windows

Page 66 O'Connorville: (*above*) an original cottage at left, facing left, has been incorporated into a larger building; (*below*) the school building altered into a private house, The Grange

pany was practicable, and that public money on the scale necessary was subscribed to many railway and mining schemes. But O'Connor gave no clue as to whether the company was to continue or not. He wrote as if its future were no concern of his.

CHAPTER 6

FAILURE FROM WITHIN

THREE years now followed in which something was always about to be done, and nothing was done, to save the company. The veteran Thomas Wheeler made the most hopeful effort, but the largest part of all efforts went on getting one's share money back or picking up a bit of land cheap, or proving one had been right, and on venting frustration and disappointment in furious rage of accusation. This was encouraged by the Press, which tempted the allottees with seeing their names in print, and sent reporters, often incognito, round the estates to collect spicy items.

Four main parties were concerned: the allottees, who understood two things, that they could pay no rent, and that they must get a title to their land; the mass of unlocated shareholders, who wanted no one to get a penny before the final divi, and all the back rent of allottees to be paid in to swell the common pool; the directors and staff who wanted to extricate themselves from sharing responsibility with Feargus; and O'Connor himself, who wanted all his past expenditure repaid before the divi, and his expenses paid for libel actions and recovery actions arising out of his position as director of the company.

Feargus was faced with paying for two libel actions, the cost of getting the Winding-Up Bill through Parliament, falling circulation of the *Northern Star*, three sets of mortgage payments or annuities, and with building the estate at Great Dodford. Most of these were the company's liabilities and not his own. But the company had no cash, and subscriptions had fallen right away to £33, with £50 to the bank, in the week of 19 August. His children, the members of the company, had become his enemies, and so he felt them to be.

Feargus was noticeably broken, his red hair fading to white, and his ability to attend to conversation much interrupted. He made no effort to meet the world of his day, even in dress, but wore the old-style stockings, buckled shoes, brass-buttoned coat and white hat while rambling on his solitary walks round shops and markets. He had lodgings in Notting Hill Gate Terrace, and also spent time with his sister Harriet who lived in Colham House, Hillingdon and later in 18 Albert Terrace, Notting Hill.[34] His biographers say that he was drinking brandy heavily.[35]

W. P. Roberts seems to have renewed his connection with the company, and his influence over O'Connor. He certainly came out of the whole story as a leading landowner of the allotments, though the part he played is not known in real detail. He held a meeting of shareholders in London in August and brought forward propositions to locate members by bonuses (ie cash payments) instead of by ballot, owners to pay for property by instalments, and roughly to double the price of shares.[36] At this point, perhaps under his influence, Feargus went through the motions of formally separating the bank from the Land Company, and called a conference for 30 October.

He went on a speaking tour of Scottish branches, and had a personal triumph as reported in the *Northern Star*. Edinburgh greeted him with long-continued cheering, and the branch wrote a poem in his honour.

The October conference was the first sinister sign of lifelessness in the company, for it made no positive approach or beginning. It agreed with what O'Connor had already written, that the company must be registered under the Joint Stock Companies Act, the lottery be given up and location be by payment, or bonus, from then on. It denounced the refusal of the allottees to pay rent as defrauding the company, and idleness.

O'Connor went round all the estates, jollied the allottees along, tried to persuade the angry and disillusioned to stay, reviled the Press, and remitted all rents for another year. Demands poured in from the branches to turn the idle so-and-sos out of the land and houses, and let people get in who would do some work. It did not pass unnoticed that allottees who refused to pay the company any rent were often letting their land or houses to others, even non-members, and drawing good rent for them.

In January 1849 the directors (under O'Connor) began a long-drawn-out effort to compel the Registrar to register the company under the Joint Stock Companies Act. They made application in the Hilary Term 1849 to the Court of Queen's Bench for an order compelling the Registrar to register the company or to show reasons why he would not. For a year the two sides went on sparring, while an extension of the provisional registration was granted.

While the case hung suspended, building continued at Great Dodford, and sowing and planting on the other estates. The purchase of Mathon had to be completed by 29 September, or the property would be put up for sale again, and Feargus was trying hard to whip up subscriptions. He roared and cajoled in the *Northern Star*, but the spirit was gone and the money did not come in. In February next year he wrote that he had sent back all the subscriptions for Mathon.

He proposed sales of the estates to terrify the allottees into paying their rents. Charterville was now recognised by the authorisation of a post office. James Beattie was leading a malignant dissident group there. Loyal Cullingham and Doyle kept a pro-O'Connor party alive at Snigs End. Price, the bank manager, was in charge of O'Connorville, and wrote that all that was needed was £1 a head to buy pigs. At Lowbands the schoolmaster, O'Brien, was fast making a following for himself instead of for Feargus. At Great Dodford, location day was 2 July, and more complaints broke out from there almost at once. Sporadic attempts were made by individuals to sue O'Connor for their share money on the grounds that the company was illegal and exploded. Judges were cautious and mostly discouraged these efforts, though one or two pleas succeeded.

Another conference was announced for August 1849 at Snigs End, to decide whether to wind up the company or not. Feargus announced the formation of a new society, on 27 July. It was to be the National Freehold Benefit Friendly Society, with shares at £15, the same directors as the National Land Company, and the same Roberts as solicitor and O'Connor as treasurer. The office was still 144 High Holborn, and the bank was the National Land and Labour Bank. Tid Pratt was said to have agreed to register it as a Friendly Society.

At the same time, Feargus wrote to Queen Victoria, beginning 'Well Beloved Cousin', referring to his city of Cork and his ancestral home, his sacrifices and patriotism, and ending 'I remain Your Majesty's Cousin, Feargus, Rex, by the Grace of the People.'

Early in August 1849 the last land conference was held at Snigs End, where a cheerful situation was reported, even if no one had paid any rent. Deputies from other estates came, as well as company delegates, though these had no power to vote. All the grievances were aired: failure to pay up £200,000 on share money, houses standing empty while 390 members awaited locations drawn in the ballot, no leases made out. The conference promised location to the 390 on the next estate. Feargus was now indifferent to the whole business. He said he could not give leases until the future of the company had been decided by Act of Parliament, or the Press would jump on him as making away with the land. He gave an account of £1,200 received by him since the 1848 report from sales of material or allotments. A *Northern Star* report of May 1851 says that Mr Grey, the accountant, was at this conference and confirmed the claim.

The calculation of rents on each estate was going on slowly. Mr Grey had brought some order into the accounts, and the results were announced in November 1849. Everyone was to pay six months' rent on 12 November, and no more till the following year. Then O'Connor-ville and Lowbands would owe $2\frac{1}{2}$ years' rent on 1 November 1850, Snigs End would owe $1\frac{1}{2}$ years' rent on the same day, and Charterville would owe $1\frac{1}{2}$ years' rent on 1 September 1850. Six months' rent varied as follows:

4 acres, between £7 10s (£7·50) and £6
3 acres, between £6 10s (£6·50) and £5 8s (£5·40)
2 acres, between £5 10s (£5·50) and £4 5s (£4·25)

O'Connor took boat for Ireland in November, but the Irish had forgotten him, and there was no reality, except in Feargus's fancy, in an alliance of English and Irish working classes under him, so he was back in London in December. Secret conversations had begun about recovery of the Charterville estate by Weaving and Pinnock, the mortgagees. Feargus now spoke with a new threat. He reckoned he had paid £1,000 in interest on the mortgages on Snigs End and Charterville, interest which was supposed to be paid out of the rents. From now on he would cease to be the buffer between the allottees and the mortgagees. Interest would be paid direct by the rents, and Mr Roberts, the company solicitor, would collect the rents and sue or evict every non-paying allottee.

All the unlocated members were in favour of ejecting non-paying allottees, and many wrote to say so. But everyone was shaken when in January 1850 the mortgagees of Charterville issued sixty-eight orders of ejectment against the allottees for non-payment of rent. Forty-one of them petitioned Parliament in February, saying they would pay rent if they received a title to their land. In panic, a faithful few on the estates wrote in, among them Cullingham and Doyle, saying they feared to pay rent because it would make them tenants of their dear old friend Mr O'Connor, whereas they hoped to obtain a title to their plots and be independent. It was the heart of the gospel that had been heard by those without hope, and to which they still clung.

In February Feargus started an action for libel against Bradshaw, editor of the *Nottingham Journal*, for writing that he had 'wheedled the people of England out of £100,000 with which he has bought estates and conveyed them to his own use and benefit'. The defence produced very damaging evidence, although the jury recorded that O'Connor's personal honesty was unimpeached.

One more northern speech tour in March, and the end was upon him. On his return, Feargus was questioned in the House as to when he was going to introduce the Bill to wind up the company. On 30 March 1850 he announced in the House that he would introduce it after the Easter recess.

He still concealed the fact of failure from himself by the hope that a decision against the Registrar in the Court of Queen's Bench might effect the registration of the company under the Joint Stock Companies Acts. But on 8 June 1850 the *Northern Star* published the final blow— the decision of that court, under Lord Campbell, to uphold the refusal of the Registrar to register the company. Grounds for the decision were: the company was not a joint stock company; it was not run for the profit of the company; profits and advantages on an allotment would belong to the owner, not the company; the rent was not a profit but a further subscription to buy more land.

Nobody was really surprised by the verdict of the law, though there was a general renewal of anger and recrimination. Roberts took

O'Connor up north in July on a speaking tour, perhaps to keep him on the move and away from London. They remarked on the apathy which met them everywhere, but to Roberts, making his careful anodyne speech after each of Feargus's, this was no doubt more welcome than being torn to pieces. On their return, Feargus announced that his suit for ejectment at Charterville had succeeded at the Oxford Assizes, and now the estate could be sold, thank God. He went off to Paris to see his uncle Arthur, who was ninety-one and had lived for fifty-one years in France; he made no effort to detain Feargus with him.

On 9 July 1850 a petition to bring in a Bill to wind up the company was presented to Parliament, signed by the four directors and O'Connor.

Unexpected support for the Land Company came from the economist Harriet Martineau, who lived at Clappersgate, near Ambleside, in Westmorland. In August and October she wrote two long letters to the manager of Guiltcross Workhouse on the capabilities of $2\frac{1}{4}$ acres of land to support, in security and full, varied diet, her small household of five, with the labour of one man from the workhouse. These letters were quoted in the *Northern Star*. She gave an immensely successful picture, every practical detail worked in, but free from those money fantasies which made Feargus's sketches of allottees' life incredible.

At the same time Price wrote a strong defence of the conduct of the Land Bank, to refute accusations by 'The Whistler' in the *Manchester Examiner*. When he took charge on 27 September 1847, the bank had fourteen benefit societies' accounts, and eighty-seven had since opened. No person or society asking for his money back had failed to get both principal and interest on the day the money was due; there had been no swindle, no breaking up. He was continuing to transact business and to open daily, with the same staff of clerks and the same manager as in 1847.

Feeling grew that Feargus and Roberts were taking a cut out of the funds before the divi. Newspaper attacks and rowdyism at meetings increased during the autumn of 1850, no doubt inflamed by the fact that O'Connor now referred all matters of cash to Roberts to deal with, repeating that the mortgagees could now screw the rent out of the Charterville allottees instead of out of himself. He did, however, make a successful trip to his constituency at Nottingham, 'to resign his seat', as a result of calumny and persecution. Like the Shakespearean crowd when Caesar refused the crown, the Nottingham crowd, with 'a considerable number of females', sighed for him and voted a resolution asking him to continue as their Member. The same citizens later had a rowdy meeting, with scuffles and shouting, to force all allottees to pay rent or get out. On 16 November a notice appeared, signed by Roberts, that application had been made to Parliament to bring in the Winding-Up Bill in the next session.

Disintegration was proceeding to chaos, as concern for the divi sharpened. Share sums were small, but men were prepared to murder one another for 26s (£1·30), as any newspaper would show. Beattie, from Charterville, was tramping the countryside with support from the Press, including the *Illustrated London News*, to raise funds to start an action in Chancery against O'Connor. An O'Connor Defence Fund was started, to meet his legal costs in the Bradshaw libel action and ten other actions in which he was concerned. The publisher of the *Northern Star*, now William Rider, was in charge of this as well as of the fund for the Winding-Up Bill.

CHAPTER 7

DISINTEGRATION AND THE END

MR FAGAN, MP for Cork, introduced the Bill on 10 February 1851. On 15 February the *Northern Star* came out, and members seized the paper to read the text of their Bill. But no text was printed. The paper only stressed that allottees who paid rent would get leases for ever and those who did not would be ejected. The public had to get its information from the hostile Press. They read in the text of the Bill, among other points, that it was found expedient to abandon the undertaking of the National Land Company in order to protect Feargus O'Connor and the promoters from legal proceedings and demands for return of subscriptions. Alarms and conspiracies flared in every branch. Committees met to devise clauses to protect their particular share of the divi, and to petition against clauses which they feared would impair it. Patrick O'Brien, from Lowbands schoolhouse, actually wrote to Fagan asking him to introduce a compensation clause to save 120 families from being destroyed, 'who have been decoyed from their homes and regular avocations' by Feargus O'Connor. O'Brien did not blench at asking for compensation for those who had received all the benefits bought by the other 70,000 members, nor at jumping on the bandwaggon to hound his countryman and friend, to whom personally he still owed money. It stands to the credit of the city of Exeter branch that they wrote sternly of O'Brien, who came from Exeter, recalling that, far from being decoyed, he had petitioned O'Connor personally to get him on to Lowbands estate. Three allottees of Charterville were at present imprisoned in Oxford gaol for payment of costs for the action by the mortgagees to recover rent. The possibility of unpleasant consequences all round after the removal of the company's protection began to penetrate the inexperienced minds of branch committee men.

They continued to stir up the storm, but now began also to look for shelter from it.

The groundwork of their ideas was that the estates must not be broken up and sold off at a loss. The deposits in the Land Bank must also be kept together and used for the members. The directors and the lawyers were not to get their hands on them. All kinds of curious schemes were put forward, but the only one that actually got under way was Thomas Wheeler's National Land and Labour Loan Society. At a public meeting in the City Chartist Hall in London on 23 April, the proposals were explained. Shareholders were asked to deposit their share scrips with the new society, so that it could buy a great deal of the old company property. If the estates sold at a high price they would increase the assets for the divi, and if at a low price the society could buy more of them. Later, Wheeler said that they had £20,000 in sums under the price of one share, £1 6s (£1·30), which would not be included in the divi. They must begin again, buy the estates back, gather the shareholders and make a better plan, and combine manufacturing with agriculture. A few weeks later the name of the new society was changed at the suggestion of Tid Pratt to the National Loan Society, and enrolled as such, with the security of the law.

Meantime, Feargus got wind of the plans to have the Bill altered in committee. He knew himself to be at some risk of unlimited liability towards the company. He was ill again during April and May, but ordered himself sufficiently to execute a covering movement. In April he served the directors with a notice that on 31 March 1851 he had signed a deed making over absolutely to his private solicitor, Marshall Turner, the debt of £3,299 which in the year 1848 was found to be due from the Land Company to himself, and all further debts or sums due to him from the company, and that in consequence of this deed he had ceased to have any personal pecuniary interest whatsoever in the company which could be made available to the bank depositors. The directors had swallowed this, but on 17 May a notice appeared in the *Northern Star* that by the unanimous decision of the directors of the Land Company the bank would be closed until Mr O'Connor was repaid the £3,000 or £4,000 which he was owed. The notice was signed by the bank manager, T. Price.

The directors, Dixon, Doyle, M'Grath and Clark, refused to

swallow this. In plain terms they denied any hand in the business or any knowledge of it except the deed of 31 March. O'Connor had had sole responsibility and direction of the bank since 1848. Certainly the directors were no match for Roberts and Feargus. However, they were roused now, and went on to object to the amount assumed in the notice to be owed to O'Connor. Since August 1849 he had 'received several thousand pounds on account of the company, of the appropriation of which we, in common with the shareholders, know nothing'.

Feargus was recovering, and came back fast at them. A directors' meeting had complained that the rent of the bank office and the salaries of the manager and two clerks were injurious to the company. Therefore, of course, the bank must be closed. O'Connor was liable for the salaries from 1850 but not earlier. He had given an account of his money transactions at the conference in 1849. Mr Grey had then said he was owed £1,200, which, added to the sum the Select Committee had named, and interest and legal expenses on both, made £5,320. Interest on mortgage payments and rent and taxes on the company office brought the total of the company's debt to him to £6,320. He had paid into the bank in 1849 and 1851 £3,606, and his travelling expenses during the life of the company were £2,000, which made £5,606. So he was owed altogether £11,926. On the other hand, he had received from sales of horses, goods and stabling, and from rents £4,930. So the company owed him only £7,000.

This was the kind of accounting to which the House of Commons had become accustomed at the hands of O'Connor. Its members, however, were business men and could deal with him, while they recognised that the shareholders of the Land Company could not. The result of Feargus's move was that when the parliamentary committee met on the Bill ten days later, with counsel for the promoters and for the allottees and shareholders, it decided to strike the bank's expenditure out of the preamble and throw all its expenses on to O'Connor. Wheeler's new Loan Society received the blow that the £20,000 to which they had referred would count among the assets of the company, and could not be the perks of the Loan Society. The society and other small movements withered away after this.

Clark, a director, wrote to the *Northern Star* advising members of the company to employ counsel to examine O'Connor's claims before the Master in Chancery. He said that the Charterville allotments, sold by the mortgagees, were selling at a huge loss, £46 per acre. The cost of the land alone was £32 per acre, which meant that for the house, preparation of the allotment, and share of the cost of building the estate and schoolhouse, only £14 was paid.

On 19 July the Bill was passed, and on 7 August received the Royal Assent. The company was to be dissolved and wound up by an official manager under a Master in Chancery, following the procedure laid down in the Joint Stock Companies' Winding-Up Act of 1848. The company should be deemed to have been a company within the provisions of that Act. All property and assets were vested in the official manager as tenant, and all responsibility for payments or repayments lay with him. Assets were to be sold and invested in Exchequer Bills. Costs of the Act and all charges to which the company or Feargus O'Connor as chairman or general manager might be liable, would be paid off first, before paying out the divi. The promoters would be protected from legal proceedings and demands for return of subscriptions. There was no inclusion of the bank.

Any allottee who had no conveyance would be invited to prove his title and take a conveyance, and pay such sum as rent for past occupation as the Master should decide after making allowance for his work. The title was to be fee simple in possession, subject to payment to the company of a perpetual fee-farm rent charge for the allotment, to be fixed by the Master. The conveyance should be to the allottee and his heirs for ever, on condition of paying the rent charge. If he failed to pay for a year, the official manager had the right of re-entry or of taking the property back. No allottee who kept his allotment and had a conveyance should be entitled to any dividend from the assets.

Roberts said later, in an affidavit, that shortly before the passing of the Bill O'Connor left England without telling him or Chinnery, and leaving no instructions. Roberts therefore assumed responsibility in O'Connor's name. The official manager was clearly a vital figure. Lobbying began at once among all the contestants. The branches wanted a man who understood local views, and were suspicious of London fellows. Twelve nominations were made, mostly counting less than 500 votes. Three had notable slants, Price the bank manager, with 700 votes; Ernest, who was put up by the Charterville party and claimed that the allottees had peculiar interests which needed representation, and Ainger* who was put up by Roberts with a circular which said that those who could not write their names need only put a mark. Ainger collected 2,000 of these votes. Grey, the Government accountant, was nominated, proposed by Thomas Wheeler. William Goodchap, from a legal firm in the City which was accustomed to winding up companies and was totally unconnected with the Land Company, was also nominated. He recorded an objection to Ainger, Price and Ernest, as involved in the affairs of the company.

O'Connor was absent, and according to his sister was in Leghorn. Roberts applied to the Master in Chancery for the order to wind up the company in O'Connor's name, without saying he was missing. During September the Master in Chancery, Humphrey, called a shareholders' meeting at his office in Southampton Buildings to hear the claims of candidates. Such a crowd arrived that he had to order an adjournment to the Vice-Chancellor's court at Lincoln's Inn. There he conducted a meeting which became extremely warm. Candidates objected to other candidates, and when accusations began to fly the Master adjourned again until 23 September.

O'Connor was still missing, and Roberts was still in charge of affairs. In the interval many stories and complaints had reached the Master, who arrived in a stern mood. Arguments began again at once. It was said that in canvassing for Ainger, 'a vast quantity of ale and spirituous liquors have been consumed' amounting to bribery and contrary to the usages of the High Court of Chancery. The courses pursued had been very improper. Roberts's counsel urged that it was necessary to make speed, as many poor people were involved. The Master requested that Roberts should provide a full, clear affidavit on why he had procured the order for winding up the company in the absence of Mr O'Connor. He adjourned the meeting till 30 September.

Feargus suddenly reappeared in England, and the Master invited him to be present at this meeting. Roberts's affidavit was then read. It stated his long connection with the company as solicitor appointed by the general body of shareholders, and his responsibility in Mr O'Connor's absence. An affidavit from Chinnery supported it, giving details

* This name is also spelt Angier.

of his search for O'Connor. This was followed by an affidavit from
Feargus himself, recognising and approving all that Roberts had done,
and saying his absence was due to ill-health. Feargus sat heavy and
silent. Whatever anyone thought of the origin of this affidavit, the
Master would not argue with it. He said that the connection between
Roberts and O'Connor was not clear. He would make an announcement later.

On 4 October William Goodchap was named manager. He was free
from involvement in any of the company's interests, and he demon-
strated the best of law by acting with justice, promptness and benevolence. He started work at once. At each place he invited every allottee
to come before him, either to claim a title and agree to pay rent, or to
relinquish his land and claim compensation for loss in respect of it. Any
subscribers to the company might attend all sittings. The history of
Goodchap's work belongs with the estates.

From now on the story of the National Land Company is dispersed
into the affairs of each estate. The final account is lost. No report to
Parliament was required by the Winding-Up Act, the case was probably transferred to the bankruptcy files, and since it hung on well after
the sale of the estates in 1857 and 1858, interest had moved away and I
have found no paper which reported it. The final divi, if any, is not
known. I have tried, too, to trace William Goodchap, without success.
In fact, I have found no later history of any Land Company character
except Philip M'Grath, of whom Gammage says in his *History of the
Chartist Movement* that he went into business in an assurance company
and lived in London.

Was the Land Plan, if properly organised, a possible one? Are smallholdings valuable or workable? Do they contribute to the national
economy and the national life, on which the personal life depends?
These questions are asked in every period, and each settlement venture
relates to the conditions of its own time. Of the Land Company, they
were asked particularly in connection with Charterville, in surveys of
the agriculture of Oxfordshire, and in connection with Great Dodford
by Birmingham radicals. I have taken a brief glance at them at the end
of their stories.

O'Connor's responsibility is complete. Insufferable as are 'verdicts'
upon one historical period by another, this one has the ground of seeing

the case as the people concerned saw it. O'Connor claimed that he alone invented, produced and operated the Land Company, and we now can agree that this is true and that he so made it that it destroyed itself by its own method of existence, the lottery. But without the lottery none of the 70,000 poor would have subscribed their savings. Without the craziness of O'Connor the estates would not have been bought, and without his energy the 250 houses would not have been built. No more is due to him. He made and he killed the Land Company. Later happiness on the estates was due to English social development unconnected with O'Connor.

While the company ministered to his need for admiration and success, he lived wholly in it and for it. He had always chosen to be on his own, and when breakdown threatened he had no business backing and no social or political group which could support the company. Neither did he have the law, for he had chosen to do without it. That he became insane is not wholly relevant. His choices were made long before Land Company days—when he broke with the Chartist leaders, with the Whig party, with O'Connell, and with the schoolmaster's daughter, and when he agreed with his father to hold himself above the common world around him. This central choice, continuingly renewed with each change of circumstance and opportunity, moulded his history and drew on his insanity.

*   *   *   *   *   *

Curiosity and piety both ask for one more conclusion to be told. Feargus was back in England, and had to give evidence frequently before the Master in charge of the winding-up. He had sold the *Northern Star* in January 1852. In February the paper reported that his mental state made proceedings before the Master painful and impossible. The other directors, too, needed counsel to help them order their evidence. The editor expressed surprise that the solicitor of the company, who had made so much money out of it, had not engaged counsel to watch over and help O'Connor and the directors. A good accountant could sort the mass of material which lay on the table before O'Connor at enquiries while he sat there and said he knew nothing of it. His behaviour encouraged those who said he had taken the money and now refused to account for it.

Roberts seems not to have helped Feargus at all in public, whatever he may have done in private. At a long meeting in early February 1852, Roberts resisted the request of the court to produce the bank books and the title deeds of the company's property which he held in return for loans to O'Connor. Only when the Master said that his fees would be the first debt paid by the company share-out did he relax his attitude of a wolf snarling at the entrance to his cave.

In February Feargus made a row at the Lyceum theatre and assaulted a policeman, for which he spent seven days in Coldbath Fields prison. News began to get round that he was neglected and in want, and working-class generosity sprang up again. A fund was started in March, and allottees and members subscribed their small sums. By April people were speaking of a commission of lunacy. Feargus smelt it, and secretly took the train to Liverpool. A friend followed him, and early next morning saw him slip out from his hotel and board the *Europa*, which was due to sail for the United States of America. He spoke to Feargus on board, down in the saloon where Feargus was sheltering from chance eyes on the dockside. He described him in the *The Star of Freedom*; 'the eye dulled, speech rambled to twenty different subjects'. He left him standing vacantly in the ship's saloon.

At the beginning of June he was back again, and made another scene in the House of Commons. He was arrested and detained in the Palace of Westminster. Feargus considered himself as a state prisoner, and regarded his confinement with grave pride. The House formed a committee to consider his needs, and called in Dr Harrington Tuke, a mental doctor who kept a hospital or clinic for the insane at Chiswick. There Feargus was conveyed in the middle of June, still thinking himself a great man in honourable confinement, willing to lodge with Dr Tuke.

From then on he was mostly forgotten. His sister, Miss O'Connor, visited him, and periodically made trouble with Dr Tuke. On 22 February 1853 *The Times* published a letter from the doctor asking the paper to correct reports appearing in the Hammersmith papers. He wrote that O'Connor had no idea that he was under restraint. His solicitor, nephew and sister visited him regularly, and other friends now and again. 'The amount of money belonging to Mr O'Connor is much exaggerated.' The nephew, Roger, also wrote to *The Times* in Feb-

Page 83 Lowbands school building: (*above*) the almost unaltered front;
(*below*) the back, now the modern entrance to a private house

Page 84 Smallholdings today: (*above*) the original aim of the Land Company achieved; (*below*) five neighbours in a sylvan setting

ruary, defending the doctor and the clinic from complaints made by
Feargus's sister. Both he and Dr Tuke thought Feargus 'would much
lament any forced change of residence for him'. At this time Feargus
was moderately happy, played with children, sang 'We'll rally around
him', and recited Chartist verses in his own honour, and lived the part
of a great man in adversity. But as months went by his condition
deteriorated. Next year, 1854, the first signs of epilepsy appeared. All
that year he grew worse, and became completely helpless, often in
great pain. He lingered on for many months. In August 1855 his sister
removed him from Dr Tuke's care to her home in Notting Hill, and
there on 30 August he died.

Chartist feelings flared up again, forgetting the Land Company split
in the recollection of Chartist campaigns. William Lovett arranged the
funeral, and on 10 September big crowds followed the coffin to Kensal
Green cemetery.

That autumn a meeting was held in the Exchange Hall, Nottingham,
to propose a monument to O'Connor. Aldermen were present, Ernest
Jones spoke, and a statue was agreed upon.[37] Resentment and grievance
boiled over among radicals and Land Company men. They might for-
give Feargus, but a statue was too much. A poem appeared in Nottingham, indignant that a statue should be put up in their town to a worth-
less man simply because he was dead.

> Has Sherwood's new member nought better to say,
> That because poor O'Connor in Kensal Green lay,
> That Nottingham workmen, altho' he did cheat 'em,
> Should erect him a stone in their own Arboretum?
>
> They said that all statues to be understood
> Should only be raised to the great and the good,
> That the finger of parents might point without shame,
> To the statue of one we deemed worthy of fame;
> And not with a blush for the men we did honour,
> As would be the case with the one to O'Connor.
> Shame, shame on ye all who supported the motion,
> That Tories and Whigs should pay their devotion,
> At the Demagogue's shrine who the people deluded,
> With schemes full of wind and of all sense denuded;
> Who dealt in sedition both wholesale and retail,
> And left the land planners their fate to bewail.[38]

Accusations grew wilder and more bitter, especially from Leicester men. Trouble went on until a group from Nottingham and Leicester took the Free Trade Hall, Manchester, in May 1859, for a public hearing of the accusations.[39] The meeting started with threats and shouting, the people passionately reliving the misery of hopes held out to hungry men and then proved unworkable. All the sufferings of the Midland cities were blamed on the Land Company. But, slowly, truth worked through. A Leicester man said the frame-workers were miserable, but not because of O'Connor; they died in Unions, but not because of O'Connor. Ernest Jones spoke, and gathered up the evidence. He had parted from Feargus long ago, but that was put aside. As he spoke, the audience came round to him. At the close the meeting declared O'Connor's character clear, unimpeached and unimpeachable. It was generous.

Work on the Nottingham statue proceeded, and in August 1859 it was finished and a ceremony held before it in the arboretum. Ernest Jones spoke again. The words on the statue risked no controversy. They simply said, 'Feargus O'Connor Esq, M.P. This statue was erected by his admirers 1859.' The obelisk over the grave in Kensal Green held a little more echo of that pulse of feeling, dangerous, daemonic, which had shaken Feargus and his rough listeners ten, fifteen years before:

> Reader, pause,
> thou treadest on
> the grave of a patriot.
> While philanthropy
> is a virtue, and
> patriotism not a crime,
> will the name of
> O'CONNOR
> be admired and this
> monument respected.

PART TWO

THE ESTATES—1846 ONWARDS

CHAPTER 8

HERONSGATE OR O'CONNORVILLE

THE estate of Herringsgate, or Heronsgate, later called O'Connorville, is called by all these names and spellings in contemporary reports.[40] The OS 1-in map calls it Heronsgate. The estate lay 2½ miles from Rickmansworth, 6 from Watford, 15 from London. It consisted of 103 acres of neglected farm land, freehold, with lime soil and cherry woods and no great obstacles of marsh or hills. The owner, William Hunt, had died, and his solicitor Thomas Fellows sold the property.[41] Chorley Wood Lane ran past the estate, and the Grand Junction Canal wharf at Rickmansworth was three miles away.

The price was £2,344, but three annuities of £20 each were subtracted from it. Fourteen acres stood in wheat and ten in oats. On 14 March 1846, £1,860 was paid, in Chinnery's presence, by a cheque signed by W. P. Roberts.[42] Purchase was in O'Connor's name, but Roberts retained the title deeds on grounds of alleged lien, or claim. In later evidence Roberts said that he provided a mortgage of about £1,372.[43] This was done without the knowledge of anyone in the company except O'Connor.[44] After valuation of the produce on the land the full price was finally paid.

The ballot for allotments on Heronsgate was announced for 20 April 1846, Easter Monday, at Manchester, for everyone who had paid up on his shares. There was a rush to pay up £2 10s (£2·50) on shares. By 20 April, 1,487 people were eligible for thirty-five cottages and allotments. 157 held two shares, eligible for the thirteen 4-acre holdings; 580 held one and a half shares, eligible for the five 3-acre holdings; 750 held one share, eligible for the seventeen 2-acre holdings. The draw was to be at the old Manor Court Room, Nicholas Croft, Manchester. O'Connor was to be in the chair, and the Manchester committee of the

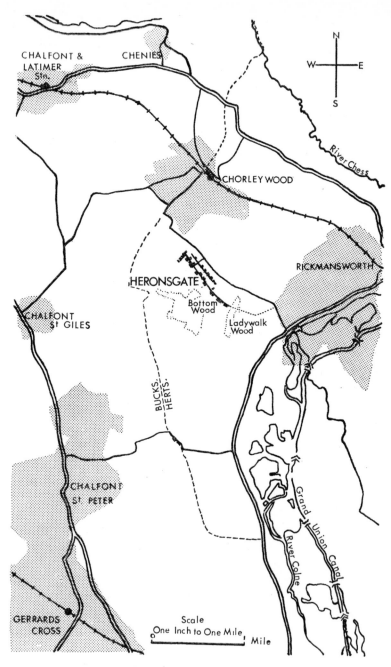

4 Map showing the position of O'Connorville (Heronsgate) estate

Land Company and the directors were to conduct the business. The notice was signed by Feargus O'Connor, Philip M'Grath, Thomas Clark, Christopher Doyle, Thomas Wheeler, secretary.

A draw would be held for each size of holding, which meant three boxes of tickets and three of blanks to be prepared. As many blanks were taken out as there were prizes in each section, and replaced with slips marked Prize 1 or Prize 2 and so on. In the ticket boxes, the tickets had to carry the name of the shareholder and the number of his share certificate. The boxes had to be fixed to revolve on a wheel to shake up the contents thoroughly.

During the month pressure built up among the 1,487 eligibles and among everyone who knew them. Paying up on a share could continue until the close of Saturday, 18 April. If a house and land for a poor knitter were possible, anything was. Among underfed and uninformed men and women, craving and excitement leaped from one to another. Hundreds did not sleep that Sunday night, but by one o'clock were walking in to Manchester. First light found the small lanes and approaches to Nicholas Croft full of fustian jackets, quiet and tense. Some got into the hall, hundreds stood outside, still, awed by the mere chance of heaven.

Inside the hall there was the same tenseness. On the platform stood the boxes, guarded by members of the Manchester branch committee. Feargus's chair was in the middle. At a table sat Tom Wheeler to write down the results, and the names of the incredible winners. Feargus spoke. He told them of the grass and trees on their estate, the clear unsmoked sky over it, the birds no freer than they would be themselves, the little house, the yard behind and the neat gate, the plates piled with bacon, greens and carrots. He spoke of children in the field or at school instead of in the mill. Sharply, painfully, they wept.

The ballot began. First, for the 4-acre prizes. One man stood at each wheel, another stood ready to draw. The man at each wheel revolved his box, through several silent minutes. At a movement of O'Connor's hand he stopped. The man on the draw put his hand into the ticket box, pulled one out, and read aloud the shareholder's name and certificate number. A quiver in the crowd showed where the ticketholder stood. A man at the prizes box put in his hand, and held up a blank. Again, and again, with every blank, the hopes of everyone else strained higher.

LOT 4.

A CAPITAL

FREEHOLD ESTATE,

With extended to press ... lled

HERRINGSGATE FARM,

Most advantageously situate in the Parish of

RICKMERSWORTH,

HERTS.

COMPRISING A

Commodious Farm House,

With Barns, Stable, Cow House, Cart Lodge, Cattle Shed, and other Outbuildings, Yard,
Garden, Orchard, and the following enclosures of excellent

Arable, Meadow, and (small part) Wood Land,

CONTAINING ALTOGETHER

103A. 1R.-30P.,

LITTLE MORE OR LESS.)

Lying very compact, as will be seen by the Plan.

No. on Plan.	Description.	State.	Quantity.		
			A.	R.	P.
1	Homestead, Yard, Garden, Orchard, &c.	Arable	3	0	25
2	Pike Field	Arable	10	1	13
3	Sheep House Field	Ditto	4	3	15
4	Wood	Wood	9	1	25
5	Hop Garden	Arable	11	3	34
6	Rick Yard Field	Ditto	7	3	35
7	Cherry Walk	Ditto	7	3	11
8	Little Field	Meadow	4	0	1
9	Chalk Dell Field	Arable	6	0	39
10	Long Field	Ditto	6	3	37
11	Ten Acres	Ditto	12	0	6
12	Upper Coney Burrows	Ditto	8	3	38
13	Lower Ditto and Dell	Ditto & Wood	9	2	31
			103	1	30

The Tithes have been commuted, and the Rent Charges apportioned on this Lot in lieu thereof are
£17 3s. 0d. and £5. 8s. 6d. per annum.

This Lot will be sold subject to three Annuities of £20. each, (payable weekly) to three persons,
independently of each other, of the respective ages of 62, 63, and 67 years ; and the exclusive right of
sporting over this Lot is reserved during the life of a gentleman aged 58 years

Land Tax, £2. 16s. 2d. per annum   Quit Rent, £1 16s. 10d. per annum

5   Sale notice of Herringsgate (Heronsgate) farm,
which became the O'Connorville estate

The first prize was shouted out! David Watson of Edinburgh. Thomas Smith of London followed, and Thomas Bond of Devizes, and at last a Manchester man, Joseph Openshaw. A surprise came next, a woman winner, Barbara Vaughan of Sunderland. There followed Thomas Meyrick of Worcester, Alfred Crowther of Ashton-under-Lyne and six more 4-acre winners. Next came the draw for five 3-acre holdings: William Oddy of Bradford, Isaac Jowett of Bradford, James Short of Bilston, Benjamin Knott of Halifax, and George Richardson of Westminster. Then came the 2-acre draw, for seventeen prizes: Philip Ford of Wotton-under-Edge, William Mann of Northampton, William Mitchell of 'Whittington and his Cat', London, John Firth of Bradford, Ralph Kerfoot of Rouen, George Hearson of Leeds,* George Ramsbottom of Ashton-under-Lyne, Michael Fitzsimmon† of Manchester, were among them. George Hearson of Leeds disappears and Charles Smith of Halifax has taken his place by the next issue of the list.

Probably some of the winners lost their elation as they faced those acres and the prospect of no wages. Wages might be slavery, but they were regular. O'Connor caught their mood in his first columns in the *Northern Star* of 23 May 1846.

> 'From Paradise—No. 1'
> Hereditary bondsmen, know ye not,
> Who would be free, FOR SELF MUST TILL THE LAND.

The rent—dreaded point—he dealt with at once. It would be about 5 per cent on the cost of building a cottage and preparing the allotment, and O'Connor said now that this would be about £6 a year for the 2-acre man and £11 10s for the 4-acre man. Each man would be given a cash loan to begin with, £15 for 2 acres, £22 10s (£22·50) for 3 acres, and £30 for 4.

O'Connor and Cullingham settled in the farmhouse on the estate in April. While Feargus planned the lay-out of thirty-five allotments and the school, Cullingham recruited workmen. They tramped over every field, wet to the knees in April rain, plotting the acres. They went to Watford and Uxbridge and chaffered with building contractors.

Messrs Beeson[45] contracted for three, but most offers were too expensive, and O'Connor turned to wholesale suppliers of drainpipes,

---

* This name is spelt Hearon in the Select Committee's list.
† This name is also spelt Fitzsimon.

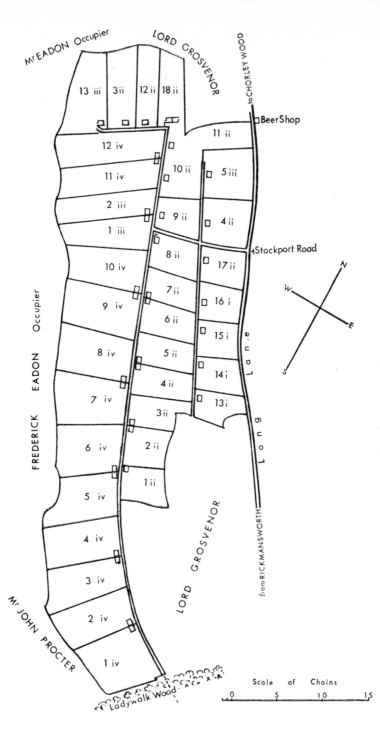

6 Plan of O'Connorville (Heronsgate) estate

ironmongery, timber and building material. Every bit of timber found
on the estate was used, however great the trouble.

First, four main estate roads were made, measuring 1½ miles, all 9
ft wide. Then labourers were set to make paths giving access to every
cottage from the road. Then the building campaign opened—making
mortar, digging foundations, cutting timber. Mortar needed vast
quantities of water, and this was scarce on the chalky Hertfordshire
soil. The one spring and pool were cherished, and a well was dug near
the works centre. Oak timber was bought for roofing, and deal for
wainscots and walls.

Clearing the ground came next, heavy work grubbing out roots of
old hedges and felled timber, filling in ditches, demolishing sheds and
wheeling away stones and rubble. Anything that would sell or could be
used again was saved. Roots were stacked for home fuel. Feargus went
to the canal wharf and ordered ten boatloads of London stable dung at
60 tons a load; 103 acres would get 5 tons 17 cwt each. One of the
early pleasures of the estate was finding a patch in the centre of the
estate where sand could be dug, 'enough to build a town'. On 23 May
they read in the hill streets of Wigan and Heddon Bridge, 'On my way
I saw a Cow that had just calved, a black cow without horns, and I
bought her. She gives 28 quarts A DAY! ! ! What say you to that?'
Milk was not delivered down these hill streets, being 2d a quart.
Twenty-eight quarts a day between thirty-five houses meant more than
a pint a day each. They looked at their children, and marvelled.

Cullingham was overseer of the skilled men such as carpenters and
masons, and dealt with the outside suppliers. He found an overseer for
the labourers in Mr King. Joiners, smiths and bricklayers were under
another man, and horses and field-workers under another. Later sug-
gestions that the workmen were Irish immigrants are not borne out by
any evidence. Men worked in gangs of six, and O'Connor experi-
mented in operating day work or task work. The men soon found that
they could earn immensely more by task work than by working so
many hours a day. They were on the job at 5 am on these May morn-
ings, and knocked off at 7 pm. Over a tested 5 days, 12 men earned £6
between them, and 7 men earned £5 12s 6d (£5·62½).

Cullingham kept the cash book. Each overseer told him the payments for his men. Anyone who at O'Connor's instruction sold any

produce off the estate, tiles, stone slabs, old iron, brought Cullingham the receipt and the money. He told O'Connor how much cash was needed for wages, and by Saturday the amount was obtained in correct change. 'Standing between you and Mr King', said O'Connor later, 'I paid the money.' Cullingham called out the amount as each man came up, O'Connor paid it, and Cullingham wrote it down in his book. When O'Connor and Cullingham had approached building contractors, the price offered per house was around £230. Managing for themselves, each house cost just over £100.

Feargus enjoyed every moment of it. He was up on the builders' scaffold all day.[46] 'My pale face is turned into a good, sound sun-burnt ruddy complexion,' he wrote. 'I can jump over the gates without opening them. I am up every morning at 6 o'clock, and when I look out of my window at the prospect, and think of the number my labours will make happy, I feel myself a giant.' The fever was in Ashton-under-Lyne, people in sweating-rooms, cellars and tiny houses, working all hours in the stinking 'rattle-boxes', or cotton mills. At Heronsgate there was no fever, but bright eyes, straight frames and brawny arms of farm workers earning 12s (60p) a week, and £1 at hay and harvest. Let everyone pay up for the next ballot in July.

Relations with the neighbourhood were mixed. The main landowners round the edge of the estate were Lord Grosvenor and Mr Frederick Eadon, who made no objections. With their tenant farmers O'Connor and Cullingham maintained a careful peace, abstaining from politics and Chartism, and keeping to economics and employment. But in a few weeks local farm labourers asked them to open a district branch of the Chartist association. Feargus was told that a parson three miles away had said in his sermon that all labouring folk should look to have a house and a bit of land of their own. Building contractors were contemptuous and hostile. When local people raised doubts about the wild men from the north, O'Connor pledged them for good behaviour, and told the neighbours he pledged *them* for good encouragement.

By June 200 men were at work; carpenters, sawyers, bricklayers, sand-diggers, wall-builders, plasterers, road-makers and carters. More wells were dug, for the soil held water poorly. A mile of straight gravel walk stretched from the trees on one boundary to Lady Walk Wood on the other. Houses were rising on either side, 'most beautiful, in fact to my eye most heavenly'. Already Feargus preferred the 4-roomed houses to the 5-roomed; a smaller house meant more spent on the land. 'My own dear fustian jackets, blistered hands and unshorn chins,' he cried in his column. No one before had built houses for poor men except on condition of making the man his servant.

People continually visited the site to admire or to find flaws, and wrote to their local paper about all that struck them. Some were Land Company shareholders. They fingered the seasoned oak ready for roof beams, and strong deal for doors, and gaped, 'Eh! but that's rare stuff!' They tramped or got lifts from the north, not able to believe the printed word of the *Northern Star*, came into the blossoming June countryside of Hertfordshire, and walked up and down the estate roads only a little more able to believe that such a paradise could fall to working men. Three men tramped all the way to ask O'Connor for work. They arrived in a useless condition from fatigue, and none of them had any notion of land work. O'Connor was angry, paid their fares and sent them away, and filled his columns with instructions in capital letters that no one else was to come.

The black cow was a sure favourite with visitors, and came up to have her head scratched. She was soon named Rebecca after the 'Rebecca riots' over tollgates in South Wales in 1842–3. Visitors hoped to get a drink of milk, but O'Connor insisted they pay for it. She was the people's cow, and her milk was the people's, and the people must have their return.

Two houses were nearly up. O'Connor took personal charge of the bricklayers, and used no contractor. In the second week in June Cullingham gathered all the workmen round these houses, and contrived two long red, white and blue flags. As bricklayers on the roofs raised the chimneys on each house, the workmen burst into cheering, and the flags were flung out and tied to the chimneys. Haymakers in all the neighbouring fields stopped to have a look, and some ran over to ask what was up.

In the same spirit, O'Connor and Cullingham planned a demonstration and procession for 17 August 1846, when more results of their labours would be for show. Money was coming in fast, but also he was spending a good deal, and wanted people to see what they were getting.

On 6 July he declared a half-holiday for all estate workers, and organised a cricket match on Chorley Wood Common. The bricklayers, with Feargus, played the carpenters and sawyers. A tent was put up, and local people collected to watch. The oldest inhabitants had seen nothing like it, and said so frequently. The day was showery, but play began at 1 and went on till 7.30. The bricklayers won by 28 runs. After the match, 60 working men from Heronsgate sat down to a substantial supper. Speeches were made by Henry Cullingham and two others, and O'Connor's health was drunk. A return match was arranged. The hilarity continued to a late hour.

O'Connor was using the visible achievement at Heronsgate to build up an image of labour as capable, civilised, cheerful, good. The public image of it was very different, and many groups of Chartists dealing in violence and conspiracy exulted in this. But the main strength of English feeling was working for a better social order by lawful change. O'Connor's method was wise, and his image welcome. Only seven years ago General Napier had told the Government 'the Chartists have what they call a rocket, which they believe will, if thrust into a window, blow the roof off a house. Their arms are chiefly pistols, and they have cast a vast quantity of balls. . . .' Nobody would want cells or plantations of this activity set down in their parish. Now O'Connor reported of the people's estate, beautiful Chartist villas, more like retired tradesmen's than the present houses of workers, made of the best materials, with the comfort, convenience and happiness of the occupier studied. 'The mind has not been forgotten, as each house is fitted up with a neat and elegant library (bookshelves).' Any man could elongate the middle window to a door or even a porch on to the little lawn that adorns the front, and he would have a residence that 'the choicest sprig of fashion' might envy.

O'Connor and Cullingham organised a public meeting on Chorley Wood Common, on a Sunday afternoon in July, to invite questions and discussion. Cullingham was in the chair. Five or six hundred people were reported as attending, yeomen in their chaises and gentry in carriages. Cullingham spoke of the need to restore an independent working people, free of the terror of unemployment and of the degrading effect on mind and body of the work offered in factory, mill and mine. He stressed the desire of the poor lacemaker or pattern-maker to work and not to come on poor relief. A poor man could not buy land. But poor men had co-operated to get and build Heronsgate estate, and would co-operate to work it.

Cullingham's audience was sympathetic, but not convinced. Other co-operative schemes of land settlement had been known, and two acres had never yet succeeded. But Cullingham was as honest and plain as O'Connor was spirited and attractive, and the meeting went well.

A local man named Gay, of Rickmansworth, thought enough of it to challenge O'Connor to a continuation, on Fair day, on a piece of open ground called The Fortune at Rickmansworth. Again a big crowd gathered. Gay struck at once at the basic condition of the Land Company—that it was a lottery. O'Connor might call it co-operation, but Gay said that the whole subscription, £15,000, of one section which he understood had 6,000 members, would only locate 128 of them, at the £127 which O'Connor claimed to be his cost for each location, and forty-seven years would be needed to locate all members at this rate.* However, following the meeting, a branch of the National Land Company was opened at Chorley Wood.

Now all energies were bent on presenting the estate for the exhibition on 17 August. Tree and bush roots were stacked for fuel, and the surplus sold. 'Not a tile, not a lath, is allowed to go to waste,' he wrote. Had skinflints complained of his buying Rebecca? She had earned £8 of her price of £16 in less than 8 weeks. He felt justified in hiring ten carts and horses and forty labourers for the exhibition.

Up in Manchester the Land Company branch held a second ballot for choice of allotment on the estate. The houses in each acreage section were numbered consecutively on a plan, and the winners in the ballot would occupy them in the order of winning. O'Connor and Cullingham saw the danger that the allottees would turn up at the demonstration, camp in the sites which they had drawn, and become an extreme nuisance by starving or wanting special treatment. O'Connor thundered forth in the *Northern Star* that NO ONE would be located until the directors' plans were completed. A month's notice would be given.

* Gay's or newspaper reporter's arithmetic. £15,000 ÷ £127 = 118 locations and 51 years would be needed.

After weeks of transport organisation, 17 August arrived. The metropolitan committee had borne most of the burden, as most of the transport was organised from London. Horsedrawn omnibuses, called vans, were ordered to leave seven different points at different times from 5.30 am onwards, to assemble at the western end of Oxford Street, or the Marble Arch as we should know it. Every passenger had booked a ticket beforehand, costing the substantial sum of 2s 6d. It is a fair guess that among them were the London men who had won an allotment in the ballot, Thomas Smith, John Westmoreland, William Mitchell and George Richardson.

All the vans arrived on time, and took up positions on the park side, each van decorated with banners and carrying a board with the name of its district. Private vehicles waited with them. As the clocks of London struck 7, the procession started. The banners and streamers rose, and people in the street spelled out 'Labour's Procession to Labour's own Land, purchased with Labour's own Money!'

Feargus was already at work. He and his staff had been woken by the firing of a cannon at 4 am. No one knows where they had got this from. By 4.30 they were out of doors, rigging up booths and tents or putting a finishing touch to piles of manure at yard gates. The first visitors arrived on foot at 7 o'clock, and the flow never stopped, on foot or by horse. The morning was dry and fine. Vans arrived from Oxford, Yorkshire, Lancashire, Exeter and Plymouth. A four-horse stage coach came from Reading, blowing its horn and streaming a green silk banner. Gigs, carts and waggons crowded in. The band arrived and began to play. But all were waiting for the London contingent. Not a great deal of interest was shown in the streets of London, but when, towards 11 o'clock, the procession approached Uxbridge, 17 miles from Oxford Street and only 7 from the turn to Heronsgate, they found things growing more lively. Outside the Crown Tavern the way was almost blocked and every viewpoint crammed. On, with increasing excitement, through Uxbridge, past New Denham mills, to the Rickmansworth turn, through the woods beside the river Colne, along the rich valley, joined now by people on the lookout for them, and then, off the high road, into the lane to Heronsgate.

Within a mile a shout went up at the sight of new cottages on the left of the lane, bright and clean, with neat slated roofs. As the leading van turned in, a cannon went off, the band and choir struck up the Chartist Land March, composed and written by Mr Whitmore. A chestnut tree at the entrance was swathed in a red, white and blue banner proclaiming the name of the estate to be O'CONNORVILLE. Beyond it, Rebecca was tethered, also clothed in red, white and blue.

The history of poor people can hardly show a day of purer happiness. People wrote of it to the *Northern Star*, and the *Daily News* reported it. There was dancing in a huge booth, food and drink in others, recitals and singing in another. Groups of minstrels walked about, and people joined with them in singing 'The People's First Estate', 'Beautiful Villas' to the air 'Land of the Free', and 'No Longer to be a Slave' to the air 'The Mariner's Grave'. The words of 'The People's First Estate', by John Arnott, were on sale at 1d. There were donkey racing and ninepins (skittles), and best of all the meeting of old friends in the labour and Chartist movements.

Most people went first to look at the cottages, the centre of every hope. The *Daily News* said they were very neat and well-built, most were roofed and all the walls were up, none occupied except one by O'Connor while seeing to the work. The school house was in preparation, 75 ft in length, with a 4-roomed house in the middle for master and mistress and two schoolrooms, each 24 ft long, one for boys and one for girls. One of the crowd wrote that the cottages were substantial, roomy, airy, well-lit, with oak plank floors and good cast-iron grates. He spoke to a local labourer who said it was a palace compared with his, and he had no land with it.

This was a wonder almost as great as a cottage to yourself. O'Connor wrote in the *Northern Star* that 'few would believe that four acres was such a spacious tract of land'. In every mind was the slow assimilation of the fact that land was political power and economic security, and here for the first time the people had possession of land. There was an uplifting gravity in the day. The English labouring classes did not naturally see progress in terms of guns, barricades and killing. They saw it in terms of solid gain, of an advance into the more favoured classes of their world, rather than an attack upon them. Here, at the demonstration of the O'Connorville estate, they parted company with Marx and Engels.

What fun they had! 'Rebecca, tastefully dressed out for the occasion,

G

was the only living thing that appeared dissatisfied.' The situation was declared heavenly, picturesque and healthy. Every corner of houses and allotments was inspected, the wells and sand-pits, drains and paths. Everyone rejoiced, ate and drank, sang, talked politics in groups, exchanged family gossip. By 3 pm they had all gathered round the hustings under the trees for the speeches.

Mr Knight was in the chair, Thomas Clark spoke, and Ernest Jones read a poem.

> See in here the cottage, labour's own abode,
> The pleasant doorway on the cheerful road,
> The airy floor, the roof from storms secure,
> The merry fireside and the shelter sure,
> And dearest charm of all, the grateful soil
> That bears its produce from the hands of toil.

Then came their leader, their father, Feargus O'Connor. He spoke to them of 'cottages, land and capital' as the principle of Chartism. The Land Company could make it a reality for every working man. It was giving the people what modern society had taken away from them.

> I am neither leveller nor destructive—I am for the altar, for the throne and for the cottage; but I wish to see the altar the footstool of God, instead of the couch of Mammon. I wish to see the throne based upon the affections of the people, instead of the caprice of an aristocracy. I wish to see the cottage the castle of the freeman, instead of the den of the slave.

He told them he had never travelled a mile, eaten a meal, or received a fraction of a farthing for any service, from any party or individual, but he had been the instrument of bringing real bliss to his people.

The whole crowd was united in a rapturous reception of his speech. Doyle followed, and then the chairman sent them all off to enjoy the pleasures of the day. The London vans had to get away early. A trumpet sounded at 6.45 as a warning, and again at 7 as the order to depart. They drew out punctually, passengers singing the Chartist songs, their voices sounding back along the lane. When dusk came on, two bonfires were lighted on the slopes east and west of the estate, and the cannon was fired. There was a firework display. Dancing and singing went on, the cannon went off at intervals, and rockets shot up into the dark sky until midnight. Throughout the day no accident, damage or bad behaviour was reported.

Work on the estate continued at a great rate. O'Connor spent nearly all his time there, hanging roof slates, making cement, turning compost. A workman named Dowling made trouble among the bricklayers, and was discharged. He returned, penitent, and was taken on again, only to repeat the offence, get discharged, and repeat the cycle. O'Connor tried the experiment of letting plastering and stuccoing out to individual plasterers. He found they all cheated, and as it was impossible to measure half-finished work he could not prevent it.

Walwark, a 2-acre winner, a weaver from Ashton-under-Lyne, arrived on the estate in August 1846.[47] He must have made himself useful, for he was allowed to stay. His wife was uneasy, but Walwark took to the life at once. He had brought his hand-loom, and wove gingham lengths to sell in the district.

The end of September brought early morning frost, the first advance of the enemy winter. Outdoor work was mostly done, all allotments laid out, land ploughed and harrowed, dunghill ready by each gate, tools, plants and seed laid in at wholesale prices. O'Connor wrote of the fear of winter as 'the scarecrow of the hothouse plants, taken from the heated atmosphere of the rattle-box', to persuade his readers that with better health in country life they would feel the cold less.

Experiments in smallholding schemes were being made in many places. Landowners as well as the poor were concerned. The Rev Lord Wriothesley Russell, minister of Chenies, near Heronsgate, came over frequently to study the progress and talk about plans.[48] A letter from Basle was published in the *Northern Star* on 31 October 1846, about the O'Connorville plantation. The writer said that Belgium and France were peopled with small farms, all with the great drawback that the owners lived in towns or villages two miles or so away. The people lived on milk products and vegetables. Money was not spent. In England, however, the object of the people was, not a contented life and the means of existence, but to get rich and rise in the world. Of Heronsgate, the writer considered the miscellaneous character of the inhabitants, the unreasonable expectations voiced, their ignorance of land work, the abilities of their wives and daughters. He thought it would require all O'Connor's skill and discretion to guide the colony aright. O'Connor of course had no plans for guiding it at all. By 31

October he had bought Lowbands, and by the time that O'Connorville was occupied he would be busy with several others.

The annual conference of the Land Company for 1846 was held on the O'Connorville estate in December. O'Connor announced that the estate would be occupied by the allottees on 1 May 1847. Frost and cold would be well over, and offer no danger to people used to heated work in factories. The months February to May would be used to plant crops.

Some time during December O'Connor's enemy 'Whistler at the Plough' from the *Manchester Examiner* visited the estate. He was out to find fault, and he found it. Plaster in several houses was coming off already. Looking in the schoolroom, he saw a reason why, since plasterers were sitting in there, drinking, and cheaply-hired apprentices were doing their work. The timber of the houses would soon warp if O'Connor had used unseasoned wood off the estate. He talked to workmen and to Walwark's wife, and published a number of anonymous complaints that the roads were bad, that the well held no water, that apprentices were doing the work. O'Connor dashed to the defence of plasterers and timber. No apprentices had been used, no plasterers had been drunk. Seasoned timber was used for doors and window-frames. In January 1847, James Taylor, a painter, suspected of having been one of the complainers, wrote that the Whistler was a spy and that people had told him lies.

The school at O'Connorville was finished during the winter of 1846–7. Shortage of water affected building. O'Connor said that sometimes hauling water for mixing mortar cost £4 10s (£4·50) a week. On 30 January the enchanting print of O'Connorville which still survives was on sale, 3s (15p) plain and 4s 6d (22½p) coloured. Who drew it? Did some engraver's hack in a dark office dream of the innocence, simplicity and good content which is in the print?

The allottees were now getting impatient, and, with O'Connor often away at Lowbands, efforts were made to move in before the appointed 1 May. William Oddy, a weaver from Bradford, arrived in January. A group arrived in February without means, and found their houses unfinished and no food growing in the frozen soil. There was a small crisis. O'Connor and Doyle were at Lowbands. Doyle arrived next day with money for the interlopers' fares to go back where they came from. Three refused to go. O'Connor arrived and tackled the three families.

They overcame his determination. 'I wish the Whistler had seen the delight with which they were cultivating their own spots.' Of course they were uncomfortable, since the February weather was bad, but sitting by their tree-root fires in their own kitchen grates they all swore they would rather starve than go back.

Signs of cold feet appeared among some lucky winners of allotments. Thomas Bond of Devizes sold his lot for £90 to T. Gamble of Somers Town, London. Mr G. Wheeler, father of the secretary of the Land Company, bought a lot for £80. O'Connor had to be careful. He wrote that the directors were allowed to receive offers of sale, but advised the poorest to try it before they parted with their luck.[49] He asked all those allottees who had already taken possession if they wanted to sell. Those in possession were happy. Walwark had refused his fare back to the north. Oddy had never been so happy; he had never earned more than 6s a week or lived in a house of his own. 'If anything breaks us, it will be the appetite!' said Oddy. His wife was also contented now, and so were the boy and girl of 12 and 14. They had already made 'a little paradise' of their garden, and would be an honour to the society. Heaton, another weaver whose name does not appear in the original list, and his two grown sons were all happy. Feargus gave them £4 to buy yarn to weave, and moved them from their unfinished house to one which had been occupied by a foreman. Mitchell's wife, from London, out picking up sticks for firewood with her little girl of three, told O'Connor that she would rather live on half-rations than leave. She was happy, and had never felt so well. Griffiths, from Worcester, working on his house, said a timber train would not get him out. He and his son were sleeping on straw and would not change for a feather bed elsewhere. He had written to his wife to say he was never so happy. Another ballot won a lot at O'Connorville for W. South of Cirencester.[50]

March brought in the sowing season. Carrots, turnips and swedes were being sown, potatoes would be planted. Soon the longed-for notice of location was issued, with directions to the allottees. All from the south and west were to go by GWR to West Drayton, and from there through Uxbridge to Heronsgate. All from the north were to come by the Birmingham line to Watford station and thence to Rickmansworth and Heronsgate.

Friday, 30 April 1847 was the last pay day for the allottees of O'Connorville. How great a faith they must have had, in O'Connor, in the Chartist movement, in life itself, to have been ready when the moment came to sign off from work, from the dreariness of industrial city life certainly, but also from wages, from neighbours, old folks, streets, lights, corner shops, everything they understood.

1 May was a glorious day, and gave them a good start. 'England's May Day', O'Connor called it, and certainly there had been nothing like it remembered in the history of poor folk. The houses stood ready, new and well-built, the land lay prepared and sown, lines of green barley and vegetables sprouting, and a parliamentary vote as its unseen choicest crop, all waiting for poor men who had never had house or acre or vote of their own.

> From feverish couch by o'er taxed labour pressed
> That yields man slumber, but denies him rest,
> More weary still when smoky morning breaks
> In crowded towns the pale mechanic wakes.
> But why today, at twilight's earliest prime
> When morn's grey finger points the march of time,
> Why starts he upwards with joyous strength
> To free the long day slavery's cheerless length?
> Has freedom whispered in his wistful ear
> 'Courage, poor slave, deliverance is near?'
> Oh! she has breathed a summons sweeter still,
> 'Come! take your guerdon at O'Connorville![51]

A contemporary account said:

(The settlers) arrived at Watford . . . and while the sun was still high—the travellers being all seated in vans, in readiness for the occasion, the band struck up 'See, the conquering heroes come'—the road for the whole distance, presented the appearance of a Gala Day and never was such a merry May-Day seen in Hertfordshire or in England before. At the entrance to the Holy Land the first settlers were met by many old friends and well wishers and all were conducted to their respective abodes, all anxiously inspecting their castle and their labour field, and tho' tired after a long day's journey, only terminated their research when the sable clouds of night had spread its mantle over their little domains.[52]

They began to arrive, driving in with their bundles and furniture, each looking anxiously for his own plot. The 9-ft-wide estate roads were named after towns from which many of the allottees came.

Stockport Road entered the estate at right-angles from the Chorley Wood lane, or Long Lane. It was crossed by Halifax Road and led on to the long Nottingham Road which ran down the length of the estate, named after O'Connor's constituency. Cottages were all set facing the roads. The 2-acre lots were nearest to the public lane, cottages of the 3-acre lots looked over at them. The 4-acre lots were mostly at the southern end, with their cottages on the central road. At the head of Nottingham Road, four different lots were placed at right-angles to the rest, giving the lay-out more compactness. Here was the school. A beer-shop, now a public house called the Land of Liberty (the sign now painted by Dorothy Haigh, illustrator of this book), was on the Long Lane at the edge of the estate. No hedges or walls yet divided the allotments, which were simply staked out with wooden pins. There was only one well properly functioning on the estate, and though water was free and unlimited it had to be drawn and carried.

The houses were of brick, covered with stucco. Their interior design showed that occupants were expected to be human beings and not farm creatures. They were to be able to cook, to read, to sew or work, to sleep privately, to wash. Descriptions of the time show surprise, some show resentment, and the Scottish reports show amazement.

Here were no earth floors, with the fire on the earth. The kitchen, placed in the middle of the house, had a tiled floor, an iron grate with oven and boiler for hot water. A room led out on either side, boarded and papered. All rooms were roughly twelve feet square.[53] All had windows which opened. A chimney marked each end of the roof, which sloped down at the back over the lower level of dairy, wash-house, cart-shed, cow and pony shed, all conveniently under the same roof. Joining the house were, on one side the privy and pig-stys, each with small yard, and on the other the wood shed and fowl shed. All were of brick, and slate-roofed, no timber shanties. A low wall joined the two sets of small buildings, making a good-sized yard for the house, with a neat gate out into the allotment. The whole occupied 2⅓ perches of land. The grates, the windows which opened, and this gate were the objects most picked out for delight by the new owners.

Thirteen houses were pairs, shared by two families. Each family had five rooms, built in two storeys of two rooms each, with a kitchen built out on either side, entrances through the kitchens. There was a court-yard behind with separate privy and wash-house etc for each family. Five other houses had four rooms, three on the ground and one above, and the rest were single-storey. Examples of all these types remain today on the estate. There was no mention of entrance gates to the estate, though these certainly were built and admired on other estates.

7 A pair of semi-detached two-storey cottages at O'Connorville

O'Connor arrived at 10 o'clock. He greeted each allottee, and made a point of talking to the women and children. He found the women even more delighted than the men, and the children frisking. Most people had entered their cottage by midday and unpacked a few of their belongings. In the kitchens there were a table and wall dresser, and in the living-rooms some shelves and a chimneypiece. Otherwise, of course, the houses were not furnished. People had brought as much food as they could carry, and they stood round the new kitchen table for their first meal. After that, everyone was summoned to the school-house.

Here the directors met them. The room was nearly finished, still smelt of plaster and clean wood; it was empty except for a few car-penters' benches. Doyle proposed Wilkinson (perhaps the Exeter man) to the chair. Wilkinson said that here every man would be master of his own time and guardian of his own family. The environment would help the good in every man to become better. Doyle begged the allottees to be brotherly, and to remember that the eyes of all would be on them. Then came the author of the whole enterprise. The small crowd felt themselves to be his people, and looked to him to resolve their fears and strangeness and confirm their hopes. He looked to them to carry his vision into reality. Neither side had a practical plan worked out. They faced each other at the peak of the dream which had brought them to that point. O'Connor did not fail them.

'Must I not have a cold and flinty heart if I could survey the scene before me without emotion?' he asked. Here mothers could tend their babies, instead of being dragged from them to work by the factory bell. Here men could be good and vices would wither away. Stunted and deprived as they had been, this was the word they wanted. Tears stood in their eyes.

O'Connor went on to rents, the free gift of roots, firewood and old posts for two years' burning piled at each man's gate. The allottees had a house, land, roads, a well, for ever, for £6 15s a year (£6·75). They knew that they could redeem, or buy the freehold of, their lots at the price of 20 years' rent. He urged them to industry and to family love. On Whit Monday, 24 May, a visiting day to the estate would be organised. 'I will sleep on the estate if any of my children will give me lodging (cheers, "All"),' and would ring a bell on Monday morning, 'and then you shall have the satisfaction of saying "D—n the factory bell" '.

The people settled in that night in their unfurnished cottages, with such beds or bedding as a poor man could bring in a bundle. At Almondbury, near Huddersfield, the church bells were rung to celebrate the possession of labour's first estate, and many poems appeared in liberal newspapers on Monday.

O'Connor wrote an ardent account of the day in the *Northern Star* of 8 May. Then he said, 'Is a beer shop near your land? Avoid it as a pestilence. The one enemy which can ruin settlement life is drink. It leads to poverty, crime, disgrace.' Don't become poachers. Don't take the first step down. Don't allow religious discussion, especially not in the schoolhouse. Don't let a religious man come among you. He poured out advice on horticulture. Don't allow ONE WEED. Take care of every spoonful of manure, it is gold. Keep the birds off. Begin a compost heap of weeds, suds, waste, and turn and stir it. Combine, and buy a boat-load of manure, £24 for dung and carting. Be early and pick up the worm before he picks up your seed or cabbage.

Visiting day came in three weeks. A notice went out that several allottees would be happy to provide hot water, tea and salads at moderate charges. Three vans came from London, two with banners 'Men of Marylebone' and 'The Land the People's Birthright', and there were people from the north and south and the Midland towns, as well as from the neighbourhood. The day was brilliantly fine, and the people in their best clothes, the new white stuccoed houses, and the springing fields and gardens, made for general joy. A flag was flying from the school tower. A friendly farmer lent South's Field, joining the estate boundary, for tents and vans and horses. Everyone examined Chartist villas, Chartist crops, Chartist pigs. Barley was up, and broad beans, peas, cabbage, and potatoes. Neighbours exclaimed at the im-provement in appearance of their friends after only three weeks in clean air and healthy occupation. George Richardson had already planted bushes of currants, gooseberries, raspberries and apples.

At 2.30 the meeting was held in South's Field. First the crowd gave three cheers for 'the happy homes of honest industry'. Then a speaker reminded them that at that moment 20,000 people were walk-ing the streets of Manchester destitute and near starving. Cochrane, parliamentary candidate for Westminster, spoke next, and urged them to let no religious tenets be taught in the fine new schoolhouse. Every man must be free to worship God according to his own conscience. O'Connor said that people were accusing him of getting a share out of the company. His share was getting up at 4 o'clock that morning, driving ten miles to Gloucester, from there by GWR to Slough, and from there by gig to O'Connorville, and that was all the share he ever would have.

Then came a big event—dinner for all, provided by Mr Toovey of Watford in the schoolhouse. The schoolroom was decorated with green boughs; at the top table were O'Connor, Cochrane, Allsop, and the secretary to The Labourer's Friend Society. Doyle and Wheeler sat at other tables. What a meal! Roast and boiled beef, veal, lamb, meat pies and salads were picked out for mention. Drink is not named. There were more speeches, and O'Connor offered prizes of £7, £5 and £3 for good gardening, ability, ingenuity, sobriety, affection for wife and children, and happy homes.

Eight o'clock came suddenly before anyone noticed. There was a scramble, and a race to the railway station at Watford. O'Connor and Cochrane gave lifts in their gigs. The station was besieged. All the spare carriages had to be put into use, and even the first-class carriages were brought out to make a monster train to take the crowd back to Euston.

In spite of all the hopeful omens, James Greenwood, from Heddon Bridge, Lancashire, sold No 31, four acres, this month for £80 to a London tradesman who wished to retire and settle with his savings, and wanted what amounted to freehold property. Strong opposition was shown in the company. The people's money, not the allottee's, had bought the allotment, and they saw no reason why he should make a capital gain out of selling it. Members were incensed to think that the house and land, meant for Chartist supporters, might go to a retired tradesman with savings. O'Connor defended Greenwood in the *Northern Star*, saying the directors had no right to prevent a sale.

Staff of the *Glasgow Saturday Post* visited O'Connorville in June. They admired the schoolhouse, in two storeys with a pinnacle in front with points to the four quarters and a vane. They went round the allotments and talked to the owners. Thomas Eaton (who does not appear in the original ballot list), 'an industrious, cheerful weaver from Wigan', said he had been offered £40 for his 'land ticket'. This would have been a little fortune for him, he admitted, but money was soon gone and they would be as helpless and miserable as ever, so he refused to sell. Greenwood's London tradesman, however, was at work fencing in his land. Another allottee, perhaps James Cole of Bradford, though he had refused £75 for his 4 acres, was only holding out for more. He was 'a hearty little bachelor from Yorkshire' and was busy planting potatoes. The Scotsmen passed a joke that he ought to marry and make himself comfortable. 'He was na gaun to do that, he wud improov and haad on till he got eitty twaa pawnd for his prize.'

Comments were flying to and fro in all the concerned newspapers. Some were hostile, some were anxious for the fate of the unskilled city poor who were expected to live through the winter without money, on crops which almost certainly they would not be able to raise. O'Connor was now contesting Nottingham in the parliamentary election, and criticism infuriated him. 'Do you suppose, sir,' he wrote in the *Northern Star* in July 1847, 'that I will make dunghills from daylight to dark; that I will plough the ground, and buy the seed, and sow the seed; that I will turn horse-jobber, and cow-jobber, and bailiff, and pay-clerk, and surveyor, and land purchaser, and receive only insolence as my pay?' He denied that factory workers were unskilled at land work. Weavers had the best cultivated allotments, and some had as many as six pigs. Hard workers would succeed, and lazy ones had the means to sell.

Certainly some of the allottees applied a business sense to their problems. They co-operated to buy coal and groceries at wholesale prices. Lambourne, a tailor from Reading, a 2-acre man, over 50 years old, tackled the more fundamental problem and tried to find regular buyers for garden produce either in London or locally, men who would send round to collect it. He worked out a plan for making artificial manure, carried on his tailoring, and raised pigs. A Manchester reporter talked to him and said that he had 'a very pretty young Berkshire sow, which he had procured from a well-bred stock in his native county. This he showed us with just and natural pride'. He had come to O'Connorville with £3 of his own and the company's £15 aid money, so with winter dinners in view a black Berkshire breeding sow was the best possible investment. Lambourne said he had no doubt of ultimate success on his holding. A 4-acre man found his house 'too good', and converted the upstairs rooms into a barn for storing barley. William Mann, shoemaker of Northampton, a 2-acre man with a wife, had a sow, seven piglets and a cow. He said he could have sold five times the amount of milk. Mann continued his trade as shoemaker, and paid to have the heavy work done for him on his land. The man who had drawn the first ticket in the ballot, David Watson of Edinburgh, a confectioner, had half his 4-acre holding planted with vegetables and half with barley. His wife and young child worked with him, and by September, on this quick-growing light land, they were lifting their own potatoes for dinner. He agreed that he had a hard uphill course in front of him, but what he liked was the independent character of the life. He was confident that he would manage it. He planned to have the barley land ploughed again in the autumn, and eventually to have a man working for him on the 4 acres.

They were all interested in the opening of the school. Twenty applications for the post of master had been received. What their children were to be taught, and how much the parents would have to pay for it, was a vital concern. Ernest Jones wrote in his poem *O'Connorville*,

> See there the School, where no false doctrines cloy,
> But wisdom teaches duty to enjoy,
> Nor clothes religion in a harlot's dress,
> How rich to dazzle! but how poor to bless![54]

One worry at this stage was the delay in getting up the outbuildings. Most men had harvested their barley and wanted to thresh it, but had nowhere to store the sacks of grain. Hornby went to O'Connor at the Land Company office and offered to build sheds if he could have the materials. O'Connor gave him an order for timber and felting from Osbourne's of Uxbridge,[55] and also an order on his personal account from the *Northern Star* office for £70 to pay each allottee for his labour in building the sheds.

In August the Bethnal Green, London, branch visited the estate. They started at 6 am 'in a splendid four-horse van'. It was probably on this visit that Mrs Baine of Southwark presented the estate with four dozen cups and saucers. As a result, the allottees resolved to organise tea in the schoolroom every Sunday for any visitors or for themselves, between 3 and 5, at 8d a head. C. N. Smith was the organiser, probably Charles Smith of Halifax, on the second list of the ballot. The last visiting day of the year was arranged for 5 September.

At the annual Land Company conference at Lowbands in August, a report was made on O'Connorville. Renham, an allottee not on the original list, had seemed as if he would never make good as a farmer, but he had earned money helping the plasterers and now he was resolved to succeed. One man was said to have received £40 aid money and bought two heifers. Probably this was meant as an example of how wisely an allottee could lay out money, but it raised a howl. The man was named as William Oddy, and he immediately became an object of odium. The report, he said in a statement to the *Northern Star*, was 'in every way calculated to do him serious injury'. He came to O'Connorville on 1 January, with £2 from his own district, and was given £22 10s (£22·50) by the company. He bought:

	£	s	d	£
2 young cows	9	0	0	9·00
4½ bushels barley	1	18	6	1·92½
4½ bushels seed potatoes	1	5	6	1·27½
Peas, beans, seed		15	0	0·75
3 apple trees		3	0	0·15
Furniture and bedding	3	5	8	3·28½
Timber from the Co.		8	2	0·40½
Ploughing, harrowing		9	11	0·49½
Food for cows, rake, scythe		16	9	0·84
	18	2	6	18·12½
Balance to keep him and wife	6	7	6	6·37½

It is clear that in this society to be respectable you had to be poor. One who certainly qualified for the highest peak of respectability was Tawes, who was taken from the workhouse at Radford, a cotton-working slum near Nottingham, to his allotment (not by the original ballot), in what must have been to him an operation like the angel's in releasing St Peter from prison, was given, in sixteen weeks, aid money in the amounts of £6, £6, £3, and 'now has his cottage, outbuildings, the fresh air of heaven, four pigs fattening in the sty, vegetables, potatoes and barley'.

Tawes was the object of an unfortunate interview. A man visited the estate in the autumn, looking for work mending shoes. From the fact that he wrote his experiences to the *Mercury*, one of O'Connor's enemy newspapers, he may have gone as a journalist trouble-maker. He asked for Tawes 'of Radford workhouse'. He seems to have made Tawes uneasy by suggesting that he was now living a life of plenty. His story was that Tawes apologised for having nothing to offer but potatoes, and said he had had them for every meal and now had not enough left to last the winter. The wife took a small saucepan and boiled a few potatoes, and put more on to cook while they ate, saying that she had not got a saucepan big enough to cook for all. She had scarcely any utensils or furniture in the house. Dinner was potatoes and salt. The visitor offered Tawes apples, which seemed a great gift. He asked about the publicised prosperity and pigs in the sty. Tawes and his wife and children wished they had never come. The pigs were 'little 'uns, 4–5 stone each'. Tawes said the aid money was too little to lay out well.

Since they came, they had had 1 lb of butter and no cheese or anything else to put on the bread.

> 'Why,' said I, . . . 'I expected to find you all in the midst of plenty, and that you would have found me some jobs at shoe-mending.'
> 'Ah,' says he, 'O'Connor tells a many lies about the land and cottages.' They all seemed alarmed for the next winter.

Tawes agreed that the land was full of stones, but said it was good soil. A bad thing, he said, was to fetch water and coal, and 2 or 3 miles to a shop. O'Connor had not been to the estate for three months. The potatoes, he added sadly, were smaller than at Nottingham.

The visitor went on to the next house. The man, Ramsbottom, was out, but the missus said she had nothing to offer. She showed a piece of a loaf which must last the week out. She had come from Manchester, and wished she was back there. She was alarmed at the thought of the winter. They had sold part of their barley and three pigs. There had been a many lies about this place.

O'Connor sent this *Mercury* letter to Thomas Wheeler, at O'Connorville, ex-secretary of the company. Wheeler investigated, and reported the story very differently. Tawes only had potatoes because he was that day out of meat and was too busy to go to Rickmansworth to get it. The man left an apple on the shelf against their wish. Tawes had plenty of pots to boil in, but he was busy getting in barley; wood fires need a lot of attention and his wife only put on a small pot to fit the grate well. Wheeler added that Tawes and the family did not look hungry. When Wheeler had dinner with him they had a cauliflower 36 inches in circumference.

Wheeler went round other allottees. Ramsbottom, he said, had the worst allotment, and three of his pigs had died, but he did not complain or wish to be back in Manchester. Wheeler did not believe the story that his wife said they only had bread for the rest of the week. It was unlikely that a woman would ask a stranger in to dinner, especially as the man was covered with vermin, as Mrs Tawes had seen. Wheeler said he himself was pretty comfortable, and had plenty of potatoes. Most people had two or three hogs, some had as many as ten, and six or seven had sows with big litters of baby pigs. Only about three had sold their barley instead of keeping it for flour to eat. Barns were being built now. Few of the allottees would have fared better elsewhere.

Three had cows, three had a horse or two; there was a donkey on the estate, two goats, and ducks, fowls and rabbits in abundance.

At the end of this summer O'Connor gave Wheeler £15 out of his own pocket to be distributed as 'premiums' among the allottees. He said the qualifying points were not to be principally the cultivation of land, but to be the best beloved and sober man, best father, best husband. The awards would go to the men best loved by their families before the men who were only good cultivators, and the opinions of wives would be asked.[56]

8   The kitchen of a cottage at O'Connorville, drawn by the owner, showing the original features of brick wall, tiled floor and dresser

By November the testing time had come for the allottees. Whatever they could grow had been grown or not. If they had raised livestock they had smoked bacon to eat, duck eggs (for hens would not lay in winter on poor food), a rabbit, perhaps goat's milk. They had flour ground from their barley or wheat, if any, and root vegetables which would store. The potato and turnip were now life-givers instead of a makeshift. Mist and cold settled down, and the roots and posts burned welcome in the kitchen grate. A good wife could now save the fight, for what the man could do was over for the time. A wife who could bake bread, make dumplings with gravy, stew bones and butchers' throw-outs into soup or faggots, get out into the fields with the children and pick rose hips and crab-apples for sweetening and jam, get 2 or 3 hours' a week cleaning at a house near by, bring home old clothes from the ragshop and rabbit skins from the poulterer to line jackets and breeches, sing and tell stories by the fire in the evening, and never pine for the street and the corner shop—a wife like this could bring the family through the winter. But did Tawes have one? Did Oddy?

O'Connor went to see them all in November, knowing that the time would be rough. Sewell, one of the company's trustees for property, and William Russell of Paisley came with him. He wrote first in the *Northern Star*, which was read in every house on the estate, that he felt his offered premium for the best-kept allotment could not be distributed fairly. Soil differed; people had arrived at different dates; some could afford hired labour. He suggested using the money to establish a corn mill which would serve everybody. He was sending five tons of seed wheat by rail.

When he arrived he met a plumber and several allottees sinking a pump in the well near the estate entrance, where the water lay very deep. 'Our old Chartist' Wheeler's house near by was a cheerful sight, with a neat little veranda and shrubs. O'Connor had dinner with him, and they ate cold pork as well as their vegetables.

O'Connor went into every cottage, except Ireland's (not on the ballot list), who lived in London and only came down on Saturdays, and Oddy's, which was locked, as he and his wife were working on a distant part of their land. He gave a report on the condition of the people, on the number of livestock, and on changes of ownership. It names nine originals who were prepared to carry on. Mitchell the chairmaker looked a different man. He and his wife had fourteen pigs. Ramsbottom had three. He said he had never been so happy and would never leave. Tawes, who must have been scared stiff to meet O'Connor after all the fearful things he was supposed to have said, made his peace. He said the man who came was a scandalising vagabond, who expected to find meat pies and fruit pies in the allottees' houses. O'Connor introduced William Russell, and told Tawes that

H

Russell had brought £50 in his pocket to buy Tawes's allotment, and send him and his wife safely back to Nottingham. Here was a moment of truth. Mrs Tawes stepped forward, and said he should not take it, nor any amount of money. She would not leave. 'The money would soon go, and then we should go to the workhouse again.' She could always get work here. She took O'Connor to the outhouse and showed him four pigs.

David Watson was another who lost and recovered his nerve. He admitted he had advertised his four acres for sale, but said that was because he had his father with him and thought the land was not enough to accommodate them both. But now his father had gone, and he was happy. He had five pigs, and had killed one weighing 32 stone, 448 lb of ham, bacon, lard, pig's head brawn, black pudding, trotters, bacon-bone soup.

Lambourne was thankful for his state, and to see his children healthy. He knew what could happen to young ones in streets and mills. Mann the shoemaker and his wife were never so happy. On his two acres he had his cow and five pigs. Smith had grown a mangel-wurzel 32 inches in circumference, 'which had puzzled the farmers'. Evesham, an old man, was digging. O'Connor strode out to him and shook his dirty, calloused hand, a hand such as O'Connor loved.

'Why, how do you get on?' he asked.
'I am a boy again,' said the old man.
'How old are you?'
'74.'
'What were you?'
'A weaver.'
Well, what do you like, weaving or digging best?'
'Why, digging, and I learnt it sooner.'
'How do you feel?'
'Why, happier than ever the king felt in his palace.'
'What would you take to go back to the weaving again?'
'Why, they often ask me that, and I always say £250.'
'What, for your two acres, surely you'd take £200?'
'No, not if you paid it down on my hand, and the reason why I say £250 is, because that would be a lump of beef on the table that would just do for me to cut at while I lived.'

Another moment of truth.

Richardson, a cutter, showed O'Connor two rooms covered with the finest onions he ever saw, and some vegetables still growing, turnip or swede presumably. Richardson said

> Kosciusko was never half so happy in his retirement. Look at my wife there, 82 years of age, that doesn't know what it is to be sick now, but was always poorly before.

Fitzsimon, the Irishman from Manchester, was he complaining and unhappy?

> They're bothering me here, writing, but I never mind them; we're too well off for them. Come till I show you my two pigs. I'm obliged to keep them separate, for they fight—this is the one I brought from Manchester—isn't she a fine baist?

Newcomers to the estate were listed as seven. Pimm had bought Openshaw's 4-acre lot for £90. He had a waggon, cart and horses, and took produce to a London market for the allottees. No one else mentioned this service. Keens, Gamble, Hornby and Ireland had bought plots. Williams, a young man but an old Chartist, bought four acres for £80. He built new outbuildings and employed bricklayers and carpenters to do a good job. Wheeler had bought his two acres. Thirty-three men had pigs, in quantities of between one and fourteen. One visitor spoke of 'the lovely girl I have just seen straw-plaiting by the cottage door' for hat-making. Without commenting on the prospects of the allottees, O'Connor said after this visit that he would pay the rent for O'Connorville from next May, when it first became due, until November, out of his own pocket. The allottees could pay him back by degrees.

If winter was hard in Hertfordshire, it was far worse in Lancashire or Scotland. The allottees formed a group among themselves, Watson, Neill, Pocock, Barber, Heaton, Ramsbottom, Griffiths, Wheeler, Barbara Vaughan, and Jowitt, to encourage the spread of Chartism, meeting every Tuesday night at Jowitt's house. They invited anyone from the estate to join them, and anyone from outside who was interested. They sold the *Northern Star* locally and gave the proceeds to Chartist funds. On Christmas Day 1847, a public meeting on political events was held in the schoolroom, followed by a social. The schoolroom was not yet fitted out, nor a schoolmaster appointed.

Spring weather in 1848 brought sickness to the allottees' stock. Several pigs were lost, and William Oddy's cow died calving, a fearful loss of £12 value. The *Northern Star* opened a subscription for Oddy, to be collected by Wheeler. Hammersmith branch sent 2s at once. The allottees started a seed-loss fund, and advertised it. Other farms in the district had had a bad spring too, and many farm workers or temporary men had been laid off by farmers who had started threshing by machine, a modern tendency which Chartists held in fear. Manure was now scarce for dressing the soil for spring growth. Doubts about the Land Company estates caused the Poor Law Board to send an inspector, John Revans, to judge whether the settlers were likely to come on the parish rates or not. He started at O'Connorville in March 1848. His findings are in Chapter 7. Nine originals had now sold up and gone.[57] On 10 June Barbara Vaughan advertised her allotment, No 6 of the 4-acre plots. She offered 1 acre of wheat, 1 of potatoes, 1½ of barley, oats, peas, beans and cabbage, and the rest turnip and garden produce. John Neil, an original allottee, advertised his 2-acre lot near the school.[58] 9s 8d (48½p) was received for Oddy's loss fund, and 9s 6d (47½p) for the seed-loss fund. More cheerfully, a public soirée was announced to raise funds for a clock for the school.[59] The allottees decided to raise a band, and J. Williams, as secretary of the group, advertised for music or instruments. A Whitsun visiting day was arranged, very popular with local innkeepers. Mr Farrell advertised in the *Northern Star* that visitors would be welcome at the George and the Falcon, Uxbridge.

By now the many weaknesses and dangers inherent in the Land Company had resulted in the parliamentary enquiry. On 27 June the *Manchester Examiner* published a report of a visit to Heronsgate, copied from the *Economist*. It made the point that no leases were yet granted, nor rents fixed; that not enough produce was grown on any allotment to pay rent and keep the man; that there was no market for successful produce. Those men with a little capital looked the most hopeful, but it was clear the rest must soon give up. Eight were seeking to sell, and probably would not even plant the land for next season. But four men with a little money and some method were doing well. One of these said that the working class would fail and the allotments would come into the hands of industrious men of the middle class. The paper commented that the allottees were not frugal, but kept up the indulgences they had had when working for wages. The endeavour to unite the character of labourer and capitalist was not good.

The directors had now chosen a schoolmaster from the many applicants, Mr M. D. Graves, with the initials MCP after his name. He now had to get pupils, and he advertised in the *Northern Star* of 1 July 1848. He called the school O'Connorville College. He had been twenty years in the scholastic profession. He was going to conduct an agricultural, horticultural and model farm school, and also provide general education. The children of grocers and cheesemongers would be boarded and educated, and Mr Graves would be willing to receive goods in lieu of cash. Terms, for everything except stationery, 16 guineas per year. The school would open on 10 July. The advertisement did not address itself to the parents on the estate, or give the fees for day pupils.

The Select Committee began to sit in June 1848. The cost of the estate was given as £2,344 purchase money and £6,700 for buildings and work on the land. £384 was made by sales of crops or materials off the estate, and £500 was deducted for the schoolhouse, which the schoolmaster was expected to pay for. After other adjustments the figure was £8,700, for 103 acres and 35 houses.

The fine summer was producing crops to which all the allottees were looking forward with high hopes; Thomas Wheeler's plot with vegetables, fowls, ducks and pigs; Richardson awaiting his fruit harvest of apples, pears, gooseberries and currants. The estate had been part of the parish for a year now, and the people were accepted as ratepayers. An article in *The Labourer*[60] speaks of this.

> We are going to attend a vestry about Church rates and guardians and overseers, and we shall have a vote. . . . Will for the first time in his life went to have his word about church rates, guardians and parish officers, and strangers in broadcloth shook him by the hand as he stood at the church door.

He even found himself canvassed for his vestry vote.

In July Thomas Smith from London advertised No 32, a 4-acre allotment in the centre of the estate. A fortnight later, John Hornby advertised No 7, 2 acres, a house with veranda before the door, gates and railings in front, outhouse 24 ft by 12, a loft and boiler of 24 gallons, brick water tank, cemented and with trap-door cover and pipe to the house, and large manure tank. His 2 acres held wheat and potatoes, turnips and mangel-wurzels, with fruit trees and a hedge. He asked £75 down.

On Monday, 30 July, the Select Committee's findings were read aloud to the House of Commons: that the National Land Company was an illegal scheme which should be closed down, in its present form, and a better-designed company started if the directors wished. O'Connorville allottees showed no consciousness that this affected them. O'Connor made a move in August to attract the settlers, by easing the method of repaying money owed to the company. By now, a 4-acre man owed a year's rent, £30 aid money, and about £20 loan. The allottees said that there was no means of selling their produce, as no market existed within reach of any transport the men had.

In September George Richardson advertised his holding, saying that ill-health was the cause of his leaving. He claimed to have 700 fruit trees bearing. He asked £90 for a 999 years' lease. Barbara Vaughan offered No 6 again with no reason for leaving. Next, Howes offered with his allotment a run of water, barn and cowshed, donkey and cart, five hives of bees, and eighteen pigs.

The main body of the allottees went on with their lives, taking little notice of visitors or enquiries. It had been a good summer, and Harvest Home was held in the school in September.[61] The room was decorated with dahlias, evergreens and banners. Mr Graves, the schoolmaster, exhibited the pen-and-ink sketches which had won him a prize from Queen Adelaide and a letter from Queen Victoria. The estate band played, John Hornby was in the chair, and gave the toast, 'O'Connor, and may the people be speedily located on the land.' Old Thomas Wheeler read a poem which spoke home:

> So friends and neighbours you are come
> To celebrate our harvest home—
> And have a little feast today
> (But at a price which scarce will pay)—
> And spend an hour in harmless glee
> With music, dance and harmony.
> ....
> This being their first harvest season
> They thought they should but act with reason
> To spend a night with friends and neighbours,

> At this, the close of harvest labours.
> And though our friends who come from town,
> May scarcely get their supper down,
> And think one course is hardly right
> Of simple food on such a night,
> Yet beef and carrots, parsnips and potatoes too,
> With 'hunger sauce' will surely do,
> For though quite simple is our meat,
> Our trimmings they are fit to eat.
> 'Just gathered, fresh from off the groun','
> Not pulled about by half the town,
> Or piled together 'gainst a wall
> And messed about upon the stall.

A discussion of National Land Company policy and progress followed. The estate recorded its opposition to location by bonus or extra payment, the doubling of prices of shares, the expelling of non-paid-up members, the admission of any more members to the company, and 4 per cent rent, claiming that 3 per cent was all that was warranted by the poverty of the soil and by the fact of being the first estate and therefore experimental.

Between then and the Winding-Up Act of 1851 the story of O'Connorville is chiefly the efforts of O'Connor to get some rent out of the allottees, and their resistance, their continuing round of the rural year with May Day, haymaking and harvest feasts, meetings in the school and rumblings of unease over the tenure of their holdings. One or two allottees failed to pay their rates and distraints were levied on standing crops. But on the whole they remained staunch supporters of O'Connor, except in the matter of rent. In the middle of his troubles in the House of Commons in July 1851, they held a demonstration in his favour, and sent him an address of sympathy and gratitude.

After the Act, the official manager, William Goodchap, went round the estates to settle rents and convey the longed-for leases. W. P. Roberts had bought many of the ground rents. Goodchap arrived at Rickmansworth in late August 1852, and held his enquiry at the Swan Hotel.[62] He was assisted by Mr Roxburgh as counsel and assessor, John Tucker, solicitor, of the firm of Tucker & Sons; Mr Woodthorpe, surveyor and architect, and Mr C. Roche, of Symonds & Roche, representing the allottees or occupants, who attended in quantities.[63]

Goodchap found that most allottees could prove their titles. There were 37 allottees and a population of 170 persons. The cottages were mostly in bad repair, the produce of the land very poor. The allottees declared their inability to live on their allotments because of the poor quality of the soil and the isolated position of the estate, three or four miles from any town or transport. Some held it was impossible to live on three or four acres; some that they had been duped by the idea of enjoying a bit of land and community of labour; some that they had only themselves to blame, as they had not used common sense when taking on the experiment; most thought that O'Connor had held out preposterous expectations and had broken faith with them, but that they 'would not believe him to be a rogue until it had been proved'. They wished to stay on the estate if they could have leases and be let off back rent.

The Wheelers, father and son, presented a case for reduction of rent owing to the poverty of the soil. As everywhere, Goodchap showed benevolence to the allottees, and found that the amount of rent paid and the sums allowed for improvements more than covered the liabilities of past rent. He induced those who had more claims than debts to relinquish them on condition that no rent was charged against defaulters.

In 1855 O'Connor died, and one must believe that many of the allottees joined the long procession to Kensal Green cemetery, and that subscriptions went from all their pockets to the monument which speaks more of the people's idea of him than he was able to sustain.[64] But who would by this standard escape censure?

The estate was sold by auction in 1857. Next year, three of the original settlers were left, Meyrick, Ford and another (see illustration on p 65). Both Meyrick and Ford had come from rural backgrounds, Worcester and Wotton-under-Edge in Gloucestershire. Being so close to London, the estate houses were soon snapped up and rebuilt or altered, some by people who carried on their smallholding character, and some by well-off people who enjoyed the privacy given by large grounds round the house. Poorer occupiers provided domestic or garden work, and found customers for their own produce.[65]

From Mr Fordham of Mill End, Rickmansworth, I have learned the following points of O'Connorville's history. The school was con-

IN THE MATTER OF THE

JOINT-STOCK COMPANIES' WINDING-UP ACTS, 1848 AND 1849,

AND OF THE

NATIONAL LAND COMPANY.

O'CONNORVILLE ESTATE,

Near Rickmansworth, in the County of Hertford.

MR. A. BOOTH

WILL SELL BY AUCTION,

On WEDNESDAY, MAY 27th, 1857,

AT

THE SWAN INN, RICKMANSWORTH, HERTS,

At One For Ten o'Clock, precisely, subject to Conditions to be then produced.

In such Lots as may be determined upon at the place of Sale, unless previously disposed of by Private Contract, of which due Notice will be given,

FEE FARM RENT CHARGES,

AMOUNTING IN THE WHOLE TO ABOUT

£280 PER ANNUM,

Amply secured upon 35 Allotments, which are held by the Allottees under separate Conveyances, executed by the Official Manager under the direction of the Master charged with the Winding-up of the National Land Company. Each conveyance contains a proviso for re-entry in case of the Rent-charge being in arrear for the space of 12 calendar months,

Also, A BRICK-BUILT SCHOOL HOUSE with 2A. 0R. 31P., more or less, of

FREEHOLD LAND,

Of which the purchaser will have possession.

The Estate has been well Cultivated under Spade Husbandry for several years past, and is in excellent condition. Each of these Allotments has

A VOTE FOR THE COUNTY.

The Estate is situate 3 miles from Rickmansworth, 7 miles from Watford, and 10 miles from St. Albans, and is one of the Estates purchased some years ago on behalf of the NATIONAL LAND COMPANY. It comprises altogether

103 ACRES,

OR THEREABOUTS,

And has been apportioned among, and is chiefly in the occupation of, the Allottees.

Printed Particulars may be obtained of W. GOODCHAP, Esq., Walbrook House, Walbrook, London, Official Manager; of Messrs. TUCKER, GREVILLE, and TUCKER, Solicitors, Saint Swithin's Lane, London; of WILLIAM ROWELL, Esq., Solicitor, Rickmansworth; of Messrs. PARKER, GOLDINGHAM, and PARKER, Solicitors, Worcester; and of

Mr. ABRAHAM BOOTH, Auctioneer and Estate Agent,

1, CARLTON HILL VILLAS, CAMDEN ROAD, LONDON.

9   Sale notice of the O'Connorville estate

verted into a private house, called at first Heronsgate House, and now The Grange. The first big change was the arrival of religion. A school and chapel were built near the entrance to the estate. In 1865 subscriptions were raised to enlarge the chapel. W. P. Roberts's name was on the list. St John's Church was the result, reopened on 16 October 1886, on the crossing of Stockport Road and Halifax Road. Mrs and Miss Roberts gave gifts to furnish the church. The estate first became part of the Swillet and Heronsgate district and in 1875 part of the parish of St Peter, Mill End, and in 1940 joined with West Hyde parish.

W. P. Roberts continued to practice as a radical lawyer, defending and advising trade unions. A short account of his life is in the Manchester Local History Library. He retired to Heronsgate House, and lived there until his death in September 1871. He is buried in Chorley Wood churchyard. His second wife lived on at Heronsgate. He had a son and daughter.

Trees and hedges grew into features and screens dominating the houses, yet still the whole estate was controlled by the 9-ft-wide lanes, through which now the Jaguars and Austins creep. All is a leafy hidden delight. In many of the enlarged houses the original shape of the cottage can clearly be perceived.

By the happy revival of interest in English local history and culture since the 1939–45 war, study of the old estate has very much increased. The Land of Liberty inn connects itself with O'Connorville, though I fancy the licence is older than 1846. Many residents now take pride in possessing a print of O'Connor or of the view of O'Connorville, cherish the decoration over the entrance door even in alterations, and try to maintain points of physical continuity as well as recalling the history of the estate.

CHAPTER 9

LOWBANDS

LOWBANDS and Applehurst farms, 170 acres of arable and pasture, were sold at Worcester on 27 October 1846. O'Connor was out in the country looking at farms, and nearly missed the sale. He drove up after it had begun, the inn staff ran out to hold the horse and hurry him, wet to the knees from his farm explorations, into the sale room. He raised the last bid of £8,000 by £100 and the farms were his.[66]

They lay in Worcestershire, in view of the Malvern Hills, in a wild and remote district, nine miles from Gloucester, nine from Tewkesbury, four or five from Ledbury. Past them ran the Ledbury road to the south, the Tewkesbury road three miles to the north, and the Herefordshire & Gloucestershire Canal four miles south-west, touching Newent and Dymock.

Unlike Heronsgate, there was plenty of water from streams at the edge and on the estate itself, good road and building stone dressed and ready at 1s 6d per ton. Lime was half the price up here that it was at Heronsgate, and sand in plenty was to be had for nothing but fetching it. For labour—parish relief in Lowbands averaged 8s a week, and Feargus proposed to offer 10s. The soil must be immensely good; the very name of Worcestershire meant Evesham, market gardens, strawberries and plums.

The ballot for allotment on the next purchase had already taken place, and was reported on 1 August 1846. Among the winners was Christopher Doyle, a director of the Land Company and a foremost worker on the O'Connorville estate. Of the forty names of winners, only London, Reading and Monmouth had the luck from the south. Northampton, Nottingham, and Leicester represented the Midlands, and all the rest were from the north of England.

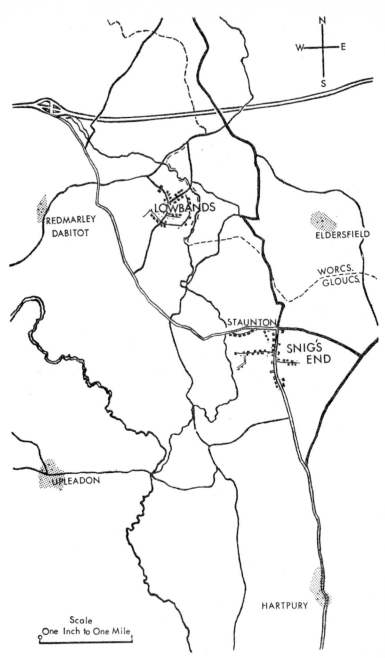

10 Map showing the positions of the Lowbands and Snigs End estates

Possession of Lowbands was on 12 December, and O'Connor wrote: 'upon the 14th, as Sunday is the 13th, the stones will be walking from the quarry, and the 8s paupers of Worcestershire will be throwing up their hats for the Land and the Charter.' A map of Lowbands estate was engraved and a copy published in the *Northern Star* on 14 November, with a warm delightful letter to O'Connor's dear Fustian Jackets, Blistered Hands and Unshorn Chins.

On 26 December 1846 he wrote one of his most winning pieces of reporting. He and Chinnery were on their way to the solicitors at Cirencester as the people's agents, to carry out the completion of the purchase of

> our second estate. I had a very small lump of co-operation in my fob, which reminded me, every time I thought of it, of your overwhelming power. The size was imperceptible, though it consisted of Eight Bank Notes of £1,000 each, gathered in shillings, sixpences, and pence.

Much of it, he knew, was snatched from gin and beer shops. He had bought the assets, timber etc on the estate for £665, and meant to sell it all for £2,000.

There was a good farmhouse on the land, ready for occupation during the building of cottages, and in January 1847 O'Connor moved over there from O'Connorville. 'I travelled here on Tuesday with Rebecca and my old bailiff and family, who never saw a steamer (locomotive) before, and already all have conspired against us, except the elements.' King was the assistant at O'Connorville who was usually referred to as bailiff. The owner of the chief stone quarry forbade his tenant to sell stone to the Chartists. The owner of the chief sandpit, which had been open to all for a hundred years, refused to allow them to have sand. O'Connor was told that local farmers had agreed not to send their teams to work for him, and a neighbouring landowner threatened to stop up a road to prevent their access. Landowners were G. Dowdeswell, Lord Beauchamp, of whom Feargus later spoke well, Charles Ireland, Sir Edward Lechmere, Captain de Winton, and Mr Ashton. Obstacles inspired O'Connor. 'Read that, Whistler, and chuckle,' he wrote, 'but read this, and tremble.' Bricks were 17s a 1,000 cheaper than at Heronsgate. Sand was found on the estate. In six hours from writing he would have a clay kiln on fire, burning clay to make road material, the finest in the world. 'Tyrants, Informers, I despise you!'

So he and Rebecca settled in at Lowbands, and very likely King and Henry Cullingham with him. Christopher Doyle stayed on at O'Connorville for the time as deputy manager. The directors were true to their word in asking the allottees for their individual choices of cottage. Thomas Rawson of Manchester wrote to the *Northern Star* that Mr M'Grath had written asking him what size of house he wanted on his 4-acre lot.

The plan of a 3-roomed house with outbuildings came out in the *Northern Star* of 13 February, as soon as O'Connor had settled in. He said that every allottee was 'entitled' to a 4-roomed house with no outbuildings, or a 3-roomed house with all these built on at the back. Living space in the house was less important than space for the working life which was to support it. The choice of four- or three-roomed house was circulated to all those people successful in the ballot, with Feargus's pressure behind the choice of three-roomed.

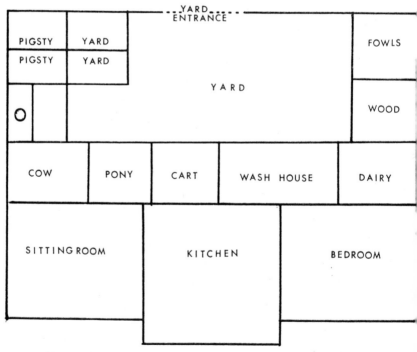

11 O'Connor's ground plan of a cottage, from the *Northern Star*, 13 February 1847

As well as Rebecca, he brought two cats and a dog. Rebecca, famed for her 28 quarts a day in summer, still gave 8 a day on winter keep and in snow. Feargus was at his fullest capacity now, inspired by the solid success of cottages rising at O'Connorville, and by work on a new estate. To his people, chilled and underfed in slum streets, he wrote of the good days coming:

> no factory bell to fear in the morning—no bastille (workhouse) on the confines of the village grimly waiting to receive them, the insatiable grave of honest industry. But, blessed change operated by democracy! the schoolhouse rises in its place—and the mother, instead of sending her children to the mill, there to brutalise the mind and waste the young form, sees them go to school with a light heart, to brighten that intellect which God gives equally to all!

That same week there were 5,000 people out of work in Bradford alone, and drifting crowds of Irish beggars blocked the stairs and entrances to shops and offices, clubs and restaurants in Manchester. From Hinckley they wrote to the *Northern Star* that the framework knitters were more than wretched, they were desperate. O'Connor's words spoke straight to their condition.

Every allottee chose the three-roomed house plus outbuildings, and Feargus went ahead at once. Gloucester contractors quoted £230 or £240 for each house, so he rejected them and organised the work himself. He found lodgings for workmen in Redmarley or Staunton. It took hard work in congeniality and coin-jingling, but he won the suspicious villagers round. He laid the estate out comfortably round open common land called Forty Green. On one edge he sited the school, near paths. He cut his 9-ft lanes roughly round the green and grouped his houses on either side of them. He got the men on to clearing land for roads, burning clay, laying out building sites, preparing land for draining and plough. Earth dug out from each foundation was mixed with lime and made the basis of a manure pile at every yard gate. The wonder of plentiful water made a pump possible in every back kitchen. The map drawn for the High Court of Chancery in 1853 showed the estate as twenty-three allotments of 4 acres, eight of 3, and fifteen of 2, with a 10-acre water meadow.

On 8 March the ballot was held to decide the order of location at Lowbands. Ten houses were up, under Cullingham's direction, and the

12 Plan of Lowbands estate

carpenters' work on the whole lot was nearly finished. Outer walls were 14 in thick and stuccoed. Every house had a path to the road. O'Connor had bought ten horses, for which he claimed that coal, beer, timber and whisky men were bidding. 'Weavers' pence beat their pounds.' Seventeen horses were at work hauling stones to build houses 'for men that never had a house in their lives', and fifteen in-calf heifers were grazing, so that there was a good source of dung as well as of labour.

Under Cullingham the mason's work was contracted to Griffiths, and plastering and stuccoing and slating to Jones. A contractor named Perry came several times to O'Connor's London office and tried to get a building contract out of him. O'Connor said that his estimate for merely building the outside of a cottage was as much as he, O'Connor, could complete one for and turn the key in it. The stonework was of good quality. Face and sides of the house were of chiselled stone, the corners all jointed, quoins and arches cut. Building like this proved too slow, and O'Connor said that instead of cut stone the masons put imitation quoins of Roman cement on fronts, sides and chimneys. This enabled them to build six in the time formerly taken for one.

Griffiths was a man of many parts. When O'Connor asked for tenders for sinking wells, he tendered 2s a yard less than the next lowest tender, and said he would find and haul the stones from his own quarry at 2s a perch. All his sons would work on the job. Three quarries were used up on the building. O'Connor hired the company's horses out to contractors, and earned 9s a day with each horse for hauling stones, 7s 6d hauling sand, and 8s 4d lime.

The schoolhouse remains in good condition today, very handsome and surprising across hedges and fields. It is owned and occupied by a private family. It faces away from the lane, towards wild country and the Malvern hills. The roof throughout is of octagonal slates. The stucco is still good, lined all over to suggest big blocks of stone, but in fact the building is largely brick. A couple of stone steps led up to the schoolroom, and perhaps kept winter wet out, as the land slopes down slightly to the wall. I was shown over the house in 1968. The upper-storey rooms are a good size, even the two little top rooms, and each is well-lit by a lozenge-shaped window, the front one framing the line of the Malverns. The house was later called The Towers.[67]

I

One of the schoolrooms remains unaltered, and is used as a store-room. It has the same height and size and shaped ceiling as in the school I also went over at Snigs End. The massive bottom of the dresser which was built in every house remained, with two deep drawers. Sliding doors had been added to this one. The original schoolroom door was there in 1968, with latch and big wooden lock.

Honeychurch and Wright built forty wells for Griffiths. Perry circulated a complaint against Griffiths on low wages and profiteering with the people's work, but got nowhere with it. O'Connor replied that he meant to take Griffiths with him to all building sites. There was also building in brick, and mention is made of bricks being loaded on the wharf, which may have been on the Herefordshire & Gloucester-shire Canal, or at Gloucester on the Severn.

In March, men were busy digging the land and sowing wheat, as well as building houses. Although O'Connor was fiercely against ploughing, he allowed a first ploughing from grass. He preferred a fork to a spade, and particularly one type of fork, weighing $8\frac{1}{2}$ lb with tines 14 in long. He claimed that after digging with this fork he need plant only 8 lb, or just over half a stone, of seed to an acre, instead of the local farmers' 14 stone sown broadcast at 2s 6d a stone.

On 28 May 1847 O'Connor held a visiting day. Two van loads of people came out from Stourbridge to see the new estate. Chartism had been unknown in this Lowbands area until then, but the building of the estate had started branches in the neighbouring villages, and £30 a week was coming in to the Land Company. Branches everywhere had been voting for O'Connor's resolution to hold the summer conference of the Land Company at Lowbands, and of course they all agreed. On 25 June he announced that the conference would open there on 16 August. He had to find lodgings for delegates, and go round every house in the remote district, except parsons'. Parsons were devils, he added as usual.

On the day the conference opened, the allottees would be located in their houses and a demonstration would be held to celebrate. Feargus kept one of the houses for his own use as a building base. One delegate for every 500 shareholders was due to come, and with 30,000 members this meant a possible sixty people to be housed on or around the estate. O'Connor was standing for Parliament at Nottingham in the election in July, but he had energy enough for anything. Potatoes were in on 12 June, ¼ acre to each allotment, with cabbage and swede. Now the ground was being prepared for more swede and turnip, stand-by with potatoes for the winter. O'Connor said that farmers in the parish were astonished at his experiments with crops. His fork-dug wheat was standing 4½ ft high, each ear 5 in long. A man, wife and five children could not consume in 6 months the produce of ¼ acre of it. The old bailiff, Ellis, had dug O'Connor a root of potatoes for his dinner, and there were 50 potatoes on it; the largest weighed 1¾ lb. Peter, a Negro, had counted them as Ellis turned them up, and roared, 'Oh Massa Ellis what a sight!' This was news that made good reading for the underfed crowds in Manchester or Glasgow. O'Connor felt with them, and exclaimed, 'I would rather be the founder of the Land Plan than monarch of Europe.'

Travelling instructions were issued on 7 August 1847 for the journey to the promised land. All from Manchester or north of Birmingham, and all from 80 miles south of Birmingham, were to go to Birmingham by rail; thence to Tewkesbury on the Gloucester line or to Gloucester, 13 miles further, where there might be more certainty of getting means of carriage for luggage or themselves. All from within 30 or 40 miles of London were to go to Euston Square station, and thence across London to Paddington, and book to Gloucester. Each man must find out exactly when his train left his own district, and how its arrival would fit in with the third-class train departure from Birmingham or London. Everyone should bring all his luggage with him, in spite of the cost—because Thomas Richardson from Warrington left his furniture at Warrington station on Monday week to go via Birmingham to Tewkesbury, and has been every day to Tewkesbury since then, with no news of it.

Mr Aston, a neighbouring farmer, lent a field free for the gathering, on the condition that no intoxicating liquor was sold. O'Connor announced that he would help the police and anyone else to duck every drunk who entered. Coffee would be available in the schoolroom and in the marquee, which would hold 500.

Although only forty names were on the ballot list, O'Connor said that forty-five cottages awaited them, made of the best materials, with a back kitchen with a pump, a privy, a dairy and outbuildings, and a walled-in yard with gateway. At every gate was a stack of firing for two years, and ten cart-loads of stable dung for the land. Every house had crops planted—food on the plate every day without having to find money for it. There was land prepared for wheat, clover and tares, stacks of manure, road access to every corner of the estate, three entrances with big gates on stone piers and wickets beside them, and a magnificent schoolhouse. Twenty-two horses, better than any distillers' dray horses, were in the estate stables, providing labour and manure.

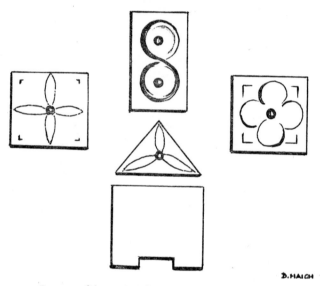

D.HAIGH

13   Patterns of decorations found on Land Company cottages.
The top four designs were used as roof ventilators

Many allottees had already arrived. Feargus wrote that there were twenty or thirty little children from the alleys and back slums of London and manufacturing towns, who now had bright eyes and blooming cheeks and appetites. He signed himself 'Your fond Father and honoured bailiff.'

Monday, 16 August dawned hazy. The high shoulder line of the Malverns was clouded, and by 9 am rain was falling. But country people were used to that, and crowds of waggons, carts and carriages filled all the ways leading to Redmarley. People came by train to Gloucester or Tewkesbury, and on by road. A local paper[68] estimated that between 5,000 and 6,000 people were on the estate, all the separate parties carrying flags and banners and headed by their own bands. In that lonely countryside of fields and trees and streams, the neat crescents of houses and cultivated plots were unanimously admired. It was indeed an outstanding achievement for eight months' work. Cows on Forty Green and crops on each allotment delighted the allottees and surprised the locals. O'Connor's cultivation of potatoes in a trench interested everybody. Lowbands crops were declared much better than those in Redmarley village gardens.

The *Gloucestershire Chronicle* observed that the new allottees 'judging by appearances, are by no means fitted to buffet with the hardships and privations of a country life'. However, privations did not begin today. Provisions were offered in the big marquee by William Dixon of Manchester, and several allottees offered tea and cold food. All the morning people toured the houses in the rain, while the bands played. The Land Conference met in the schoolroom. *Berrow's Worcester Journal* reported that the crops were not promising and that 'several of the fortunate (?) allottees appeared quite crestfallen and as gloomy as the weather'. However, as expected, the weather cleared up in the late afternoon, hustings were put up and the meeting began at five. O'Connor, burly and ruddy, held the scene. He congratulated his people on their improved intellect. They were building home colonies to obtain a legitimate influence by achievement of the franchise. He himself, now as Member for Nottingham a 655th part of the House of Commons, would proclaim their principles. The Whigs said they were too ignorant to be given the vote, but when had the Whigs built schools like this one to teach them? He reminded them that the rain would swell the allottees' potatoes, and said he was shortly moving on to develop another Chartist estate. In the evening the cottages were 'illuminated'.

The liveliest send-off for an allottee was from Barnsley, the home of Thomas Aclam, described as 'middle-class' and therefore unusual. He left home in an open carriage, with four greys and two postilions, decorated with Chartist evergreen rosettes and ribbons, through a street wedged with cheering people, while the church bells were rung for him. Barnsley brass band and Chartist committee marched in front, and behind came two other carriages. The train drew out to music and cheering.

The conference went on all the week. A hundred and forty delegates came, and complained afterwards that they were very uncomfortable, but there are no details of how they were lodged. However, everybody had a good chance to see the houses in use. Builders' and carpenters' work came in for special admiration, as being both good and cheap. Mr Woolf Moss and his opposite neighbour had an awkward corner; O'Connor called it the only bit of lean on the estate. He promised them some help, and adjustment of rent. The company's aid money was paid into the hand of every allottee during the first day or two. On Friday night a supper was spread in the schoolroom for all the delegates. Like all good blow-outs in popular esteem, it specialised in meat. Saddles of mutton, hashed mutton, veal, hams and tongues are listed. August was not, of course, the season for pork, and beef was always a luxury. 'All vegetables in season' came at the end of the list. With or without alcohol (there is no evidence), the party went on till 4 am. O'Connor left at 2, as he had to go to Lancashire in the morning.

Ledbury and villages near by organised a visit to Lowbands on the Wednesday of this inaugural week. Some came to see the houses, some the cultivating, some the Chartists. After the conference was concluded, the organisers held a public meeting to explain the Land Company. They had plenty of speakers on hand, and the subject was hot news locally. Farmers and their wives and daughters came on horseback, argued and listened, village people came and calculated to a halfpenny what could be raised, eaten and sold off the allotments. Most of them reckoned the thing to do was to get hold of a house and land and sell it.

The *Northern Star* lists of the result of the ballot for Lowbands are confused in their headings and not easy to understand. So it is not extraordinary that poor Mr Graham arrived from Hull at Lowbands with all his goods, under the impression that he had won an allotment. He was lent £5 to pay his way back, and O'Connor turned the edge of a bleak human situation by saying that the £5 could be refunded out of Graham's aid money when he was in fact located. Feargus took the opportunity to say that the company had acquired bigger funds than was anticipated, and every member had been located for a smaller rent and with more privileges than was planned. The rent was reduced 'by 1¼% on the first £100', one of O'Connor's personal bits of accounting which made comprehension so difficult.

The *Nottingham Mercury* had been taking an interest in O'Connor's expenditure on the estates. In particular the buying of horses for Lowbands, nearly two dozen of them, drew its fire. The cost and keep of horses was one of the main incentives to men to use steam and machines. O'Connor broke out into a financial defence of his horse-actions—an example of his whirling methods which roused everyone's suspicions.

First, on 16 October 1847, he printed this account for the buying of his horses.

	£	s	£
23 horses	915	0	915·00
carriage of horses by rail to Gloucester	38	19	38·95
(£1 3s per horse by 9 hour train, or			
£1 18s „ „ „ 5 „ „)			
wheelwright	181	0	181·00
cart	11	0	11·00
tax-cart	7	10	7·50
big cart	8	10	8·50
other cart	7	0	7·00
implements	41	0	41·00
saddlery and harness	54	0	54·00
	£1,263	19	£1,263·95

Next week he published feed costs.

> March 27th to July 17th, beans, hay,
> straw, oats, clover hay   £94

He reckoned haulage costs for estate work at £650, which was thus saved on the £1,264 purchase money and the £94 feed money. 'And now the Company has the horses, healthy, shining and prancing.' And eating their heads off, as every horse-owner would say when he read it.

He went on. The papers accused him of spending money on a cart and horse for the bailiff.

> Ha! ha! my eye, Timkins, I wish you saw the turnout, and our bailiff going to fair and market in it—a butcher's trap Timkins, and a shabby one, all cost £7 10s, a hired pony, Timkins, 20 years of age, and harness tied up; but our bailiff is a disgrace to us, I'm ashamed to meet him, going to Gloucester with those swells of farmers.

Or he might go jobbing for carpenters. 'Draw my coat over my head to hide my shame!' And the letter-bag he was attacked for buying costing a pound—for 100 letters at a time, many with money in them. And the watchdog! For scattered property! And it cost each 50 members ¼d. Bailiff King and Bailiff O'Connor and the watchdog are there if anyone gets off the road into the estate. There is no chain, O'Connor never chains anything. One contractor asked £248 per house without outbuildings! Up to 15 August just under £59,000 had been received by the company. On 16 August, £34,930 was in hand thus:

London Bank	£21,310
Gloucester Bank	6,030
Half notes and bank orders	890
Paid deposit on Mathon	2,000
,, ,, ,, Minster Lovell	900
In meadow and timber, Lowbands	1,100
Cows, horses, implements, carts	2,000
Registration deed, conveyancing of Minster Lovell	700

This left £24,070 which had been spent on the two estates, O'Connorville and Lowbands, about £284 for each house and ground, the school counting as four houses. At O'Connorville he had given £127 as the cost of each house and allotment, but he did not now refer to that.

He had just sent three stunners of horses in one of Goatman's waggons 43 miles to Lowbands with 3½ tons of seed wheat. The allottees need not pay for it till after the harvest. The allottees had combined to buy a horse, and also to buy a boat to carry their potatoes by the canal and the Severn to Birmingham. There were wharves on the Herefordshire & Gloucestershire Canal at Newent and Dymock, and this idea might have worked. But I find no more mention of it, and it may have been a proposal which came to nothing. Loyal Cullingham wrote to the *Northern Star* defending O'Connor against charges of waste. Four tradesmen at Gloucester made kitchen ranges, and sent them as patterns to O'Connor before he gave an order. He bought the best with the people's money. True, but an increasing number of the people wanted quantity rather than quality in houses. The allottees of Lowbands rallied to O'Connor. A meeting was called, and every member came. Mr King proposed a fund for the purpose of prosecuting the proprietor of the *Manchester Examiner*, O'Connor's most persistent enemy.

Everybody paid 1s towards it, except one female who paid 6d. £2 2s 6d (£2·12½) was raised and sent with a long address to their father and he10.

In October, O'Connor bought another estate three miles off, at Snigs End. Great excitement was aroused locally by this advance of Chartism to their doors. One estate was a local interest; two were suddenly a threat. In November Mr West came to the west country on a Chartist tour, and spoke at Gloucester. The meeting was large and lively, concerned at the new purchase following on Lowbands. There was a persistent series of interruptions, led by Samuel Bowly, a Quaker, who was operating a small land scheme of his own. He insisted that O'Connor was not sufficient security for the Land Company funds and property, and it had no other. Henry Cullingham defended O'Connor in a speech which was clearly most effective. He led a sharp attack on those Gloucester tradesmen who had received large payments from O'Connor and yet were not at the meeting to defend his honesty. Bowly was bowled out, in fact, as the report said.

Mr West then came on to stay at Lowbands and see the estate. He spent the night with Mr and Mrs Renham, and on Sunday visited round the estate. Renham, of Westminster, and Ford (not on original list) had fine pigs and ducks. Aclam, from Barnsley, and his wife were in the best of spirits and health. He had three pigs. John Lee of Manchester was called Farmer because his land was in such good shape. His winter wheat was in and trenched, and he had the best pig on the estate, weighing 14 score. Two good sons, a wife and daughter helped him. He had been twenty-one years in factories, but here at Lowbands he meant to live and die. John Dennis, from New Radford, was busy making a rabbit hutch. He had potatoes, cabbages and winter crops. His wife said to West, 'Tell them when you go back to Nottingham that though I am turned three score and two, I would not go back for £100.' Edmund Kershaw from Rochdale and several others came along to Dennis's cottage and talked to West there. He noted that they all greeted each other very friendly. William Addison of Manchester and his wife had good potatoes and were cherishing a huge one promised for a friend, Rankin, who was still in Manchester. They also had a goat in milk, and pigs. Their boy, who might well have been sweating in a factory or mill, was the picture of health.

William Charlesworth of Stalybridge was eating his home-grown dinner. He said he had left a good business behind, and was thoughtful.

'Do you think it will answer?' asked West. Drily Charlesworth replied, 'I'll try,' and went on with his dinner. William Souter and his wife were very cheerful. He too had pigs, and was taking cultivation seriously, learning and experimenting.

At the same time Mr Morgan from Worcester, a shareholder in the company, was looking at the estate. He was a joiner, and had come to look at the woodwork. He declared himself well satisfied, and ended his visit by asking each man if he would sell his lot. Edmund Kershaw said '£200', probably to a general laugh.

One or two men were depressed about failure of turnips and some cases of potato disease. But on the whole winter crops looked well, most people had a sack of flour in the house and another of meal to fatten the pigs, and by this first week in December they reckoned they were well into the winter. Wind came tearing over the land off the Malverns, and there was a lot of rain, but northern winters had been worse, and smoke-laden as well.

James Helliwell went home to Hebden Bridge for New Year 1848. A Chartist tea was held, and 160 sat down in the Association Room. The tables were decked with evergreens, and twelve huge potatoes which James brought with him of his own growing, 1 lb 2 oz to 1 lb 10 oz each. All winters were bad in the north, and this was a wicked one. Up from Hebden Bridge to Todmorden, where work on the branch line to Burnley had stopped for winter weather, hundreds of emaciated men and women tramped the narrow hill roads of the town, sent from one relieving officer to another when relief money ran out. Against this kind of background James Helliwell's Lowbands potatoes spelled life and hope. At a meeting of the Greenwich Chartist branch, Mr Munroe produced six potatoes weighing over 5 lb, from Henry Tanner's allotment at Lowbands. Munroe said simply that the estate was one of the loveliest spots he ever saw in his life.

O'Connor was at Lowbands in the New Year. He held a discussion in the schoolhouse with all the allottees. 'How did you get over the back-break?' he asked William Addison. William answered, 'Well, for the first week I thought I should give it up; but my word, now I can work the longest day and never feel it.' They all wanted fruit trees, which were expensive. O'Connor agreed to plant a double row of pear trees on each side of the roads in front of every cottage. Everyone could keep an eye on a number of trees. He would also sow French furze seed round every allotment, for hedging and for winter feed for cows and horses. M'Grath said later that they planted 8 miles of pear trees and over 16 miles of furze hedging. The leafy, blossoming effect of this through the narrow lanes is a characteristic of Lowbands today.

In February, Willis came to O'Connor at Snigs End to arrange the sale of his 2-acre allotment for £40 to Mr Parker. He said he was happy, but had no money to develop the holding. O'Connor asked what he thought he needed, and Willis said, '£10'. O'Connor offered him the £10, or to arrange his sale for £40. Willis took the £10. Parker then went to Aclam, and offered £160 for his 4 acres. Aclam hesitated, then refused. 'My son is wild about the place,' he said. His wife and daughter did not like it in winter, but he decided to part with them rather than with the land. He sent them back to Barnsley until the summer weather came, when they would be glad to come back. So the first allotment became a summer 'cottage in the country'. Feargus sold his own allotment to Parker instead, for £80.

Although the winter was far advanced into February, he found food stores in some houses. Addison, a block printer, showed Feargus his 'portraits' hanging from the ceiling—Frost the Chartist leader, a gammon of bacon; Duncome the MP, a flitch; and Feargus, a ham. Next day Feargus was measuring drains in the pouring rain and sheltered at Kershaw's cottage. Kershaw gave him rashers from one of his 'portraits', eggs from his hens, and water from his pump. Kershaw's old father and mother were living with him, and an orphan girl they had befriended, now healthy, straight-backed and neat.

John Revans, in evidence to the Select Committee, said that he visited Lowbands unknown to the directors at the end of April 1848. Crops were in, but patchiness showed that the land was not treated in a methodical way. He saw rye grown to cut green, and winter tares (vetch). The crops were not bad, but not as good as in larger units cultivated by plough. He spoke to Lee and told him who he was, and why he was looking at the estate.[69]

On 12 June a visiting day was held at Lowbands, to coincide with the day of location on Snigs End. Crawford, pro-Chartist MP for Rochdale, and Allsop, the company's stockbroker, came for the occasion. Unfortunately rain streamed all day. However, the visitors walked through most of the allotments and saw them in their mid-summer growth. The difficulty of marketing their produce was the main obstacle to the allottees' success. Aclam told them he had managed to sell his half-acre of cabbages in the ground without taking them to market. His garden produced new potatoes for today's dinner, beans and lettuce for five people, with turnips coming on. Crawford talked to everybody. Mrs Graham told him that she would fight at her door with a poker before she would give up her cottage and allotment. O'Connor wrote in the *Northern Star*, 'You should see my old grey-headed children that are happy; and my youthful children that are blooming, thankful and merry.'

On 20 June 1848 Mr O'Brien arrived from Exeter as schoolmaster at Lowbands. He would teach any child whose parents would pay him to do so. Adults, too, could learn if they could pay. Although a fellow-countryman, he was to become a reed that pierced the hand of O'Connor. Lowbands School opened on 10 July. O'Brien's course included every subject anyone had heard of, and several they had not, like conic section chemistry. He would give lectures daily on the English language, and regularly on science and philosophy. He used kind treatment to secure the affections of pupils, and exercised strict attention to morals. Mrs O'Brien was also experienced and would conduct a female school.

An unusual side to the prospectus was music. 'Mr O'Brien deems it right to state that music, instead of being a barrier to progress in the scholastic way, as some suppose, he has ever found an incentive.' He taught the sax horn (trumpet, baritone, bass or contra bass), corno-pheon, bugle, french horn, trombone, ophicleide, serpent, bassoon, clarionet, flageolet, flute, guitar, violin, 'cello, accordion 'etc'. He assured his readers that no music would be taught in school hours.

The Parliamentary Committee was now enquiring into the Land Company. One of its members, Sullivan, MP for Kilkenny, visited Lowbands and Snigs End towards the end of July. His account varied greatly from Revans's depressing report, and accorded closely with O'Connor's. Which man was the more competent judge I cannot tell.

Sullivan looked at crops all the way down on the train to Gloucester and along the road to Lowbands. He went all over Lowbands' allotments and into the houses. He was struck, and genuinely so after experience of small Irish farms, with the enormous amount of produce and the superior character of the equipment. The horses (too good for a 4-acre farmer, he thought), gates, schoolhouse 'built in the most permanent and complete style' were all mentioned. He was taken with the old cotton overseer, who was as fully acquainted with gardening and had his farm in as complete a system as if he had been there years. This might have been Aclam. He found no former agricultural labourers, but all were from trades, and he named frame-knitter, tallow chandler, stocking-maker, cabinetmaker, shoemaker, cotton-spinner. Only one cow remained, for everyone found pigs more profitable.

Mr D. E. Morgans also visited the two estates, and gave some details. On Lowbands he found that the ears of wheat were double the size of broadcast-sown grain on local farms; O'Connor had claimed that this would be so when he was planting. Mr and Mrs O'Brien had just arrived at the schoolhouse and gave Morgans a welcome. He saw allottees still at work in the dusk at 10 pm.

16 August was the anniversary of the opening of Lowbands, and near the date a celebration tea and meeting was held. 120 sat down to tea, including several from Snigs End. The feature of the event was the brass band recently formed by O'Brien, which played 'enlivening airs'. Edmund Kershaw, a 4-acre man, took the chair, and proposed prosperity to the Land Plan. A fortnight earlier, on 30 July, the findings of the Select Committee had been published, condemning the company in its present constitution. Members did not realise that this was to prove the end, but were all busy with ideas on how to reconstitute the scheme and secure possession of their acres.

O'Brien replied to the chairman's toast. He was confident the Land Plan could either be legalised or altered. Persevering allottees at Lowbands would succeed in making a living and paying their rent. Such a man as Feargus O'Connor had never existed in any age or clime. At the end of his speech, O'Brien's two children, aged 7 and 5, sang 'We'll rally around him', the Chartist song about Feargus's imprisonment in 1841, and the chorus was taken up by the whole company. The chairman then rose and supported O'Connor. He said that a man would need to stick to the allotment for three years to get its proper reward in crops. After the speeches there was dancing to a quadrille band until 5 am.

O'Connor's three-year campaign to get the allottees to pay rent now began on every estate. In September 1848 he asked for the first year's rent from Lowbands. All the allottees declared themselves incapable of paying, and the story of Lowbands becomes mainly a sad, protracted account of rent deadlock, with How and O'Brien organising the allottees. O'Brien's tone about Feargus changes from this time. Six holdings were offered for sale in September and October, five 4-acre and one 2-acre. One had an acre of reed and seventy fruit trees, one an acre of wheat ready sacked, one a brick-built oven, copper, sink, and good cellar, and asked £120. Prices were rising. O'Brien said that of these six two left because of wives, two got other jobs, and two gave up through poverty. An effort was made in February 1849 to organise a market. The allottees wrote to the Birmingham branch of the Land Company at the Ship Inn, asking if members would make arrangements to buy their surplus. Since 1844 fly-boats (fast boats) had been travelling twice weekly for perishable goods to and from Birmingham via the Worcester & Birmingham Canal, the Severn Navigation from Worcester to Gloucester, and the Herefordshire & Gloucester Canal past Newent. A meeting of all the Birmingham members was called but I have found no record of any result of this sensible proposition.

All the unallotted members of the Land Company were complaining vigorously of the failure of the lucky allottees to pay the company any rent. The allottees retaliated. O'Brien forsook Feargus and became leading agitator on the estate. In December they wrote to the *Hereford Times*, over the signature of William Alder How, chairman; they had expected their allotments to be good land, drained, manured and planted, but soon found that only some were good and none were well-drained, manured or planted. This prevented them from using their aid money wisely, so that at planting time many of them had no money to buy seed. The company made a loan of £5 per acre, but few got it at the proper time. 'No pen can portray the sufferings we endured up to the harvest of 1849.' Then life improved, but just when they were beginning to do well, Feargus O'Connor sent his agents to demand six months' rent 'at the exorbitant rate of £15 for 4 acres, £13

for 3 acres, and £11 for 2 acres'. When they refused to pay, he laid
distraints on some. Thomas Lee was under a distraint, and he had spent
£138 on his allotment and only needed time to make a success of it.
None of them wished to default the members of the Land Company of
a penny, if time were allowed. They hoped a public voice would be
raised for them, to prevent the injustice of enticing men from their
usual avocations, 'after two and a half years of suffering, sending them
adrift on the world, many with large and helpless families'. Some had
paid £80 for 'the right of location'. Allottees were called idle, dissi-
pated, grumbling. But none had succeeded, even regular teetotallers.

This letter does not tally with the details of modest happiness which
have been shown at Lowbands over the two years. The suggestion that
men were enticed on to the estates was particularly repellent. Probably
O'Brien wrote the text. This was copied by the *Gloucester Chronicle* and
Berrow's Journal on 1 and 6 December 1849. W. A. How was a York-
shireman, not an original allottee, but he acquired a plot early on.

By 1851 the allottees were fairly well accepted in the parish. The
census returns of 1851 show four who can be identified as townsmen
from the north. Redmarley parish history notes say that in 1851 the
vestry resolved that four men from Staunton and three from the
estate, including How, should investigate Lowbands and ascertain its
rateable value. A meeting of the parish in vestry decided that owners
and not occupiers of tenements under £6 yearly rateable value should
be rated for poor rates, so the allottees, who had no title of ownership
yet, escaped again. The feeling of the public (not of the other shareholders) was of sympathy for the allottees, who were often called 'de-
luded by O'Connor'. T. C. Turberville published a book, *Worcestershire in the Nineteenth Century*, in 1852, and included a short account of
Lowbands and the National Land Company, 'one of the hugest delu-
sions to which the working men of this country ever lent themselves
under demagogue leadership'. The allottees 'were speedily reduced to
the condition of ruined paupers. The affairs of the Company are now
being wound up under an Act of Parliament'.

William Goodchap arrived to conduct the enquiry into Lowbands
and Snigs End for the Court of Chancery in the middle of September
1852. He opened his enquiry at the Feathers Inn, Staunton, on 14
September at 10 am. One paper gave the name of the inn as the Star.

The estate was surveyed and a plan drawn, to which all statements were referred. This shows the estate as forty-five allotments. Local papers reported Goodchap's findings.[70] All occupants had been living rent-free, some for nearly five years. The colony was well arranged, with every convenience on a small scale for homesteads. The land had been in poor state but was greatly improved by labour. Two years of back rent were remitted altogether on account of 'industry and energy', and the sums claimed for improvements were in general allowed to wipe out the rest of back rent. All allotments had belonged to the company and were now assumed by the Court of Chancery. All tenants received a title in fee, or perpetuity, subject to a rent charge or ground rent of 5 per cent on the manager's valuation of each allotment. This would confer a vote for the county. Owners would also be liable for rates in Redmarley parish. Failure to pay the rent charge for twelve consecutive months would forfeit the property. The manager would collect rents for four or five years, during which time anything left of back rent could be paid off in instalments. After that, the estate would be put up for public sale in the usual way. Through the pause of four or five years, the manager hoped to show by a good rent-roll that the estate was valuable in the land market. This would benefit the shareholders.

The enquiry was slow, patient and just. It lasted over a month, and everyone was on good terms by the end. The gentlemen of the court gave a dinner to the tenants and wives of both Lowbands and Snigs End estates, 200 people. It was not immediately disclosed that many of the title deeds to properties on the estate were held by W. P. Roberts, probably due to his lending money for mortgages at various times in the past. Indentures, or leases, were issued by him in the same form as by the official manager. Rents were collected by the agents of either the manager or 'the Manchester man' (W. P. Roberts), who stayed at a farm or inn, and drove round the estates in a gig. Present occupiers remember this, or their fathers speaking of it.

In accordance with the manager's plan, the estate was sold by auction at Gloucester in June 1858. A catalogue of the sale, owned today by Mr Parsons of Staunton, shows the following people still on the estate from my records of 1849: William Reece, Wolfe Moss, William Charlesworth, Henry Porter, W. A. How, Henry Parker, Henry Lee and Thomas Lee (perhaps sons of John) and Richard Aston (perhaps

In Chancery.

IN THE MATTER OF THE
JOINT STOCK COMPANIES' WINDING-UP ACTS, 1848 AND 1849,

AND OF THE

NATIONAL LAND COMPANY.

TO CAPITALISTS AND OTHERS.

LOWBANDS & APPLEHURST ESTATE,

REDMARLEY D'ABITOT, WORCESTERSHIRE.

TO BE SOLD BY AUCTION,

BY HENRY BRUTON,

AT THE BELL HOTEL, GLOUCESTER,
On WEDNESDAY, the 2nd DAY of JUNE, 1858,

AT TWELVE FOR ONE O'CLOCK,

IN ONE LOT,

VALUABLE RENT CHARGES,

Amounting in the whole to about £300, amply secured upon 43 Allotments,

Which are held by the Allottees under separate Conveyances, executed by the Official Manager, under the direction of the Master charged with the Winding-up of the National Land Company.

Each Conveyance contains a proviso for re-entry in case of the Rent-charges being in arrear for the space of 12 calendar months.

ALSO, A BRICK BUILT SCHOOLHOUSE,

WITH 3A. 10P. OF FREEHOLD LAND,

OF WHICH THE PURCHASER WILL HAVE POSSESSION, AND ALSO

TWO MESSUAGES,

AND

ABOUT 4 ACRES OF FREEHOLD LAND.

EACH OF THE ALLOTMENTS HAS A

VOTE FOR THE COUNTY.

The Estate has been well cultivated, under spade husbandry, for several years past, is in excellent condition, and is distant about 8 Miles from Gloucester and Ledbury; and is one of the Estates purchased some years ago on behalf of the National Land Company, and comprises altogether

ABOUT 160 ACRES,

And has been apportioned among, and is chiefly now in, the occupation of the Allottees.

Particulars and Conditions of Sale, and any further information, may be had on application to W. Goodchap, Esq., Walbrook House, Walbrook, London, Official Manager; Messrs. Tucker, Greville, and Tucker, Solicitors, St. Swithin's Lane, London; and to

Mr. HENRY BRUTON, Auctioneer and Land Agent,

KING STREET, GLOUCESTER.

K   14   Sale notice of the Lowbands estate, 1858

son of Cornelius). Two more are possible spelling variants: Shuter for Souter, Wallis for Willis. In 1861 How's house was sold, and described as brick-built and intended for a school. At a later period the women of Lowbands got work at glove-making for Dent's glove works at Worcester. They used the big schoolroom, which I was shown in 1968.

A brief history of the Lowbands settlement was written by How, or his son, for the parish history of the Reverend Millett in 1891.* He described forty-six allotments, and said that the land provided a living if you had a trade as well. 40s freeholders had the vote. A large part of the estate remained in the hands of a Manchester man after the Chancery settlement. The estate people were a poor lot, with a disastrous effect on parish morals, and nearly doubled the poor rate by 1868.

The 1876 rate book of Redmarley gives only John How and W. A. How as familiar names. They owned two 2-acre plots, three 3-acre, and two 4-acre, living in two and sub-letting the rest. How says that by 1891 very few allotments were still in the hands of the class of poor man for whom they were intended. Most of them were owned by tradesmen who used them for raising van-horse fodder, and often left the cottage empty or used it for storage. The remote situation attracted few people.

The *Victoria County History of Worcestershire* quotes Noake's *Guide to Worcestershire* that a Bible Christian chapel was built at Lowbands about the middle of the nineteenth century. Gradually most of the properties were sold individually.

On 26 June 1920, Messrs Bruton and Knowles sold the remaining portions. The sale catalogue shows a distinction between freehold cottages and those which carried a rent charge from the original days. Lot 33 is listed as 'Rent charges of £6 6s on one acre with cottage and out-buildings in Mill Lane, Lowbands, in occupation Mrs. Watkins.' Freehold cottages have much the same rent when let: 2-acre holdings at £7 pa, tithe rent 6s 11d (34½p), land tax 4s 2d (21p). All the sales were at just about £100. Good water was an item of every sale. As far as I can discover, the last of the estate properties passed into individual private hands at this sale. They were not a great catch at that time. But since the 1939 war, the immense rise in the value of land and easier transport have made these trim little houses in their huge areas of orchand land

* This MS history is in the possession of the Vicar of Redmarley d'Abitot.

ever more desirable. Main services have arrived, and the people can work in Ledbury, Gloucester or Tewkesbury while they enjoy the completest peace and privacy among rich western scenery, some of the loveliest in England. Transport, and hence jobs, and social security, have given that massive injection of money every week for lack of which the estates languished and died a hundred years ago.

Round most of the Lowbands houses I saw a few sheep, fowls, young cows, heard pigs, geese and young children and men tinkering in sheds. There were television aerials and small garages. Lines of washing blew among the orchard trees. Most people have cherished the shape of the old cottage in their alterations, though some have pulled it down and started again. At every gate I met friendliness and interest in the history of the company. Here are achieved the independence, health, dignity and security for which the estates were built, not by the Land Company—an impossible aim in 1846—but by a hundred years of effort and change in the social structure of England. How fortunate that so much of the estates survived to see it!

CHAPTER 10

MINSTER LOVELL OR CHARTERVILLE

ON 24 June 1847, four weeks after the brilliant open day at O'Connor-ville, O'Connor bought 300 acres near Minster Lovell, in Oxfordshire. It was upland meadow and pasture land, with a good farm on it, lime-stone and freestone quarries, the river Windrush on the boundary, where one could fish in season for eels, crayfish and trout. Within a mile began the ancient forest area of Wychwood, providing un-limited right of grazing cattle. But what a price, said the locals![71] £36 an acre, £10,878.

O'Connor said the sale took nineteen consecutive hours. It was at the Crown Hotel, Witney, where Mr Long the auctioneer, Feargus and the two trustees of John Walker the late owner, Weaving, a corn merchant of Oxford and Pinnock, a farmer from Chimney,* must have been at it all night. Feargus was a much heard of man; his name, though not his face, was known in every village, but doubt hung about him, and Pinnock and Weaving were trustees and meant to make sure of their money. Afterwards they swore they did not know it was Feargus O'Connor they were dealing with. Solicitors were W. P. Roberts for O'Connor (with George Chinnery as agent), and Lee for Weaving and Pinnock. They wrote into the conditions of sale a clause they were to remember: that £5,000 of the purchase price could be left as mortgage on the estate, at 4½ per cent interest.[72] So long as the interest was paid by 25 March and 25 September, the principal need not be repaid for seven years from the date of purchase; until then, the purchaser had no power to resell the estate. The £5,000 must be paid off by 29 September

* So named in an indenture of February 1851 between Weaving, Pinnock and John Walker, in possession of Lee, Chadwick & Co, of Witney.

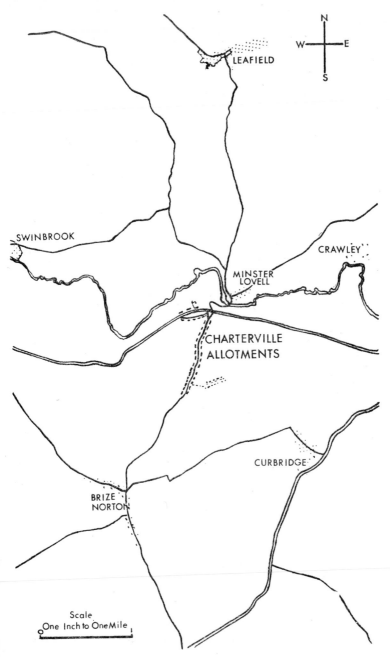

15 Map showing the position of the Charterville (Minster Lovell) estate

1854. Unremarked by anyone, the date 1854 was altered to 1848 before the deed was executed. O'Connor had no expectation of needing to resell, for he expected that mortgage interest would be paid out of the allottees' rents. Weaving and Pinnock trusted no one until the money was in their hand. Roberts kept the title deeds in his safe in Princess Street, Manchester.

A great advantage about the new estate was that two roads in it were already provided, for it lay on either side of the Cheltenham–Oxford road and of the Witney–Brize Norton road, neither of which the allottees would have to maintain. Oxford was 13 miles east, Witney 3, and Bampton 5 to the south-west. The New Inn and the White Hart stand on the main Oxford road at the edge of the estate. Part was deep soil, and part, towards Brize Norton, called Bushey Ground, was gravelly and brashy. Most was treeless, exposed, windy downland. Conversation about the river Windrush caused Feargus to seek out the Drainage Society and get a man to examine the soil and plan drains. He himself left Lowbands for Minster Lovell on 21 August. By the end of September he and Christopher Doyle were laying out allotments and lanes. The farm was sold and separated from the estate. Two hundred loads of timber and the deal for joiners' work had to be bought, but sandstone for cottages and limestone for wells and walls were found on the estate. This great benefit enabled work to go on so fast that on 23 October Feargus wrote in the *Northern Star* that forty-seven houses were up and thirteen would be up next week. He said that some loads were brought by canal. These loads may well have been bricks from the clay country of the Midlands, carried on the Oxford Canal to Oxford, thence on the Thames to Tadpole Bridge, near Bampton, the nearest wharf to Minster Lovell.

The estate was built in two parts. Fifty-seven houses stood on either side of the road from Minster Lovell to Brize Norton, with the Bushey Ground spur to the east. Eighteen more and the school were in a group with a crescent on the Cheltenham road behind the White Hart, and three more across from the White Hart and close to the modern New Inn on the Witney road.*

* The plan shows seventy-eight. Records of the time often speak of eighty, probably a rounding-off figure. Some numbers indicate only occupied allotments, some all of the allotments marked out by O'Connor, and some include patches of unused land.

O'Connor was now an MP and had to spend time in Westminster. He put Doyle in charge of the estate at 5s a week. Doyle lived in one of the farm cottages bought with the estate, and made it his works office. Feargus slept there on his frequent visits. They bought 18 pigs and 40 oxen to make manure. For wages, Doyle told him the appropriate sum needed, and Feargus sent it from London to Clinch & Co's bank at Witney. Doyle fetched it, paid the men and bills, and kept the account.[73] To the surprise of local builders, he and his men worked out of doors through the winter, so that seventy-eight cottages and the schoolhouse were sited and under construction by February.

Criticism of O'Connor's management was becoming more vocal, as members of the Land Company were scandalised by the high quality of the houses and workmanship. To inhabitants of mill town slums it was

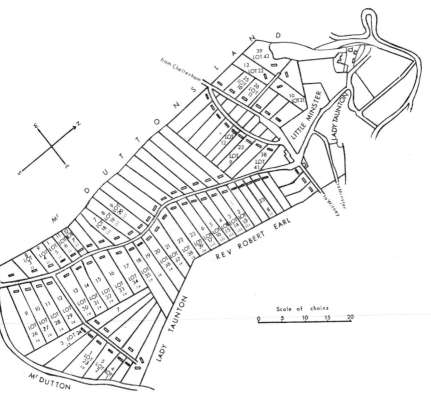

16   Plan of the Charterville (Minster Lovell) estate

a wicked waste of money. In that first November, workmen at Minster Lovell gathered for a meeting at which Henry Cullingham and Christopher Doyle spoke, supported by two workmen, Coutts and Moody. The result was a unanimous resolution that the accusations against O'Connor were false and that he was the only man in the country competent to carry on the company's business. Modern readers might well agree with them about competence and rapid progress, as work began after 21 August 1847 and on 18 December the *Gloucester Chronicle* said, 'The estate at Minster Lovell, Oxfordshire, is fast approaching to a state to receive upwards of 90 allottees.'

Mr Price, manager of the Land Bank, paid a visit to the estate in January 1848.[74] Why he went in January I cannot guess, unless with some shrewdness Feargus insisted on it, when the country was bleak under snow and the road over ankle in mud. At the entrance to the estate he was met by a shepherd in a donkey cart, with a dog. Price had to dismiss his own vehicle and climb into the donkey cart, and creep slowly through the lines of half-built houses to O'Connor's lodging. He said that it was like a room in barracks of an officer living on his pay. He noticed the good standard of horses and estate implements. The subscribers' funds were certainly being spent on the estate.

When the fiercest of winter's grip was slackened, in February, Tom Wheeler set out to walk from O'Connorville in Hertfordshire round all the estates. From Witney he walked up the long rise of two and a half miles to Minster Lovell, and passed the dreaded Union Workhouse, the only refuge of the poor who could no longer work. Across the Brize Norton road the estate made a little town, with a street a mile and a half long, a crescent and a school. The whole of it delighted old Tom Wheeler's heart and winged his pen to the *Northern Star*.

Ballots for location on Minster Lovell are the most confusing of all, as the announcements and results may have been only for certain sections of the company, and are seldom distinguished from those of Snigs End and Great Dodford which were held during the same period. Ballots were announced for August and October 1847, and for February next year (held in fact in January). The division of allotments varies a little, but roughly there were seventy-eight, made up of thirty-odd 4-acre lots, thirteen 3-acre, and twenty-three 2-acre. Not all were occupied. Winners announced in the *Northern Star* on 12 February 1848 are in Appendix 3. Of the forty-three places of origin given, twenty-nine were in the North and Midlands, one in Norwich, one in Boulogne, and twelve in the south. Receipts for the Land Company for the week of 12 February 1848, when the last ballot results came out, were just under £500, a slowly sinking figure.

In January–June 1848 O'Connor was building Snigs End at the same time as finishing Minster Lovell. Complaint continued about money thrown away on solid building, lasting material, good workmanship, above the standards and the needs of people used to cellars and lean-to sheds. In the *Northern Star* for 6 May 1848 he said he was accused of contracting out the building at such a price that it was then sub-contracted for a lower price, and the difference lost to the company. He replied that at Minster Lovell the plastering and the painting were contracted to working men. He paid good wages to the builders and had no complaints.

In the same issue, 6 May, Feargus announced boldly that a public soirée would be held in the elegant schoolroom on 15 May, and the proceeds would go towards a clock for the school. On 12 June, the day that allottees arrived at Snigs End, some would also be located on Minster Lovell, and there would be a demonstration of the houses. He had reason to be proud of his work. Within ten months, he and Doyle had built almost eighty cottages, installed eighty water tanks to give water indoors, sunk wells at the back, equipped every house with out-buildings, cupboards and bookshelves, kitchen grate and dresser. Cullingham said a contractor would have charged £4,600 to bring water to those houses.[75] O'Connor put tanks and water in each house for £3 10s (£3·50) a house or £280. The land had been cleared of fences and tree stumps ready for allotments; 15 acres had been drained, all had been ploughed and harrowed, some twice. Manure had taken the horses two months to spread, and more was stacked at each yard gate.

Doyle had no trouble with workmen. At the parliamentary enquiry he said they were good, well-behaved towards farmers and neighbours, and did very little drinking. Local people were friendly, and there was no hostility from big landowners. No workman was ever charged with poaching.

Though troubles darkened the sky, the purpose of the Land Company and its solid achievements for a few could not be defeated. June would see the parliamentary enquiry, but also two different settlements begun. Allottees arrived with less ceremony than at O'Connorville and Lowbands, in small groups throughout the summer. At Minster Lovell, June was haymaking time. One allottee, Mr Smith from Carlisle (on the Select Committee list) had rented an extra meadow for the season, and now his friends and neighbours on the estate gathered round to learn scything, forking, turning and cocking hay and making ricks. A philanthropist, Mr Russell, who lived near the estate, joined them, perhaps to teach the craft. The work done and the feed for their animals stored in sweet-smelling ricks, Smith gave the helpers a hay-harvest tea. They spread a cloth in the meadow, and carried out from Smith's house food and tea and quantities of home-brewed ale. 'Singing and dancing with music echoed through the beautiful valley of Minster.'[76] All through the long June evening they ate and drank and danced and rejoiced, free as O'Connor's dream from landlord, employer, dirt, poisoned air, poverty and hunger. 'The party was kept up till a late hour.' On parting they gave three cheers for Mr Russell, three for the Chartist heroes in exile, Frost, Williams and Jones, and then for Feargus O'Connor three times three. A similar party was given by Mr Hart of Brize Norton, who took up the allotment of poor Mr Townsend (1847 list) who had died. Mr Hart also took up Townsend's three orphan children.[77] Nearly forty couples danced at his meadow party. From about this time the estate was called Charterville, though never so consistently as Heronsgate was called O'Connorville.

Members settled in Charterville applied in July to the GPO for the establishment of a receiving office for letters, and the Postmaster General replied favourably.

The new allottees were aware of the attacks on the company, but began as supporters of O'Connor and Chartism. George Buss became sub-secretary for selling the *Northern Star* on the settlement. The allottees wrote by the hand of Henry Grimshaw, secretary, asking for the loan of aid money in three months instead of waiting through the summer for six months. Other allottees found seed already in when they arrived.

By the end of July the verdict of the Select Committee on the company was known, and the two main fears were confirmed: the com-

17 A drawing of the Charterville estate, showing the tower of the school, from the *Illustrated London News*, 1848

pany was illegal, and the settlers had no title to their land. But the lure of a house and land of one's own was strong enough to make poor men take the chance. In August 1848 *Berrow's Worcester Journal* reported all but four or five houses on Charterville occupied.

> The land is in tolerable state of cultivation, and the crops look healthy, the potatoes especially. The first view of it gave us the idea of the approach to some large manufacturing town, and altogether it has a very cheerful appearance. We noticed a few sign boards of tradesmen. . . . Everything about it looked neat and clean.

George Bubb suggested setting up a market at Charterville, and a committee was formed. Minster Lovell parish was suspicious and expected to have to support the 80 householders on the rates.

At the Land Company conference in November 1848, James Beattie, a Scotsman, began a war with Feargus which was to go on for years. At a meeting he said that there had been no cultivation on the estate since Adam, he had to employ seven men to remove huge roots and stones from his land, all his aid money was gone and he was destitute and nothing had been done to his land. To ask for rent was an insult. Feargus answered that roots had been removed and were stacked for fuel. A carter named Hall stood up and said that he had shifted them off Beattie's ground with a horse and cart. Feargus forced Beattie to admit that of his four acres he let three, for £13 a year, more than the rent which was to be asked for all four acres. Digging that tight, reddish, upland soil with a spade had been too much like work for Beattie. Shouts of rage went up in the meeting. This was exactly how the unlocated members thought the allottees were behaving. After his public set-down, Beattie occupied himself so tirelessly with his war with O'Connor that he can have had no time over for agriculture. The hardships of John Bradshaw so worked on his old neighbours at Almondbury that a public benefit was held for him in the Town Hall in November, and raised 30s (£1·50).

All allottees felt themselves under fire as the thousands of unallotted members of the company settled down to plan its reorganisation. Payment of rent was everyone's first demand. It was the only source of income for the company except mortgaging the property, and indeed that depended on a good rent record. Feargus tried to cajole the allottees with remissions and promises. John Bradshaw adopted a cunning tactic. He got thirty-two members of the Huddersfield branch of the Land Company to sign a letter to the directors in January 1849 saying his allotment was not productive this year, he was destitute, £30 must be advanced at once, as allowed at the Birmingham land conference, or nothing could be sown on his four acres for next season; they all testified to his knowledge and industry. O'Connor was able to floor them with the reply that, as Bradshaw had bought the allotment and was not a member of the Land Company, he had no claim on company money. Ten shillings from each signatory of the letter would help Bradshaw, 'though it is always much easier to ask than to give'.

Other letters came from Charterville, from different groups, some expressing gratitude for rent remission, some a sense of guilt about it, but no one paid any. Stallwood applied again to the Postmaster General for better postal service. The PMG replied that Charterville would now be served with Curbridge and Brize Norton from Witney, and on 17 March a post office was opened on the estate, with an allottee as postmaster.[78]

On 30 March an election of parish officers was held in Minster Lovell church vestry. Four nominations were required, from whom the magistrates would choose two. Minster Lovell nominated one, named Clinch, and Charterville nominated Beattie, Pickersgill and Gathard. But the magistrates struck off the Charterville nominations, leaving Clinch, and adding William Hudson of Minster Mill, who had been rejected at the vestry meeting. The Charterville residents appointed a committee to draw up a protest to Sir George Grey, the Home Secretary, asking for redress. At the Easter vestry meeting for electing churchwardens, under the Rev Bryan, George Bubb was elected from the estate, so conclusively that no poll was demanded.

At Eastertime Charterville celebrated almost a year of existence. Mrs Hill and Miss Price decorated the schoolroom with portraits of Feargus, Duncombe and Chartist heroes, flowers and greenery. Spring weather was bitter, sharp wind and rain cutting across the allotments, but a hundred came from the estate, and parties from Swindon and Oxford. Tea was at 5 o'clock, followed by speeches. 'Churchwarden' Bubb was in the chair, supported by the Rev Bryan and Mr Gimblett. The parson said they must all love their neighbours, and wish success to the land plan which had produced Charterville. It was a pleasure to him to be there. He had met with great courtesy from the members since he came to the parish. He wished success to their cultivation and expressed heartfelt aspirations for their eternal welfare (loud cheers). Fraternising with the Church was a new experience. Unfortunately, it did not last very long, for the archdeacon refused to accept Bubb as churchwarden, and so the estate got no representation, civil or ecclesiastical.[79] Its history largely proved local county feeling correct, but there must have been bitterness at the time. This broke out in August, when, according to a complaint from the allottees in the *Northern Star*, the gentlemen farmers of the parish saddled one-third of the parish rates on Charterville, which only comprised one-tenth of the parish. The Charterville overseer of the poor had been rejected and so had the Charterville churchwarden, all from 'political persecution'. Local people called it common sense, because they did not believe that the allottees would grow into lasting members of the parish, and they were right.

The summer of 1849 saw the dreaded hand of cholera in towns. People fled into the country. Bennet's brother came to visit him at Charterville. He declared the swedes and potatoes were good but the carrots were the best anywhere. His brother said he was 'thankful he was one of Mr O'Connor's dupes'. Willis too, and his wife, were full of hope. Their wheat looked good this autumn. Bathway's crops were promising; 'he had a good agricultural wife', wrote Bennet to the *Star*.

O'Connor was pressed for money. When 25 September brought Weaving and Pinnock's demand for £225 interest payment on the mortgage, which he had reckoned would be paid by the rents, his exasperation grew more hectic. Almost certainly Weaving and Pinnock were waiting for him to default. In November half-year rents were announced for all estates. On Charterville, 4-acres had to pay £6; 3-acres £5 8s (£5·40); 2-acres £4 16s (£4·80). All who had sublet must pay without remissions; anyone not paying would be ejected. Revolt was immediate. Beattie broke out into abuse, but O'Connor was used to that. Later in November he got a distraint order against some of the allottees, and a bailiff and some soldiers arrived at Charterville on a cold misty morning to seize goods in payment for rent. The whole estate was at its doors, with sticks and brooms. One man threatened the bailiff with a reaping hook. The officer had had enough. He drew a pistol and ordered the drummer to beat. Shortly afterwards he marched his men away. The settler with the reaping hook summoned him for assault, and the case was heard at Petty Sessions at Witney. After much arguing about O'Connor's right to demand rent at all, and who was the rightful owner of the property, the charge of assault was dismissed.[80]

On 1 March forty-one allottees presented a petition to the House of Commons saying that subscribers to the Land Company had been offered the standing of freeholders; they would not pay rent as O'Connor's tenants; notices of distraint implied a landlord's rights; they looked to the House of Commons for redress. Sir Benjamin Hall questioned O'Connor in the House on this petition.

In the meantime, the mortgagees of the estate, with solicitors Roberts and Lee, had been weaving an interesting little plot, all of which was patiently unravelled by William Goodchap, the official manager under the High Court of Chancery, three years later.

The rejection of his position as the founder and father of the estate so infuriated O'Connor that he sent Chinnery to Lee, the solicitor for Weaving and Pinnock, saying that he would pay no more interest on the debt but they must look for their payment to the estate and not to him. Lee then went into a huddle with his clients. At a meeting at The Three Cups in Oxford in October 1849, they decided that the contract of sale of June 1847 had ceased to exist by O'Connor's refusal to pay the interest; that power of resale was not mentioned in the contract only because no one thought it necessary, but that now Weaving and Pinnock were justified in taking all legal steps to get the interest due to them. In November Roberts, acting through Chinnery, asked Lee to help him to get the rents due, which would pay the interest. Lee suggested 'to blink the doubtful question of tenancy between O'Connor and the occupiers', to serve an ejectment on O'Connor on grounds of non-payment of interest. They reckoned the September payment would not be made. This was to be a joint business between Lee and Roberts, who would divide the profits. However, unexpectedly O'Connor paid up the interest in late November or early December. Roberts then switched to suggesting that O'Connor should waive his right of leaving the principal unpaid for seven years, and allow Weaving and Pinnock to foreclose at once and put the estate up for resale. On 6 December 1849 Lee agreed to this. But when Roberts and O'Connor consulted the sale contract they discovered that no condition of seven years existed, because the date read 1848 instead of 1854. Nobody wanted to ask any questions, and so a deed was prepared to enable O'Connor, through Weaving and Pinnock, to serve ejectments against the occupiers and to sell the estate. Profits above the 1847 price were to go to O'Connor. The deed was executed on 4 January 1850.

Following the plan, Roberts served 68 orders of ejectment, in the name of O'Connor. Thirty were defended, and the cases came up at the Oxford Summer Assizes in July 1850. Weaving and Pinnock proved their title as devisees of John Walker, saying nothing of the indenture of 4 January. They won the case and were awarded costs, but no allottee could pay any costs. Three of them were confined in Oxford Castle gaol, where they remained for twelve months and might have remained permanently.

The rest of the allottees were given until November 1850 to get out. They consulted other lawyers, and were advised to make a plea to the Court of Chancery for redress, but the expense of such a suit was beyond them. Two or three of them set out in the fine autumn weather to tramp the county with a memorial setting out their case and asking for money or personal backing. They now regarded O'Connor as their enemy, and indeed he would have had them turned out on the road with their bits and pieces round them so long as he was not there to see and be abused. The *Illustrated London News* gave publicity to the case and printed the memorial (Fig 18).

The allottees tried a bold stroke in writing to O'Connor's most powerful enemy, the *Manchester Examiner*. They told the story of the ejectment orders and the proposed plea to Chancery, and their total lack of funds to get justice done. Gathard signed the letter. They overreached themselves. When the *Examiner* began to fire all guns, O'Connor published their letter in the *Northern Star*, answered that he was now handing them over to the tender mercies of the mortgagees to whom *he* had been paying '£225 a year interest while the rascal allottees would not pay a farthing', and then brought an action for libel against the *Examiner*, which had not in truth examined the facts. Feargus said that the editor met him, with a solicitor, apologised, and said he had been deceived and now saw that O'Connor had been unfairly treated by the allottees. Willis wrote from Charterville refuting Gathard's letter.

Meantime Jackson, from Nottingham, gave up his allotment and went back home. The Land Company branch at Nottingham, Feargus's constituency, organised a meeting on 23 September for the Charterville leaders, Beattie, Bradshaw and their group, to state their case. As reported in the *Northern Star*, the meeting was rowdy and went

---

MINSTER LOVEL, OXON.

WE have already detailed the sale, at Oxford, of this portion of Mr. Feargus O'Connor's celebrated land scheme, consisting of 297 acres of land and eighty-two cottages. (See the ILLUSTRATED LONDON NEWS, September 7, 1850.) We now engrave a view of the estate taken from the Oxford and Cheltenham road, at the west end of the crescent which parts the same, commanding a view of the schools in the right-hand crescent. At the other extremity, to the right, are cottages flanking a road leading from Minster to Brigenorton; the houses being at equal distances on their respective allotments, nearly reaching the aforesaid village, turning another angle to the left, at the extremity of the straight line. The property is situated upon a hill, commanding a picturesque view of the ancient village of Minster, and the Lovel Ruins below to the left.

We understand that two or three of the allottees on the Minster Lovel estate are travelling the country soliciting subscriptions, in order to take proceedings in Chancery, to avert the threatened evictions next month. They have also published a memorial, showing that they have been induced by the representations of Feargus O'Connor, Esq., to take shares in the National Land Company, "and have had their allotments in accordance with the rules of the society, and others have given large sums of money as bonuses for allotments. That the occupants have, therefore, broken up their homes, left their respective callings, and travelled, at great expense, from distant parts of the country. That such allotments were, by the rules of the said company, to be conveyed to each occupant as freehold property, subject to the payment of four per cent. per annum on such portion of the original cost of each allotment as should remain unpaid. That the soil of such allotments, when given into their possession, was so exceedingly foul and exhausted, that your memorialists have laboriously and incessantly toiled, and have not been able to obtain therefrom a sufficiency of the commonest necessaries of subsistence. That the said Feargus O'Connor, Esq., has demanded an enormous rent of your memorialists in his own name, as landlord, thus attempting to make them his tenants at will, and the property his own, having had it conveyed to himself individually, instead of in trust for the company, with whose money the estate was purchased. That your memorialists have refused to pay such rents, but have offered to pay interest on the capital expended on their respective allotments, and remaining unpaid; declining, however, to become tenants to F. O'Connor, Esq., who has, in consequence thereof, commenced proceedings in ejectment against your memorialists in the names of the trustees of the mortgagee. That your memorialists have resisted such ejectments, gone to trial, and had judgment given against them in the Court of Queen's Bench, and, in November next, will be turned out of possession, and thereby be deprived of their capital and labour employed in the improvement of their holdings. That your memorialists have, therefore, consulted equity barristers, whose opinion is, that your memorialists have an efficient plea in, and are, consequently, advised to make an application to, the Court of Chancery for redress against such injustice; but that the costs of such proceedings in Chancery are too expensive for your memorialists, who have already exhausted all their available means in defending the aforesaid suit in ejectment. That your memorialists, therefore, respectfully solicit the assistance of the charitable and benevolent, in order to enable your memorialists to take the necessary proceedings in the Court of Chancery for their protection against the cruel and unjust proceedings of Feargus O'Connor, Esq. And your memorialists" &c.

18   Some allottees of Charterville estate protest against evictions.
From the *Illustrated London News*, 1850

against the allottees. People remembered that Beattie had let three of his acres for more than the rent of his four. There was scuffling and minor fighting, and the meeting ended with a vote in support of O'Connor and in favour of forcing allottees to pay rent or chucking them out.

Weaving and Pinnock tried to make a settlement, in view of the memorial and support for the allottees by the Press, by giving an assurance that if the allottees 'attorned' or recognised them as land-lords, they would give a lease to each man and so guarantee his tenancy. The men answered that the estate was theirs as members of the Land Company and not O'Connor's and certainly not Weaving's or Pinnock's,[81] who could whistle for their money. Weaving and Pinnock were equally tough, and many allottees were ejected. Some 'attorned', accepted the position as tenant, and paid up some rent—£20 or so instead of the £300 or £400 which Weaving and Pinnock reckoned was owing.

Lee and Roberts now began to put into effect their scheme to sell the estate so as to get the £5,000 mortgage principal, and to make some money for O'Connor from profits over the 1847 sale price. On 4 August 1850 a notice appeared in the *Northern Star*, advertising the sale of the whole estate. The sale was held at 3 o'clock on a Saturday at the Star Hotel in Witney. The *Oxford Journal* of 7 September 1850 says that between 70 and 80 of the allottees were among them, 'loud in their expressions of dissatisfaction with the way in which they had been treated'. They circulated a handbill cautioning people not to buy any of the lots offered at the sale, as 'doing so would involve them in a Chancery suit with all its tedious processes and overwhelming costs'.

Mr Long, the local auctioneer, arrived at 3.30. He ignored the crowd, and went straight to work, stating his authority to offer for sale, and putting forward the best points of the lots. At this point James Beattie arose and interrupted. The newspaper calls him 'a fine old fellow whose spirits did not appear to be broken, although the hopes of enjoying his freehold undisturbed were annihilated'. He cautioned the public not to buy and referred them to the handbill. Unperturbed, Mr Long waited for Beattie to finish, and then said that the land was mortgaged to certain parties and that they were legally authorised to proceed with the sale. He did so. At least seven lots sold for more than the reserve price, some to local people, some to the Land Company agent, Chinnery. He bought the farmhouse and James Beattie's house. Two settlers, George Carter and Charles Wilkins, bought their own for £170 and £125. But the sale flagged. There were few bids, and after the first quick sales Mr Long closed the business and departed before any argument and trouble could get started.

Weaving and Pinnock reckoned they had clawed themselves clear. The three allottees remained in Oxford gaol. Beattie himself must have gone after the sale, and was not seen on the estate again. With the removal of the Scots bully, mild men emerged again. In February next year an address reached Feargus, thanking him for the clause in the Winding-Up Bill that all who paid rent would get a title. It said that since the ejectment of revilers there had been peace. Beattie rather gave away his case against the condition of the allotments by saying in March that he was willing to pay all demands providing he got his lease, although ejected.

The Act to dissolve the Land Company was passed in July 1851, and all its estates and assets were put under the Court of Chancery. Happier days dawned, with the application of sense and a constructive attitude. By 7 February 1852 the *Illustrated London News* reported that the three allottees had been released from Oxford gaol.

Weaving and Pinnock held another sale in August next year, 1851, before the appointment of William Goodchap as manager. John Walker bought No 79 with 2 acres next but one to the White Hart Inn, and 7 acres of old quarry ground called Colonel's Hill, which was part of an enclosure. He paid Weaving and Pinnock £275 for the lot, and thought himself secure. There were others like him. The wheels of the law ground on through the affairs of the Land Company, year after year, proving the basis of the company non-legal, and therefore its agreements non-legal. All the John Walkers read the reports anxiously as the edge of their security crumbled.

The *Northern Star* of 7 February 1852 accused Lee, the Witney solicitor, of turning a family of children called Townley out to starve. Lee replied that an allottee, Hart, had taken them all into his care. I suppose the *Northern Star* was confusing Townley with Townsend, perhaps deliberately to make a story.

The deeds of the estate were in the hands of that skilled campaigner

W. P. Roberts. The Master in Chancery had to bargain with him for possession, and eventually he handed them over to the official manager. From the north James Beattie kept up his war, using every opportunity to attack anyone in charge of affairs on the estate, and suggesting that Weaving and Pinnock would bribe the official manager to secure themselves from legal action. Beattie and his kind looked for shady dealings, but the manager, William Goodchap, was not a man with whom this method would succeed.

The Chancery archives hold Goodchap's draft report to the Master in Chancery on the action Goodchap *v* Weaving, Pinnock and O'Connor, his receivership account, his cash account for the estate from midsummer 1852 to Christmas 1855, and his schedules of allotments, owners, rents and money details for 1852, 1854 and 1855, with various notes made during those years. He gives his own terms of reference and his duties. The value of the allotments now let was £256. He proposed that all vacant allotments and any that should become vacant should continue vacant during the hearing of the cause. He suggested that after paying taxes and expenses the estate value would be less than £200 pa. Gardner's *Directory of Oxfordshire* for 1852 says that Mr Tidmarsh, a local landowner, was put in charge of the estate, and a small manuscript history of Minster Lovell in the possession of the vicar also gives his name.

The Court of Chancery had instructed Goodchap to enquire into three specific points: first, whether in the indenture of 16 August 1847 there was any power of sale of the estate, and second, what amount of interest was due to the defendants Weaving and Pinnock in respect of the principal sum of £5,000 on 4 January 1850. On these two points rested the validity of any sales of allotments made by Weaving and Pinnock and O'Connor in attempts to recoup themselves either for rent or interest. Goodchap stated, 'I find that no power of sale was contained in the indenture.' He said that he did not know who had made the alteration of the date of repayment from 1854 to 1848, nor why. As the interest due on 29 September 1849 was paid in November, he said, 'I find that no interest was due to Weaving and Pinnock on the 4th January 1850.' The moves by Weaving and Pinnock, with O'Connor's agreement, to get control and to begin reselling the estate were therefore without cause and invalid.

The third instruction was to find out who had been receiving the rents and profits of the Minster Lovell estate since 4 January 1850. He reported that Weaving and Pinnock had received them to the sum of £236, had endeavoured to get possession after 4 January 1850, and had sold parts of the estate 'for the best prices that could be obtained'. His schedule gave particulars of nine contracts of sale, and submitted to the court the propriety of completing such contracts. As for the costs and expenses incurred by Weaving and Pinnock, Goodchap tranquilly remarked that whether these were properly incurred must be decided by the Court. He said that he intervened in the case of the three allotment holders who had been in Oxford gaol for debt for twelve months, and had them freed.

There follows his schedule of the allotment owners on 10 June 1852, their lots, and their rent.

Other schedules of Goodchap's show that only two of these 1852 owners were from the north or any distant part. All the rest were local people. Forty-four lots were owned by twenty-eight people. One man came from Luton, forty miles to the east, and five from Pershore or Evesham, forty miles to the west. The rest came from Minster Lovell, Witney and villages within ten miles of Charterville. Only John Littlewood of Leeds and John Bennett of Wotton-under-Edge in south-west Gloucestershire remain from the ballot list of 1848. The earliest sale date was 31 August 1850 and the earliest date of conveyance 13 February 1851. All were well behind on their payments of the purchase price. It is of course possible that the owners were not the occupiers, but had bought the land and allowed the original allottee to remain as tenant, but after the experience of ejectment orders this is not very likely. The keenness of local people to buy points to the value of a small house and bit of land. Nearly all the legal business had been done through Lee of Witney, the solicitor employed by Weaving and Pinnock, ancestor of the modern Lee, Chadwick & Co of Witney.

After the list of owners by purchase, Goodchap gives a schedule of rents and occupiers, whose names are all different from the list of owners except that of Samuel Stone. He owned five cottages and 20 acres, and he occupied No 2 in the 3-acre lots. Three names remain from signatures of letters before the take-over, Willis, Smith and Bennett. I cannot tell if they indicate the same persons. Several occupiers are clearly relatives of the owners, having the same surname of Batts, Cross and Wheeler. No women appear in the occupier list. The school house is occupied by Masfen Hart, who took on a good deal of work for Goodchap. He may have been the Hart who took the Townsend children into his care.

E. Wood was made caretaker of the estate. His expenses are recorded, including '2s 6d for rent of a room to receive rents in', and his travelling expenses, as he was not an allotment holder and probably lived in Witney. The rents, tax, insurance and poor rate were duly collected, or compassionate notes made in the 'remarks' column, 'in great poverty and unable to pay', or more drily, 'very doubtful'. A list dated 1854 gives identical names and rents as in 1852. The annual rent value of the estate is still £256, and of vacant allotments £104. A note dated 24 August 1854 at the bottom of the receivership statement of February 1857 says that the estate is of a gross yearly value of £350.

Empty allotments had to be cultivated for the benefit of the estate, and the accounts show that Masfen Hart had chief responsibility for this. Seed was bought and labour paid for. Sometimes rent which could be paid was refused or withheld, and distraint had to be used. A clerk was sent over from Witney or even down from London, and his expenses are all recorded.

On the credit side stock and crops were sold. Under Messrs Weaving, Pinnock and O'Connor any such credits had gone into the bank accounts of the three sharks. Under Goodchap they went into the account of the estate at the Bank of England. The sum was not very large. Goodchap's final statement reads:

Receiver's Statement from midsummer 1852 to Christmas 1855

	£	s	d	£
Received from rents and profits	893	4	5	893·22
Paid out for necessary outgoings and his costs and for the poundage allowed him for his care and trouble	640	1	11	640·09½
Left in Receiver's hands	253	2	6	253·12½

On 29 February 1856 Vice-Chancellor Sir William Page Wood declared that the indenture signed between O'Connor, Weaving and Pinnock on 4 January 1850 authorising Weaving and Pinnock to resell

the estate of Charterville was fraudulent and void, and sales made under it were improper. This was not, of course, the same as declaring all such sales void. Goodchap had to examine each case, sorting patiently through the mesh of little actions and agreements, sifting the simple from the devious, the honest from the fraudulent. He advised the Master in Chancery, in whose hands lay the worldly luck of the John Walkers, that John Walker of No 79 was not a party to the fraudulent indenture, and that his title was not impeachable. Accordingly, on 11 December 1858, Richard Richards, Master in Chancery, directed Goodchap to confirm Walker in his title to the purchase of 31 August 1851, in consideration of £30, for which Goodchap was to give a receipt. The title deed and the receipt must have stood between the candles on the mantelpiece of No 79 that Christmas. Many other titles were also confirmed.

From the schedule Goodchap made in 1852 it seems clear that all true connection with the aims of the Land Company had ceased in Charterville. The allottees had disappeared and ordinary members of the land-working community of Oxfordshire and neighbouring counties had moved in as to any group of cottages.

Kelly's *Directory* for Oxfordshire gives a few later statistics for the estate. The chief crop was potatoes in 1883, 1891, 1907. By 1883 there was a Wesleyan and Primitive Methodist preaching room. The school-house was not used as a school, but in 1872 a school was built at Minster Lovell, down on the lower ground, which held 120 children. In 1891 the names Buckingham and Gould are in the trade list, which may be the Goold of Goodchap's schedule of 1852 and the Buckingham of his receivership rent account. An old grievance is healed, for Jasper Taylor of the estate is surveyor and inspector of nuisances to the Witney rural sanitary authority, and surveyor of highways to the Bampton East highways board. In 1907 Henry Moby is listed as market gardener; he may or may not be a son of the Moby who is recorded as 'gone away not known where' in Goodchap's receivership rent account. A landscape gardener, two farmers and a carrier are added to the trades on the estate in 1907.

Agriculture in Oxfordshire by Orr, published in 1916, speaks of the history of Charterville after the collapse of the Land Company as a failure, and the life of its people as hard, until the twentieth century.

Then it began to fit in better with the economy of the county by the housing it provided for labourers. On the other hand a resident of thirty years told Orr that the colony was full of life and enterprise, and the land was better cultivated than ever before.

A penetrating study of the estate is made in Ashby's *Allotments and Small Holdings in Oxfordshire*, published in 1917, and incorporating the findings of the Richmond Commission on Agriculture of 1882, which examined all the Land Company estates. Ashby says that in 1867 two of the original allottees remained, but he gives no names. Far from being a failure, from 1858–87 the colony settled down to the most prosperous period in a chequered history. Local farmers were not then growing potatoes, and the soil of the estate raised good ones in quantity, with regular sale in Oxford market. In 1872 the cottagers were selling potatoes to the value of £30–£40 per acre, on holdings of 4 or more acres. In the district round the estate, wages in cash were 10s (50p) a week in summer and 9s (45p) in winter, and there was strong demand for the Charterville holdings. The sale price of a 4-acre cottage was as high as £320, a good investment for small capital. A leaseholder's interest sold for £130.

Local farmers took the hint and began to raise potatoes. As soon as bigger quantities were on the market, the smaller crops of the allotments found difficulty in selling. In 1881 and 1882 the potato disease nearly ruined some smallholders. There was a move to increase the size of holdings, and by 1882 thirty-four holdings of 4 acres had increased to thirty-nine.

But no holding was big enough to support a family with no other source of income. Some cultivators had little businesses, or were farm labourers outside the estate. Some went hoeing and haymaking for weeks together, moving up towards London. Some worked on their land before going to work, and again when they came back. They showed great strength and tenacity, and also were a sign that employment was scarce and wages low. One 4-acre man told the Richmond Commission in 1882 that he had taken a holding to better his position but had been deceived; he made a profit of £22 per acre, or, counting his own labour, was getting £29 from 4 acres. But, little as it was, it meant security.

Land value and rents continued to fall throughout the 80s. But in spite of that, the people in the neighbourhood were eager to get a free-hold or leasehold, because the place would be a man's own and he could not be turned out. Whatever happened in the world, he could eat. In fact, they were moved by exactly the inducement that O'Connor held out forty years earlier to half-fed people dependent on a fluctuating cotton, wool or steel market for their subsistence. It was an inducement which tended to seal the smallholders off from the larger ecomomic life in a bad as well as a good way, and by enabling the holders to accept low wages tended to keep wages low and be a bad economic tendency.

The manuscript history of Minster Lovell says of Charterville that around 1889 the estate was known as 'Little Evesham', which must reflect a number of successful market gardeners, as Evesham is the key name for market gardening. In 1896 a bungalow on the highway was licensed as the New Inn.[82] In 1889 sixty men (forty-two owners) cultivated the eighty original plots. A few cultivators held 10 or 12 acres, but very few lived wholly on the land. In 1917 there were sixty-nine occupiers, of whom twenty-six were owners, and twenty-five depended on their cultivation.

Markets become more and more a necessity to any market gardening success. Charterville was always handicapped. A continuing need for co-operation in transport to market was never met; consequently Charterville growers often sold at lower prices than other local growers, leaving no margin of profit; this depressed the market and made estate people unpopular.

Barley and potatoes remained the chief crops between 1877 and 1919. Fruit was never grown for market. Some writers say that strawberries were a crop, but evidence suggests that this was at Carterton, another village in the area, and not at Charterville. One occupier had a binder which did most of the harvesting; others had horses used for general ploughing, or ponies for carrying stuff to market. Efforts to form a credit bank, clearly a big need, fell through in 1914 or 1915.

Opinions on whether Charterville and its like are worth while have always been divided. Economists feel that holdings of less than ten acres tend always to keep people at a low level of both subsistence and productivity, feed only the occupiers, and contribute nothing to the growth and wellbeing of the rest of the country, on which they themselves ultimately depend. From a more local viewpoint, Ashby reported that the vicar of the parish, who knew the estate closely, pointed out that it maintained 300 people, 250 more than it would as a large farm. The people were much superior, mentally and physically, to the other workers in the neighbourhood. They worked hard and fast because they were used to working for themselves, and were better fed than others. They withstood economic depression much better than the rest of the neighbourhood. By growing their own bacon and potatoes their cash outgoings were few. Perpetual leasehold meant that the poor who could not buy freeholds could become virtual owners with power to use their own judgment and to secure the value of their improvements. These comments were sound. They do, however, reflect an attitude of non-expansion, even an expectation of economic depression, characteristic of country areas for many years before the modern era of prosperity.

In the 1920s and 30s the cottages changed only slowly. The water supply was the biggest problem. Well-owners were the lucky ones. The 6-in plan marks one well on the Brize Norton road and three on Bushey Ground. Otherwise the supply was by catchment, drained from roof or ground into a shallow storage well or tank and pumped back by hand-pump to the house. However, people with plenty of ground to raise food on were always in a better position than those who had to put their hand in their pocket for every meal. Messrs Habgood and Mammatt, land agents in Witney, had experience of the estate through those years and up to the present time. Mr Sutcliffe, a senior member of the firm, gave me some expert information. There were occasional bankrupts, but not many. Some occupiers rented more land, often neighbouring allotments behind the houses which they could manage as one piece, there being no hedges on the estate. In the late 1930s electricity was brought to the cottages. The properties remained very popular, and changed hands in 1938 at £375–450. Bushey Ground was always slightly cheaper, being far from the main road. Slowly the smallholders were sold up and replaced by owners who had other jobs. After the Second World War water was laid on, and in 1967–8 main drainage.

After the war came the spectacular rise in the value of land, and the beginning of a complete change in the estate. The plots now change

LOT 2

A STONE & BLUE-SLATED

BUNGALOW

AT BUSHEY GROUND, MINSTER LOVELL

together with approximately

Two Acres of Arable Land, the whole forming

A COMPACT SMALLHOLDING

The Bungalow comprises

> **LIVING ROOM,** 12ft, x 12ft., with Range
> **THREE BEDROOMS,** two 12ft. x 11ft., with Fireplace, and
> the third 11ft. 6in. x 8ft.
> **KITCHEN,** 12ft. 6in. x 8ft. with Range
> **LARDER**

Outside

> Stone and Corrugated-iron **WASH-HOUSE,** with Copper
> **COALHOUSE & E.C., TWO PIGSTIES**
> **GARDEN** with Fruit Trees
> **MAIN WATER**

Let to Mrs. I. R. Bayliss on weekly tenancy at 9/- per week, inclusive, but Tenant paying water rate £1 per annum.

Gross Income

Per **£23-8-0** Annum

Landlord paying General Rates

The two Acres of Land are let at a nominal rent of £1 per annum to Messrs. Lawley of Bushey Ground, who would be willing to vacate at Michaelmas, 1946, or would remain if required.

> **Tithe Annuity Payment 13/- per annum.**
> **Last Annual Payment of Land Tax 13/9.**

19   A sale catalogue description of a smallholding on Bushey Ground, Minster Lovell (Charterville estate), giving details of the house, 1946

hands for £2,500, and with extra land for twice that amount. This brings a new type of occupier and of outlook. In many places the land is used for building. By the White Hart a set of two-storey modern houses suddenly interrupts the single-storey scene. The name Charterville Close commemorates without continuing the estate. The road containing the school is called Upper Crescent, while the houses just down from it on the highway are Lower Crescent. The road was widened and the tollhouse demolished in 1950.

However, there is still much left to see. The land remains open, with not many trees or hedges. On the Burford–Witney road by the White Hart, and for over a mile along the Brize Norton road, stretch the single-storey cottages with triangular centre gable and porch, and the small decoration cut over the door. The change in character shows in some rebuilt and enlarged houses, lawns and gravel drives, garages and flower beds. But others still plant broccoli and sprouts up to the road wall, and have lorries and collections of partly defunct machines at the back. One owner raises pigs seriously, and has 300. Bushey Ground is more countrified, in the older style. Here I found a dairyman with 25 cows, still a true smallholder. In another cottage the sheds, wash-house, dairy etc are turned into a series of trim tool-sheds and workshops, using the 1848 dresser as part of the workshop, and keeping the old copper. In another the iron kitchen grate with side hobs and ovens remains. I saw one good strip of strawberry planting, plenty of small groups of pigs, poultry, bantams, ducks, not many old fruit trees, not much pasture and no sheep.

The schoolhouse is a fine building, still hardly altered. Three porches along the front distinguish it from all the other estate schools, one in the middle for the master's house and one on each side for the pupils' rooms. The roof is slated with octagonal slates, like the other schools. The little turret shown in the *Illustrated London News* print on p 159 has gone. I was allowed to go upstairs, and saw the old windows, opening inwards, and on the top floor two attics side by side, not opposite as in Lowbands school, lit by one central lozenge window on the landing between them, the two door-frames slanted to the middle of the window-pane, so that the one window lit both attics.

Modern prosperity has made a good life for all country-dwellers, with an independence near to the dream that first inspired O'Connor.

By direction of the Administrators of Elizabeth Norridge deceased

LOT 1

The stone and slated Bungalow

known as

Ash Tree Cottage, Minster Lovell

Situate on the Brize Norton Road, less than half-a-mile from Trunk Road A.40 and about three miles from Witney.

The Bungalow contains:

Porch.

Sittingroom 12′ × 11′ 6″ with range, dresser and cupboard.

Two Bedrooms each 11′ 6″ × 11′ 3″ with fireplace.

Kitchen 12′ × 8′ with fireplace, baker's oven and copper.

Scullery 8′ × 8′

Workshop convertible to another room.

Outside are stone Barn 13′ × 10′ 6″ with lean-to alongside, Coalhouse, E.C. and other shedding.

There is a road frontage of 153 feet,

and a total area of **THREE ACRES**,

being contained in Ordnance Survey No. 16K, 3·022 acres.

The bungalow stands well back from the road, is approached by a field gate and grass drive and sheltered by trees. There is a wide stretch of grass on the frontage with plenty of fruit trees.

With the exception of 2 acres of back land (arable) let to Mr.W. Luckett, of Holt Farm, Minster Lovell, at an annual rent of £1.10.0, on Michaelmas tenancy, the property is sold with

Vacant Possession

20 A sale catalogue description of a 3-acre allotment and cottage at Minster Lovell (Charterville estate), giving details of the house, 1951

Most of the Charterville people work in Witney or Oxford, at all levels of employment. I met a blacksmith's assistant chugging home on an old motorbike to his cottage and allotment, grimy and cheerful. He was as near to the blistered hands and fustian jackets as a modern man would be, yet free and independent as O'Connor meant to make at least some of the working class in his day. But of course he and all the estate dwellers are underpinned by what O'Connor could not provide, and failed to realise was necessary, the immense rise in English social prosperity and cash wages.

CHAPTER 11

SNIGS END

(For map showing position of the estate see p 128, fig 10)

SNIGS END was bought by O'Connor in June 1847. The contract and deposit were dated 5 June and the purchase was completed in October according to Feargus, and December according to the *Gloucester Chronicle*. The estate was a big one round Staunton village on the cross of the Gloucester and Tewkesbury roads, where trans-Severn Gloucestershire begins to show the red soil and rich wild character of Herefordshire and the Marches. It was in two parts: Snigs End, south of Staunton and on both sides of the Gloucester road, and Moat Lane, north out of Staunton and curving round back to the village road on the west. It was also in two parishes, the southern tip in Corse and all the rest in Staunton. The size given to the Select Committee was 268 acres. It was six or seven miles from Gloucester, Tewkesbury and Dymock, and ten from Ledbury, with the great comfort of being within walking distance of Lowbands. Water transport was available three miles away at Ashleworth quay on the Severn above Gloucester, or at Gloucester itself.

The price was £11,000,[83] and with odds and ends was given in the company notice of 12 June 1847 as £12,000. Allotments were planned to be ready by the end of May 1848. Ballots took place during the autumn of 1847.

On 8 January 1848 Feargus wrote that he was off to build 90 houses, all to be finished by April. In fact the 1853 plan shows about 81, and the school.* He planned a new publicity device, a procession through

---

* It is not always clear on a plan if a house is an estate house or one already existing. One must always allow for a slight discrepancy in numbers of allotments.

Cheltenham on his way to take possession of the estate. Handbills appeared saying that Feargus O'Connor and his splendid team of horses would pass through the town on the way to the new Chartist estate, on Monday, 10 January. The *Northern Star* reported the scene. The day was beautiful. A band led the march, and thirty horses followed with 'bright harness and light steps through the sickly town of Cheltenham'; invalids peeped out of their mufflers to see; two vans carrying people and children followed.

Local papers, the *Gloucester Chronicle* and *Cheltenham Examiner*, also reported it.

> First of all came the band of music, playing 'See the Conquering Hero Comes', next came the one-horse fly, . . . containing the local leaders of the 'People's Land Scheme'; . . . the third item in the procession was a waggon-load of household furniture, drawn by a splendid team of four horses, another, then came a waggon-load of workmen's benches for the constructing of the new houses at 'Snigs-end', next was a cart-load of wheat, next a cart-load of potatoes, then 2 or 3 cart-loads of ploughs and other agricultural implements, the next item was a cart-load of 'humans', the wives and children probably of the 'Snigs-end settlers'; these were followed by a tilted-cart, full of what appeared to be the better class of settlers, the tilt of the cart being formed in most primitive fashion of unplaned elmboards. There were, in the whole procession, 3 waggons and 8 carts, drawn by altogether 30 horses, the latter were all noble-looking animals, and we could not help contrasting their plump and corny appearance with the look of the squalid and shivering wretchedness of the 20 or 30 women and children huddled together in the open cart. The patriarch himself, Mr F. O'Connor, did not show; at least we did not see him in either the open or the tilted cart and of course he would disdain to ride more comfortably than the humblest of his disciples.

This, for a newspaper, is a reasonably objective report.

The people were unlikely to have been settlers, but were probably workmen brought for the building. The route must have been about fourteen miles, as they came through Cheltenham instead of Gloucester. The Severn lay between them and Snigs End. I guess they went straight out of Cheltenham for five miles to Coombe Hill, on the Gloucester road, turned right to Highfield and then struck off left on the cross-country track to the Haw Bridge over the Severn, built twenty-three years earlier. Five miles more on by-roads would bring them in to Staunton cross, and the Swan and the Feathers, and the toll gate out of the village. Feargus was probably not in his own procession,

Page 181 Charterville: (*above*) the front of the school building, with original porches at three entrances; (*below*) Upper Crescent, back view of a cottage showing the hipped roof line and original slating

Page 182 Snigs End: (*above*) the school building altered for use as a public house; (*below*) snug and secure, 120 years later

for his own account says he arrived on the estate on Tuesday evening, and was busy laying out roads and sites for Labour's castles.

I have been fortunate in searching out the history of Snigs End to find a direct descendant of a near-original allottee still living on the estate, Mrs Travell, of Moat Lane, Snigs End. Her great-grandfather was Mr Hawkesworth, who in very early days bought an allotment and later increased his holding. One of the properties that he or his family acquired was 26 Moat Lane, originally won in the ballot and occupied by Miss E. E. Willis. Through Mr and Mrs Travell I came to know Mr Charles Parsons, who has been all his life in the building trade in this district, and his father before him. These valuable contacts have given inside information on the building of the houses and the history of the estate.

Stone quarries were made available, probably Kimpton's and Birchall's. A lime-kiln was made on Corse Wood Hill, and stone from Kimpton's quarry was probably burnt there for lime. The laying out and construction of roads went on doggedly all through the winter. As bailiff, Feargus drove the men and himself in bitter weather, harder than a man of their own kind would have done. He lodged near the lime-kiln and was always on the work site. Timber off the estate was used in the building. The estate was double the size of Lowbands; the Select Committee list gives thirty-three allotments of 4 acres (taking two 'Kinross' to be sharing), twelve of 3 acres, and thirty-five of 2 (taking two 'Staples' to be sharing). The crescent lay-out was used here more than anywhere else.

As you approach Staunton on the Gloucester road from the south, the familiar cottages with shallow central gables appear three-quarters of a mile from Staunton cross on each side of the Gloucester road. Half-way on to the cross a lane leads to the right with more cottages, and on the left is a crescent with the former school building in the middle. Time has altered the school to the Prince of Wales public house, and perhaps thereby preserved it. The formation of the allotment outlines has been broken for a car park and other changes. Behind this crescent a long lane runs straight across the fields with a dozen houses along it. Up at Staunton cross, more of the estate lies down the village street, in Ledbury Crescent on the left of the road, coming out into the road at Bridge House. This is the main extent of Snigs End. But the other, and

M

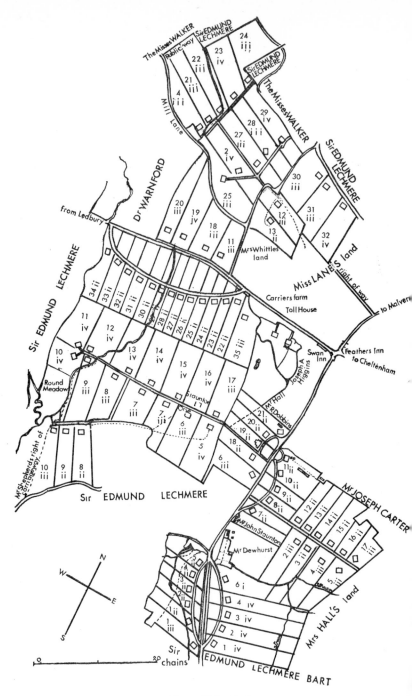

21 Plan of Snigs End estate

most secluded, attractive part, is called The Moat, from an old farm name, and lies straight over the cross and up the hill, curving down again to meet the Staunton village road opposite Bridge House.

O'Connor was plagued by members of the Land Company who arrived, he said, thirty, forty or fifty at a time, without warning, and claimed some unspecified right to be given work on the estate. He issued instructions: carpenters should apply to the foreman Mr Cullingham; sawyers to Mr Goatman; bricklayers to Mr Jones; stone-masons to Mr Griffiths; labourers to Mr King; and carters to himself. He kept the horses. Griffiths was the stonemason of Lowbands' wells.

The carpenters had portable workshops on the estate, with store room for converted timber, boarded against the weather and gated against theft. There were also portable stables for 44 horses, each stall separately boarded, a granary for beans and oats, and a room for chaff; and a gate that could be locked against theft. A portable blacksmith's shop and wheelwright shop completed the outfit. A pair of horses cost 10s (50p) a day to hire, and O'Connor's horses were better workers than the local animals. It was sensible, but it looked like extravagance to shareholders in the North or newspapers ready to make mischief.

The cottage walls were of stone, the chimneys of brick. In No 26 Moat Lane, in 1967, Cullingham's timber was as good as ever, 10-in boards in the bedrooms, and two built-in cupboards in one bedroom. In the middle room, meant for a kitchen, a long dresser was fitted, with three drawers and shelves above for china. The elm roof-timbers at the back had sagged, but not dangerously. In the front slope of the roof, of imported pine, not one beam had 'the grub'. The slates were very fine Cornish, 10 in and 11 in. A chimney at each end and one at the back in the middle for the kitchen completed a snug roof.

The kitchen flooring was solidly made. First, the hard marl which was dug out of the well was stamped down; then a bed of red Broms-berrow sand was laid; then red 'quarries', or 9-in tiles, were laid, joined with a rough mortar paste, and the surface cleaned off with sacking. This proved completely dry, unlike the usual tiled floor, and threw no damp. The dairy had an earth floor.

The height of the back wall of kitchen and living-room was 8 ft and from this the roof sloped down over back kitchen, dairy etc to 6 ft. In the back kitchen was the hand pump, consisting of a bucket with leather suckers and a handle. The kitchen grate was a good size, raised, with bars, and an oven on each side providing convenient hobs on the flat tops, and hooks for pots suspended over the fire.

The yard wall was strongly built of big stones, with the little gate 3 ft 6 in high. Over the front door, the ornament which is a feature of every house, though the shapes differ, was in fact a vent opening on the roof timbers and carrying air right through. Round this vent in No 26 was painted 'O'Connor Villa June 12th 1848' (the date of location on the estate) and Mrs Travell said this had always been there.

Their neighbour's house, Mr Toomey's, is almost unaltered. Plum trees bow down with fruit over the tidy grass baulks between the plots of vegetables, and every kind of rustic container and shed stands round the back of the cottage. Here the low roof over dairy, wash-house, etc remains unchanged, and the original door is still in place. Here were the privy and small sheds. Roofs had been replaced with iron sheets or any handy strip. Mr Toomey said the well was inside the house, and this is so in other Snigs End houses.

On the protruding front, the quoins at each side were not true supporting stones, but a set of facings in a frame. This must have been made of the 'Roman cement' which O'Connor said enabled him to build six houses for the price and time of one at Lowbands. The frames were mortared in on the corners. Now in their age the device shows up clearly.

In Ledbury Crescent across the village street from Moat Lane, many of the houses have a different shaped porch ornament. Signs of small industry as well as domestic farming show along the lane which re-mains basically the narrow 9-ft lane of all the estates. Remnants of the gate to this estate road lie in the bushes. In 1968 Mr and Mrs Lawson showed me the first house and garden of the crescent, Bridge House, for a little bridge joins the crescent to the village road. The owners came from Birmingham, and have lived here forty years. The garden, close packed with summer vegetables and flowers, the cherished details of the house in perfect repair and paint, the philosophical content and wisdom of the owners, showed them to be close to the original ideal for smallholders.

The licensee of the Prince of Wales took me over his building. As the school, it was built with only one front entrance, in the schoolmaster's house. Entrances for the children were in the side walls of their wing, with a lobby for coats just inside. As a pub, doors into the public and saloon bars have been made through the big schoolroom windows. The bars show the fine height and proportion of the rooms. Each has a fireplace.

Behind the school lay its land, and one long lane of the estate. Now hedges and fruit trees enrich and screen them all, but when the allottees arrived each cottage must have stood new and bare in its cleared ground.

In 1848 two corn mills were available, old Staunton mill up the green lane by Hill Farm, driven by Berrow brook from Eastnor Castle lake, handy to the Moat Lane area, and Pitts mill on the Stanbrook at the southern end of the settlement. The old farmhouse on Snigs End was bought by Dewhurst, schoolmaster from Leicester. He gave up his school and placed £400 in O'Connor's hand towards the purchase. In February 1848 he discovered that some of the estate was mortgaged, and became convinced that O'Connor meant to do him out of his purchase. He came into Feargus's office with a hatchet, and was about to attack him when Feargus knocked him down. The workmen hauled Dewhurst out.[84]

As the day of the presentation of the Chartist petition to Parliament approached, the *Gloucester Chronicle* reported on 1 April,

> Mr O'Connor is building a carriage at the Chartist colony, at Snigs End, in which the National Petition for the Charter will be conveyed when ready for presentation, to the House of Commons. Four of the superb horses now at work on the farm, are to be sent to London to draw it.

On 8 April the paper reported that two waggons for the petition had passed through Gloucester on the way to London. They would be drawn through the streets of London by twelve horses.

The presentation of the petition on 10 April 1848 was a fiasco. O'Connor retired from London to Snigs End, where Child and O'Donovan from the Chartist Convention came to talk over the situation with him. His weekly letter to the *Northern Star* was addressed to members about to be located. 'I now steal a moment from the bustle of politics to give you some information as to your fate.' The weather had been one incessant downpour for three months, but was now more genial. He would begin 'planting your cabbages and potatoes and sowing turnip etc next week at Paradise'. Rain would postpone location, which would be on the second Monday in June, when the crops would be growing and the houses aired.

A meeting of the directors and representatives of the Land Company was called at Dean Street, London, without O'Connor, to discuss the management of the company. This enraged Feargus. He sent to the meeting his foremen from Snigs End: Cullingham, 'overseer from the beginning'; Doyle the manager in O'Connor's absence; King the bailiff; Ross the carpenter; Jones the plasterer; Moody, a carpenter from the beginning; M'Gowan who received and banked the money. He kept back Bryan, who could not be spared as he saw to the horses. On 9 May 1848, the meeting issued a resolution, that it was clearly proved that 'sub-letting the work on the people's estate at Snigs End is carried on to a serious extent, and we hearby deprecate the same, and call upon the directors to immediately abolish the system entirely'. He defied all accusation of extravagance. Bryan had measured the work of 17 pairs of sawyers all the winter, to see to the best application of timber, at £1 a week. 'I will no longer devote every hour of my life to receive only insolence as my reward,' said Feargus. At the same time he flung himself into his newest purchase, the estate of Great Dodford, thirty-five miles or so to the north, near Bromsgrove, regardless of the protests about his management of company money.

The Moat was built in stone, by Griffiths; the rest of the estate in brick, by contract to Jones and Dowling. Dowling complained that building supplies were not regularly available, so that work was held up. On one occasion the consignment of bricks was under water when he needed them. O'Connor explained that hundreds of thousands of bricks were landed on the quay (presumably Gloucester quay, as canal transporters would use the word 'wharf') with 4 ft of water over them, and no rule of the Land Company could prevent a catastrophe like that.

David Watson, the first winner on the ballot for the first estate at Heronsgate, on 19 April 1846, and still settled there, advertised a 3-acre allotment at Snigs End on 20 May, 'nearly ready for occupation'. Speculation had now clearly entered into the motives of the rank and file. Two other advertisements at the same time for Snigs End allotments are more non-committal. They read, 'Right of location on 4

acres drawn in November ballot, allottee cannot now take up. G.
Harper, Willerby, Hull,' and '2 acres, allottee old lady, family bereave-
ment, cannot take up, Warren, High Holburn'. On the other hand,
another notice appears in the same issue, 'Wanted, 4 acres on Snigs
End, Dodford or Mathon, to lease for 5 or 7 years, at £10 pa more than
Company asks.'

At the same time the obscurity of the reporting of ballot results was
taken up, and at last a 'correct list of shareholders to be located on Snigs
End on 2nd Monday in June' was published over the signature of J.
Clark, director. Location was to be on 12 June, and on the same day at
Minster Lovell. On 3 June O'Connor wrote that some houses would be
on show, and that after locations, five more 4-acre lots at Snigs End and
six more 2-acre lots at Minster Lovell would soon be made ready. He
said that Snigs End allotments had potatoes in and some barley sown.
He had made over 5,000 tons of manure. One 2-acre right of location
was advertised for £40 a week before location. The coming arrival of
new inhabitants roused the more lively local people. William Wilks of
the Crown Inn, Redmarley, advertised that he would carry every
Saturday from Redmarley to the New Inn, Gloucester and return the
same day. Any allottee coming from Gloucester or Tewkesbury could
have his goods fetched any day of the week on reasonable terms. Mr
Dewhurst offered refreshments on 12 June at his cyder vaults at Snigs
End farmhouse. Mr Strathan advertised the Feathers Inn, Mr Lloyd the
Swan, and Mr Dobbin the Plough. All said they were close to the
estate.

The Land Company might be in trouble, and O'Connor a very
damaging leader, but on 12 June all that was good in the Land Company idea filled the day. The *Gloucester Chronicle* reported it as well as
the *Northern Star*. The delight of the new occupants infected everybody. The strong-coloured speeches of the day, the child rolling
ecstatically on the ground, the tears on a woman's cheek as her eyes
moved round the kitchen, these were convincements of the human
value of the plan, not yet blurred by covetousness or laziness.

All the morning allottees and visitors were arriving. The two parts
of the estate were very spread out, and friends could easily be missed, so
when dancing started in the school it attracted everybody. There is
plenty of room in front of the Prince of Wales today for people to

gather and talk. Probably the waggons and vans collected there for the procession. Feargus and Sharman Crawford, who was a landowner in Ireland as well as an MP, were expected, but did not arrive during the morning. Clouds were coming up, and it was clear the fine weather would not last the day. So at two o'clock the procession formed up, a score of waggons and carts, and moved off to pay a social visit to Lowbands, three miles west along the Staunton road.

Then O'Connor and his friends arrived. Mrs Travell remembers her mother, Mrs Pearson, telling her how *her* mother remembered O'Connor driving in with fine horses and postilions and drawing up at the school. Rain had begun, but made little difference. O'Connor drove round each house and gave his 'document of possession' to every allottee. I do not know what this was, but it carried no legal authority. He made no speech, and was clearly overstrained. 'All confessed that the eye had never beheld such a sight, nor has it,' he wrote in the *Northern Star*. 'It drives me mad to look upon it and to think of the impediments that have been thrown in my way in the prosecution of such a work.' He said he was pleased to be wet through because the rain went to the roots of the seeds he had planted, which would yield the allottees their harvest. No report is given of a speech by Crawford, and probably he was uncomfortable in O'Connor's company. They left before nightfall, and the local paper said that the day ended in the public houses, with fighting, but this would be said if only a dozen fellows were involved out of the whole varied crowd.

Mrs Travell's great-grandfather, Mr Hawkesworth of Leicester, failed to get a prize in the ballot, and came down to Snigs End hoping to buy an allotment. He did so later. No 26 was taken by Miss Willis, who, though not in the original list, came very soon, perhaps even at the location on 12 June. She was in fact spoken of as having won an allotment in the ballot. Her possession was confirmed in 1861, and she lived and died there. She built on a big shed and kept sheep in it. Mr Hawkesworth's grandson bought the house after her death. Henry Cullingham was another who seems to have been there from the beginning, but whose name is not on the newspaper list. Probably an allotment or two was kept back for directors' choice. Christopher Doyle stayed on after location, to help the allottees settle. He was still living there in November 1849.

John Revans came to Snigs End from the Select Committee in July. O'Connor said that he did not get out of the gig, but drove round making estimates from a distance.

By a sudden, snarling change of attitude, in July O'Connor began to attack the allottees, his children. In the 15 July issue of the *Northern Star* he wrote that the obstacle to carrying out the plans of the Land Company was really the located members, because they all thought they had the best title to the company's money. Men wrote to him and said that if this or that was not done they would write to the Press. A man from Snigs End wrote to friends in Manchester and said the work on the estate was not workmanlike. Let them all write to the papers! 'Some fellows, if I boiled the mutton, would expect me to feed them with broth.'

The enquiry into the Land Company was ended and the report was awaited every day, but O'Connor had not yet provided the papers and accounts asked for by the Committee. D. E. Morgans visited him again at Snigs End, and found him in an old farmhouse, with a 'tidy-sized cart load of papers' prepared for the government scrutineer. They were both up till 2 am. Morgans wrote that he would dearly like an allotment at Snigs End, which would be a paradise in another year, instead of the 'black smoky iron works of Glamorganshire' where he came from. He would think so doubly if he could see Snigs End and Moat Lane today. But many allottees were infected by criticism or uneasy about the legal tenure of their land. The first autumn brought six offers of allotments. One was not a company-built house, and may have been Dewhurst's, as it described itself as 2 rooms up and 2 down, joining the old farmhouse, and its rent redeemed; 2 acres of land; 40–50 apple and pear trees yielding 10 hogsheads of cider usually; a rick of clover, 2 doz hurdles, a sow and 7 piglets, a sow in pig, 2 ewes, and a strong ass and cart. An allottee wrote to the *Gloucester Chronicle*, and said all he had was two sacks of potatoes. 'We cannot expect to live off the land in a few weeks.' It was hopeless trying to sell produce. To go to Gloucester cost 1s (5p) or 1s 6d (7½p), and then everyone was prejudiced against the allottees. I wonder how Gloucester traders could know the home address of every man with a barrow of vegetables.

March 1849 was good sowing weather, and Snigs End was well ahead of last year. Doyle wrote to Feargus, 'It would do your heart good to see Snigs End now, it is a perfect paradise—all well cultivated but especially Mr Cullingham's allotment which is the astonishment of every traveller. They all stop to inspect it.' Cullingham wrote later in the summer, beginning, 'Honoured and respected Sir.' He said, 'You cannot form a faint idea of the splendour of the place.' The allottees were industrious, in high spirits, confident. His crop of peas! No money would buy his allotment off him now. 'I never knew what happiness was before.' He had had more real enjoyment in six months here than in six times the length of time. 'The days are never too long. . . . No one can tell the pleasure we feel in watching the progress of our crops.' Men who have sold out regret it now. Brown of Nottingham offered £5 more than he sold for, to come back. 'P.S. The apple trees are laden with bloom.'

Feargus was in trouble everywhere, and letters like these from Doyle and Cullingham were welcome. In July the next Land Conference was announced for Snigs End at the beginning of August.

It met in the school, in one of those big rooms now either the saloon bar or the public bar. The room was so full that people pressed against the windows. The story of the conference belongs to the history of the company. The gardens and allotments of the estate were admired. No schoolmaster had been appointed and the school was not in being. A month later the directors called another meeting at Snigs End. Doyle and Clark solemnly urged on members their duty to support the company rules in taking over or selling allotments. The meeting formally repudiated the idea that allottees did not mean to pay rent.

On 3 November 1849 the *Northern Star* published the half-year's rents required. On Snigs End, 4-acre allotments must pay £6 5s (£6·25), 3-acre £5 15s (£5·75), 2-acre £4 5s (£4·25). Anyone not paying must be ejected. This produced a general uproar, as on all the estates. Most of the allottees got into groups to sign letters to the papers groaning about their hardships and poverty. These irritated and hardened the unlocated members, though they had a better reception among the general public. A party at Snigs End, led by Cullingham, wrote that the majority of their allottees objected to paying rent because it would make them tenants of Mr O'Connor, without leases. They had believed that they were to have conveyances and own the land. If they could have a valuation of each allotment and a written

agreement of the annual rent, they would pay. Some men had sub-let
and rigidly exacted rent, even putting in bailiffs.

A vicious letter followed the digestion of this by the non-signing
allottees. They rejected Cullingham and his party. Guy was a smith in
a 'constant birth (*sic*) at Mr Waite's, Gloucester', getting 20s to 25s a
week; he took possession of his allotment without telling the directors.
Blackford was a dealer in rags who first lodged with an allottee and
then found one anxious to leave and for a mere trifle, chiefly old clothes,
got possession without telling the directors. Jos Smith was an original
allottee and a tenant, and was trying to shake off his landlord. Moody
got possession of a vacant allotment, 'But *not* without (*sic*) the sanction
of the directors.' Willis had bought two acres but had not paid for
them, and Esther was his daughter. Doyle got £2 a week for doing
nothing but his own farm. Cunningham (*sic*) got £2 15s a week during
the building, bought two acres, also had the school two acres and a
meadow belonging to the company. 'He has created the utmost contempt for the character of O'Connor here' and yet says his confidence
is undiminished. He fell out with O'Connor over a bill for flags for the
demonstration, went to London to get O'Connor to pay. He said that
O'Connor laughed at him and bought him drink and told him he was
'a fool to trouble himself so much about a trifle like that'. Cullingham
boasted round the estate, 'If he plays with me much longer about this
affair, I shall be induced to unfold such a tale with respect to this Land
Company, as will prevent his ever holding up his head in public again.'
The allottees were determined never to become tenants-at-will to
O'Connor. Not a penny paid to him reached the shareholders. He mis-
represented the accounts, and there was nothing but his word and his
bank book for the auditors. This letter was signed 'R. Jarvis, Chairman'.

Feargus never worried about whether he could hold up his head in
public or not. He waited until the news of the action of ejectment taken
by Charterville mortgagees against the allottees was published on 20
January, and the next week he published Jarvis's letter and replied in
detail. Guy had paid his rent on 1 November, Blackford and Smith had
paid all dues to the directors, O'Connor had sold Moody his allotment
and the directors had booked his £20 dues. Willis had bought from
Wright with agreement for twelve months to pay. The Cullingham

story was distortion and he gave details. Finally, the Snigs End men, like the Charterville men, had lost their 'bad landlord', and were now the tenants of the mortgagees and would all be sacked. This letter contains the last mention of Henry Cullingham, though he was named in the 1851 census return, still at Snigs End, described as a London carpenter.

The allottees must have spent a dismal Christmas chewing their grievances. Henry Oliver, of Snigs End, wrote to the *Manchester Examiner* on 31 December 1849, accusing the directors of buying up allotments cheap and selling them dear. 'The great imposter has made such a bungling affair of it, that he knows not how to get rid of it.' He begged members to get the estates valued by practical men. They would then see how shamefully 'you and all of us have been bamboozled out of our hard-earned pence'.

War now being declared, in February 1850 O'Connor sued Bradshaw, editor of the *Nottingham Journal* for libel in his reports about the estates,* and among others three men from Snigs End gave evidence for the paper. John Hudson, a framework-knitter from Leicester, with wife and two children, had previously earned 12s (60p) to 14s (70p) a week, his wife 5s (25p) to 7s (35p) and a child 2s 6d (12½p). He drew a 2-acre ticket in the ballot. O'Connor saw him and advised him to go to Snigs End. He got £5 aid money and was delighted at first. He found only potatoes were planted. He worked from light to dark. Another £5 was promised, but never came, nor any other help. He could never live on the produce of the land. In 1848 he went as one of three deputed to meet O'Connor at Gloucester to get the second £5 promised and £10 for barley seed. O'Connor told them that they must have read in the *Northern Star* that the company was short of money, Manchester men had paid none for nine weeks. Hudson planted swedes at 8d for seed and half a bag of potatoes at 3s 6d (17½p). 'I had no barley given to me.' Half an acre of his land remained unused. He had never paid any rent, it was enough to pay 3s 6d (17½p) a quarter poor rate. Dewhurst told his story, leaving out the hatchet, and said that, as the tenure was too unsure, in July 1848 he asked O'Connor for his money back. He had not got any yet. Alexander Cleland, a hand-loom weaver from Glasgow, with two sons, had been earning between 10s (50p) and a

* See Chapter 6, p 72.

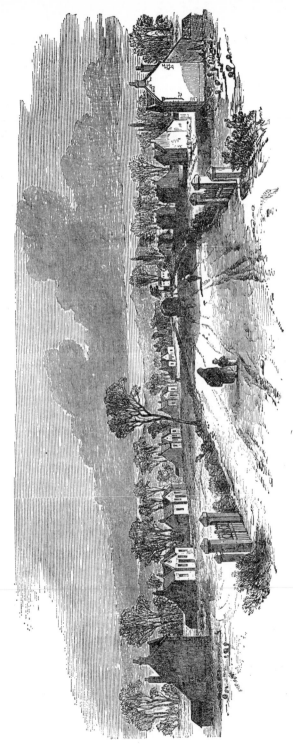

22   Snigs End estate from the road, from the *Illustrated London News*, 23 February 1850

guinea (£1·05) a week. He found only potatoes planted. He spent only £2 7s 6d (£2·37½) of the aid money on the land, the rest on his fare from Glasgow, clothes, kitchen things, and tools. He planted potatoes, swede, and turnip. His wife dug ¼ acre for wheat. He had to go to work to keep his family, and found work through one of the directors living on the estate. He always lived better in Glasgow.

The *Illustrated London News* took up the cause of the allottees, and sent a reporter to some of the estates. At Snigs End in February he spoke to a shoemaker from Exeter who had been there eighteen months and found it 'a bad place'; he had to work at shoemaking and had lost all his savings. This is the only paper I have found which said the allottees were regarded locally as 'outcasts and Chartists'.

Many appeals came in during the summer to the House of Commons to wind up the company. Snigs End and Lowbands combined to send one in August. This was signed by all members of both estates except one, not named. Feargus's reply was to send bailiffs with fifty-two writs to Snigs End, demanding rent or ejection. This is reported in *The Times* of 5 September 1850, and I know of no other information on the incident. The report says, 'The colonists, however, declared themselves "prepared to manure the land with blood before it was taken from them", and no levy was made.' The style was more Henry Oliver than Henry Cullingham. The ammunition used on both sides in this war seems to have been blank. But some of the Snigs End allottees must have been paying rent, if the list is correct in the *Northern Star* of 16 November 1850, where Snigs End is given as having paid £74 since June last year.

No longer could Feargus retreat to one of the estates for relief when the tide of trouble was roaring high. More and more the allottees and members were lined up against him in the matter of the terms of the approaching Act for winding up the company. Led by O'Brien of Lowbands, Snigs End and Lowbands allottees made two attempts in February and May 1851 to get a compensation clause for their 120 families inserted, on the grounds of having been decoyed from their homes and callings, and being rendered paupers if the company were closed.

None of the ideas of the allottees or members came to anything, but Parliament and the Court of Chancery studied their interests as closely

23   The front and back of a cottage at Snigs End, from the *Illustrated London News*, 23 February 1850

as they did themselves. The Winding-Up Act was passed, and a lull fell for a year until the official manager arrived to carry out the Act. The census of 1851 gives evidence of sixteen of the original settlers still on Snigs End estate.

William Goodchap, official manager, announced on 4 September 1852 that he would attend on Tuesday, 14 September at 10 am at the Feathers, Staunton, to enquire into Snigs End and Lowbands estates. Snigs End was stated in the *Star of Freedom* (late the *Northern Star*) to have cost £20,000, just double the cost of Lowbands. It had roughly double the number of each size of allotment: thirty-four of 2 acres (thirty-three in the location list and thirty-five in the Select Committee list), fourteen of 3 (eleven in the location list and twelve in the Select Committee list), and thirty-five of 4 (twenty-six in the location list and thirty-three in the Select Committee list); 208 acres altogether. The rents at Snigs End were fixed by William Goodchap at

2 acres—£11   8s (£11·40) pa
3   „   —£14 12s (£14·60) pa
4   „   —£17 18s (£17·90) pa

The *Star of Freedom* said on 13 November 1852 that Snigs End and Lowbands were well satisfied with the award. The first two years' rent was excused at both, and the same amounts allowed for improvements and effort. Snigs End occupiers shared in the dinner given by the court to the allottees.

An indenture survives between William Goodchap and John Fowler, of February 1854. A postal directory of 1851–6 names Dart, the shoemaker; Griffiths, the stonemason; and Smith the blacksmith among its list of tradesmen or skilled men at Snigs End or in Corse parish. What became of Henry Cullingham and Christopher Doyle? James Brand and Robert Wilson's names appear in Staunton parish baptism register, with occupation given as 'allottee'. I have corresponded with several Cullinghams, but failed to trace this Henry.

In May 1857 the estate was largely sold by auction. The solicitor W. P. Roberts, either through giving O'Connor a mortgage or by buying ground rents or some of the estate outright, became the owner of a good deal of it. Miss Esther Willis's indenture for No 26 Moat Lane, dated 24 May 1861, is made between her and Roberts and is

Page 199 Great Dodford: (*above*) the narrow estate lanes; (*below*) a cottage altered for use as a sub-post office and village shop

Page 200 Feargus O'Connor: (*left*) his monument in Kensal Green cemetery, London; (*right*) his statue in the arboretum at Nottingham

based on Roberts's indenture of 1 May 1860 with Goodchap. The perpetual rent charge payable to Roberts was £8 16s (£8·80), presumably
six months' rent.

From now on Snigs End blends in with the development of the sur-
rounding country. It was visited at several times by people studying
smallholdings. Potatoes remained the best crop, and the smallness of the
plots the chief problem. The agricultural depression of the 1880s hit the
whole countryside, and Snigs End with it. Other jobs were essential to
maintain life on the little plots. Security only came with the post-1945
social developments. Some of the Snigs End women joined with Lowbands in glovemaking,[85] but I have found no record of any common
effort by members of the estate as such. Slowly the properties changed
hands, grew larger as a man made a go of farming, or smaller as he gave
up and sold off land. On 31 July 1861 five properties were sold from
Snigs End and Lowbands, by Henry Bruton, estate agent of Gloucester. Mrs Travell has the catalogue. Solicitors for the sale were
Bretherton of Gloucester and Roberts of Manchester. None of the
names of sellers are familiar. Reference was no longer made to Goodchap's indentures but a clause of the sale agreement said 'the purchaser
shall presume that the vendor is seized of the property in fee simple'.

One set of indentures shows a long family continuity. On 25 October
1853 Goodchap conveyed 2 acres at No 2 on the official Chancery map
of the estate to George Morton at £6 8s (£6·60) rent charge, presumably for six months. In 1884 his successor, Thomas Morton, mortgaged
it. Twenty years later, in 1904, Williamson & Hill of Red Lion Square,
solicitors for the official manager, wrote to the mortgagee to ask if he
would pay the arrears due of £50; otherwise they would have to take
possession. The mortgagee refused, after looking at the property.
Williamson & Hill enquired of Morton's widow, the owner, in
Newent Union (workhouse). She was destitute and told them that no
interest had been paid for over twelve years. There was no chance of
the mortgagee getting any benefit from his mortgages. Very reluctant-
ly, Williamson & Hill were obliged to take possession. The property
was a 'complete wreck' and before they could let it they had to make
extensive repairs to house and fencing. They could only get £7 a year
rent after they had done it up, and out of that they had to pay £6 8s
(£6·40) rent charge every half-year according to the 1853 conveyance.

N

24   Sale notice of the Snigs End estate, 1857

The mortgage was transferred to the official manager, in this and other similar cases.

At least one original allottee lived on at Snigs End, for Thomas Halsale of Chorley, a 2-acre original, is named in the Staunton burial register in 1873. At some period before this the parish officers held the school building and land. It was when Corse parish built its school, in the early 1870s, that the estate school building became the Prince of Wales public house. I have found no record of the naming of the road behind the Prince Consort pub, nor of any road names. The map shows Thomas Morton as owner of several houses in the lane behind the pub.

Before the Second World War solicitors Williamson & Hill collected rents every half-year. A man came down from London and stayed at the farm near Staunton cross on the Gloucester road, and drove round in a pony trap. He saw to repairs and instructed local builders. Then, in 1920, with Lowbands, the remaining portions of Snigs End were put up for sale by Williamson & Hill for the official manager. The sale catalogue lists seven small freeholdings and thirty-seven rent charges secured on freehold lands in Corse, Staunton and Redmarley. All plots of land were held in fee simple under conveyances executed by the official manager appointed in 1851, subject to perpetual rent charges. All the rent charges referred to were in 1860 bought by and conveyed to a testator who died in 1871 and left all to his widow. At various dates after 1871 the widow entered into possession of all the properties, in consequence of all the rent charges falling into arrears. In 1892 she died, leaving the properties to trustees who sold up in 1920. Notes on the lots for sale show Mr Hawkesworth as owner of several properties on which a rent charge was secured. An unusual occupier was a naval lieutenant.

From 1920 to the Second World War smallholdings did not prosper. Mr Travell saw the cottage next to him pulled down, and another near by left empty. Twelve acres were farmed by one man, but even that was not enough to live on. But since the war, what changes! Money has poured into the countryside, via house and land prices, growth of transport, full employment, high wages. Now along the narrow estate roads there are no more derelict properties and crumbling cottages. Among the orchards, hedges, pasture, green rows of cultivation, pig sheds, lorries, small workshops, there is security and independence. The houses remain largely recognisable, even when built on to and done up in spick and span black and white paint. There is great interest in the Land Company, and a wonderful assortment of information. An old man said to me in the road, 'All built by Irish labour, you can see the huts.'

CHAPTER 12

GREAT DODFORD

IN the winter of 1847, when he had bought Snigs End and was building Charterville, O'Connor inspected yet another estate—Great Dodford, near Bromsgrove, in his favourite Worcestershire. He was told that it was the site of an ancient monastery, and decided at once that this meant the soil must be of the best in the region. With snow on the ground, he could not rest from driving round in a hired trap, walking over the estate, kicking up the heavy, frozen earth, eyeing the timber, running up sums in his head. There were 280 acres, and the owner, Mr Bomford, was willing to sell at roughly £10,350. A mortgage of £5,000 remained on the property. Ballots were held. On 8 January 1848 the *Northern Star* announced that O'Connor had bought the estate, six miles from Kidderminster and Dudley, three from Bromsgrove, twelve from Birmingham. It was near to half a million people—'don't you think a fat pig or a cabbage will sell there?'

O'Connor employed a drainage specialist, as he had for Charterville, and drainage trenches were dug over the best ground, £7 an acre for labour costs. He decided this was not soil for intensive market-garden work, but for plough crops or grazing. The divisions must be bigger, 4 acres and upwards to each allotment. All the timberwork for floors, roofs, window-frames and doors was prepared in the carpenters' shops at Lowbands.[86] As the Select Committee settled down in June 1848 to enquire into the company, the Dodford cottages began to go up, in the same design as on all the estates. Forty were built, most with 4-acre allotments, a few with larger plots. Wells were dug in the stiff marl. Work began in April or May, under Christopher Doyle.

O'Connor described his life, racing over to Dodford to work and back at Snigs End at midnight to sit up and write his defence before the

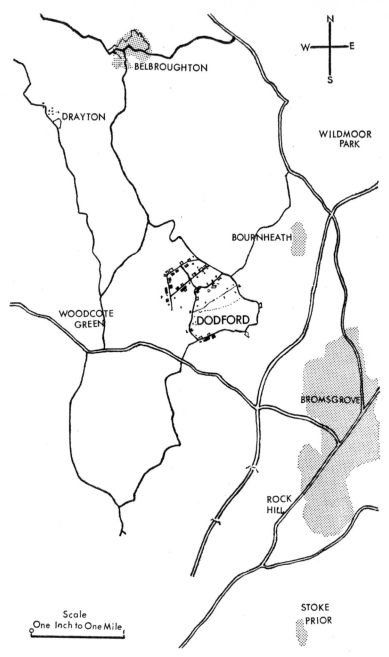

25 Map showing the position of the Great Dodford estate

Select Committee. Sometimes he took the train from Tewkesbury, an hour and a half's journey. More often he got up by lamplight and drove to the new estate, starting out on the Worcester road with the moon going down and candles lit in the trap lamps. Probably he crossed the Severn at Upton an hour and a half later, in first light, and turned the horse left on to the Worcester road soon after. At Worcester he would pull up and ease the horse, while he drank brandy and steaming hot water, swallowed three or four eggs beaten up in port wine, and watched the poultry and green stuff being brought in to market. He went off again on the Droitwich road, skirting the town and crossing the Salwarpe. Past Upton Warren by 11 o'clock, he turned off the Bromsgrove road towards Dodford. Through Little Dodford, he left the Priory down in the valley on his right and urged the horse up the rising road to Great Dodford. He pulled up at a farmhouse, and a fellow came out to take the horse and give him a hand down, stiff from six hours in the driving seat.

Feargus knew his business after building four other estates, and on Great Dodford the houses went up fast and well. When he was in London at the Select Committee's hearings, Mr Grey, the committee's accountant, asked for elucidation of the accounts, and Feargus brought him down to stay at Great Dodford early in July to work through the papers. In the same month the Land Company held its yearly conference at Great Dodford. The estate was the nearest of all company properties to an industrial area. Representatives of Chartist groups from Midland towns attended: Birmingham, Kidderminster, Wolverhampton, Dudley. It must have been one of the first Chartist gatherings since the collapse of the demonstration for the Charter petition in April. Members drove on to the estate all the morning, and had a look round, ate what they had brought with them, gathered for the meeting at 2 pm.

Doyle and M'Grath spoke for the company and reported on the Dodford work and finances. Stout-hearted Chartists from Midland mines and factories spoke up for the cause in adversity. The figure of O'Connor was seen crossing the estate from the farmhouse. Shouts broke out. 'Everybody rushed to see their "father", and when he mounted the van he was received with welcome and long-continued cheers.' The *Star*, reporting the scene, carried advertisements for sale of three of the unfinished allotments at Dodford, one by a man settled at Lowbands and not wishing to leave.

By the end of July the parliamentary enquiry had come to its fore-seen decision, and the Land Company was condemned in its present form. Subscriptions were falling off so fast that there was no possibility of further estates unless the company was reorganised and the general public subscribed to it. However, houses were up on Dodford and the company still existed. As the lottery system for locating members was now forbidden, Feargus proposed that members should be chosen for location by the bonus or advance they offered on the capital value of a house and allotment—in other words, by auction. This marked the end of the company's pull on the masses, as the poor no longer had the common hope of chance. The Land Conference in Birmingham in October that year, 1848, agreed unanimously to the bonus method, though one quarter of the new estate should be assigned to the winners in the last ballot. Unlocated winners in a ballot were to get compensation of £15, £22 10s, and £30 according to winning a 2-, 3- or 4-acre ticket. It was announced in November that location day for Dodford would be 12 May 1849. Some families must have arrived before that, because three were reported in *Berrow's Worcester Journal* on 8 February 1849 as being in the greatest distress and applying for parish relief.

Bonus money came in slowly, and location day had to be moved on to 2 July. Even then, the forty houses lacked their pumps, and no wheat had been sown, for want of money. However, they were good little houses as you can see them today, most of them grouped on a gentle hill, designed exactly like all the other company houses, with a well to each. Much of the land bought remained untouched, from lack of money. Ten acres were sold before location day. Christopher Doyle was in charge of the remaining work and of settling the new owners in. More than forty people had offered bonuses, but £55 was the lowest successful bid. Ground rent was to average £8 a year, with the first year's rent held over till November 1850. Settlers had the right to redeem their ground rent at 25 years' purchase. Thirty-six people got plots by bonus, and three by luck in an earlier ballot. One plot was reported as sold previously. All bonus money was returned to un-successful competitors before the day. The average successful bid was

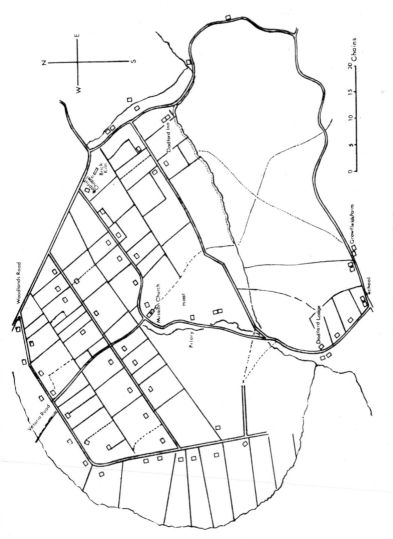

26 Plan of the Great Dodford estate

£75, which indicated people well above the money level of the weavers or frame-knitters on other estates. Perhaps this made them more fussy, for they were described as surly fellows who had little appreciation of O'Connor's efforts on his visits, and a few Scotsmen who were even worse.

They started complaining at once. Poor Doyle must have had a shocking time. By 7 July a list of the complaints was in the *Northern Star*—no pumps, no wheat, poor crops, no covers to the wells, so that all their children would fall in. They don't sound like country people. Their grumbles irritated their public, and Alexander Shaw wrote at the end of the first month in possession that none of the complainers had meant their remarks to be taken so hard, and asked that Doyle should continue to look after the place. A complete list is not known, but Peter Searby's article on Great Dodford in the *Agricultural History Review* of 1968 gives details of the twenty-five settlers known by the 1851 census returns, and seventeen are named in the schedule for the Act to wind up the company. They came from north and south, town and country, and fifteen of the twenty-five were farmers or gardeners. Carpenter, grocer, hatter, mason, East India Co pensioner, pawnbroker and plumber were others. Whatever the settlers' complaints, twice as many plots could have been sold, so great was the hunger for independence and a little bit of land of one's own. At least one wife wrote to O'Connor to thank him; Elizabeth Dewhirst, wife of a farmer from Yorkshire, wrote in her first week, beginning the letter, 'Dear and honoured Patriot'. She went on, 'I found all as I expected, with the exception of the pumps. My cottage has surpassed my expectation. With diligence and labour my labour-field will become a paradise.' She hoped he would receive the letter as a father. O'Connor promised that all the pumps would be put in, turnip sown, and wheat in the autumn. He claimed in the *Northern Star* to have had fifteen letters from Dodford people thanking him for pumps, guano, turnips, and time to pay rent, and begging him not to wind up the company. He referred to John Wooden who had a rough allotment where, later, bricks for building were burnt, 'but he is a land worker and says he will show them what to do'. The brick kiln is marked on the plan, near the Baptist Chapel. O'Connor signed himself on 27 July as the 'much abused, hunted, and persecuted friend of the ignorant, ungrateful, social and political spellbound slaves'. After location, more pieces of the original estate were sold, as the schedule of 1851 shows, and also Dodford Priory.[87]

The first winter was fearfully hard. Potatoes and bacon dwindled, there was nothing to sell and little means of earning money to buy. But somehow they managed to keep alive while food was growing. Some walked into Bromsgrove to work, some brought home knitting or sewing for shops. Dodford was more fortunate than the other estates in being nearer to a centre of population.

O'Connor was desperate for money. He held all the company's properties in his own name, and had mortgaged many portions of them. Interest was due on the mortgages, but threats and blarney had both failed to get any substantial rent out of allottees on any estate. Feargus had therefore to pay all interest and expenses out of his own pocket. He put the estate of Great Dodford up for sale. *Berrow's Worcester Journal* of 18 April 1850 carried the sad story.

The sale was on 15 April, at the Golden Cross inn, Bromsgrove. Feargus arrived in the morning and drove out to the estate for a last look. Eighty acres were still unallotted and the rest was divided into smallholdings, looking delightful and productive in the April sunshine where any cultivation had been done by the owners, but often overgrown with shaggy winter grass, and only pear blossom answering O'Connor's hopes. Back at the Golden Cross, where loungers were standing about relishing the settlement's failure, he drove the trap straight into the yard and went in at the back door to the private room which his solicitor had reserved for him. He could hear the hum of voices in the market room, and every now and then the shout of Fetherstone, the auctioneer, but he sat by the fire without moving.

The solicitor looked in to tell him that Lot 1 had gone for 205 guineas (£215·25); 6 acres and a house—it had cost O'Connor £450. Bidding was slow. A reserve price of £160 or so had been put on the next five lots, all 4-acre, but the solicitor popped in to ask O'Connor's authority to sell at £135, and Fetherstone worked hard to get it. All the rest went unsold for lack of bids. The soil was heavy, bidders did not like the division into small units, with perhaps uncongenial neighbours so close. Men who had the money would not want to live in this simple style, and men who would welcome the life had not got the money. The narrow estate roads had to be kept up by the occupiers, and so were very bad. The total of the sale was £647. Lots 4, 5 and 6 were sold by private contract afterwards. Bromsgrove tradesmen filed suits for recovery of debts from O'Connor.

On the anniversary of location a trip was made by the Birmingham and Dudley branches. The rural setting and evidence of allotment life were so pleasant and interesting that another trip was planned during the summer. An occupier, H. Green, wrote to the *Northern Star* at the time saying that twelve months had made them adepts, and few land workers worked so hard or so well. He said that on occupation 2 acres of each allotment had been planted with beans, peas, potatoes and cabbage; two bags of guano had been provided and 2 lb of turnip seed. It would take three years' work and then they would be flourishing. John Wooden, with the worst allotment, also wrote, thanking O'Connor and saying that time and exertion would put difficulties right. 'Contrast it with the day labourer, who has only about 7s a week after harvest, and often no work, while I shall have the necessaries of life, and a comfortable home, and can bid defiance to stern winter.' Another sale of parts of the estate was announced for August.

The census and the schedule to the 1851 Act for winding up the company show that many settlers had given up. Neither John Wooden nor H. Green were there. Six cottages were empty.[88] The official manager, Goodchap, visited the estate to fix ground rents and give titles to property, after the Act. Ground rent (or rent charge) was fixed at 4 per cent of the capital value of plot and house, and plots were valued at between £25 and £40 per acre and houses at £120. The average capital value was £275. The rent charge was lower than on all other estates because the entry bonus was subtracted from the capital value. O'Connor was questioned in the Vice-Chancellor's court before Master Humphrey in February 1852 about the sales he had made since the passing of the Winding-Up Act which handed all the company property over to the High Court of Chancery.[89] He had by then paid off the mortgage of £5,000 on the estate, and the sales seem to have been allowed.

Being within range of Birmingham and other large towns, Great Dodford was an object of interest observable by Radicals and social thinkers. In the 1880s, surveys of it were made by C. D. Sturge, Alfred

Harwood and Jesse Collings among others, and the results were published in the Birmingham papers and used as examples for or against smallholdings, independence of poor men, franchise, rents, rates, and kindred subjects. Dodford men had a vote, which was one of the springs of the smallholding movement. Otherwise they were in the same situation as all rural landworkers in the county, but better off by owning their little houses and their land. Ground rent was low, and even if the week's money in hand was only 7s 10d (39p) as Sturge calculated it, there were all the perks of owning one's own bit of land, the poultry and eggs, rabbits, pork or bacon, honey. Many settlers kept bees.

But one settler, John Wallace, had been gardener to the Earl of Plymouth at Tardebigge, a few miles away, and was a man of some knowledge.[90] The stiff red soil of Dodford was very awkward, so that a special strong fork known as a Dodford digging fork was made for it in Stourbridge. Wallace decided that potatoes and cereals were no good on Dodford land, but, with manure, it could be converted into market garden soil, in particular for strawberries. This was the opposite of O'Connor's judgment, and proved to be right. Dodford entered on a long period of security, even prosperity. The markets of Birmingham and Midland towns provided an ever-growing market. The strawberry crop was picked with a handy local supply of spare labour from two villages where nail-making was the domestic industry, and in the June weather the respite from forge work was always welcome. The strawberries were packed in wooden boxes and loaded on carts, some owned by settlers and some hired, which went off in the cool of the evening for the 13-mile ride to Birmingham. Buyers met them in the small hours, paid cash, the boxes were handed over, and carts returned to Dodford at 6 or 7 am when everyone was getting up. On the second Sunday in July, when the best of the crop was picked, Dodford Strawberry Wake was held, when local people came in and bought and ate all they wanted.

Besides strawberries, flowers and summer vegetables were grown. Primroses in the spring, wallflowers in May, peas, garlic for Lea & Perrins's Worcestershire sauce factory, were grown and sold. Manure was expensive and laborious to cart, but the results were worth it. The market lasted over the turn of the century, through the First World

War, when strawberries were wanted for jam, and only dwindled in modern times with rising competition and the pull of higher wages in industry.

In the 1880s Jesse Collings used Dodford to press his programme of smallholdings, 'three acres and a cow'. He did not seem to realise that Dodford's survival was due to market gardening, a very different thing from peasant farming. Its success had in fact been introduced by a gardener, not a smallholder or farmer, and anyone who knows country life knows the difference. In 1883 the Allotments & Smallholdings Association was founded, with Collings as president and Frederick Impey secretary. Impey wrote the first pamphlet, *La Petite Culture*, using Dodford as its image. He and Collings sensibly pointed out that had Dodford been in a foreign country instead of at our own door in England, a great deal more would be known and thought about it.

In 1885, of the original settlers of 1848, Benny, Shaw, Robinson, Dewhirst and Ash were still there, and two widows, one niece and two sons.[91] This was a good number, and, with Snigs End, the largest survival of the estates. During the work of a Royal Commission on the depressed condition of agriculture in the 1880s, a commissioner visited all the Chartist estates. At Dodford he found most men with a secondary means of support. A nailmaker worked on wet days and at night at his forge, and grew wheat, beans, peas and fruit. One was a brick-maker, but there is no mention of John Wooden, who found brick earth on his allotment and built a little kiln and lived by making and selling bricks. One had returned to his trade of builder after two years' experience of agriculture, and worked on building bridges and stations for railways, but continued to maintain his farm, and raised pigs, hens and strawberries. It was this man who replied to the commissioner's questions about O'Connor that he 'liked to hear O'Connor when he spoke the trooth, but Furragus didn't often do thart'. Alexander Shaw wrote to the *Birmingham Messenger* in the bad times of 1885 that Dodford had been a good bargain for the neighbourhood.[92] Dodford men had been a main cause of the abolition of church rates. They had summoned the surveyor of roads before the Bromsgrove magistrates for neglect of the parish road leading to Dodford, and had got him fined £5 with six months' notice to repair the road.

Dodford people have paid their poor rates, road rates, and Queen's taxes, have also been large employers of labour during the summer months, and at election times the great majority marched under their banner with the inscription 'Dodford Independent Electors. Ready? Yes, Always Ready'. . . . For this and such like doings they were dubbed by a neighbouring parson as the 'tag, rag, and bobtail' and by a local farmer as the 'poor devils of Dodford'. Commercially, the good old town of Bromsgrove is none the worse for Feargus O'Conner (sic) locating his Chartists within two and a half miles of it.

Dodford people did not continue anti-Church. In 1900 they were celebrating the opening of a new church room and collecting funds for Dodford Church. A song written for the occasion and sung at it is happily preserved in the Sturge collection. The descriptions must have been family memories.

> And yet again the scene is changed,
>   'Location Day' arrives,
> O'Connor's boys come settling here
>   Like bees from busy hives.
> The gay procession wends its way,
>   The waggons and the gigs,
> 'Fergus and Freedom' flaunts aloft,
>   'Less parsons and more pigs.'
>
> Sing of the land they bought and let,
>   Sing of the poor men's share,
> Sing of allotments fair for each,
>   Sing of the acres square.
> Sing of the ring of axe and spade,
>   Sing of the fields they dug,
> Sing of the muddy roads they made,
>   Sing of the homes so snug.
>
> Sing of the days when luck was gone,
>   Sing of the winter cold,
> Sing of the hungry children's cries,
>   Sing of the sticks all sold.
> Sing of the men who went away,
>   Sing of the men who stayed,
> Sing of the days when luck returned,
>   Sing of the garden trade.

Strawberries carried Dodford into the 1920s; by then industry was within reach, and although it drew men away to work it also enabled them to go on living on the little plots and using the land one way or another. Now Dodford, like all the estates, is a centre of snug, independent rural life.

I last visited it on a chill October day. Coming off the M5 past Droitwich I took the by-roads which keep west of Bromsgrove through up-and-down farm land towards Great Dodford. Soon the familiar shape of the Chartist cottage appears along the road. The main part of the estate lies on a little hill in one compact area bounded by Woodlands Road and crossed by Victoria Road. The hill faces southeast, and north or east winds strike chill across it. Cottages are built all along Woodlands Road, on each side, and look out over wide, spreading woods on the west and all the easy Midland farm land on every other side. It was a dull day, with grey sky and yellow leaves. The little houses looked comfortable and well kept; some greatly altered but keeping the character, most hardly altered at all. The triangle and lozenge appeared as porch decorations. Brickwork was pointed, roofs and gates good, paint fresh. All had outbuildings, some for a car, some for poultry and geese, a few sheep, young cattle, and one for a large quantity of pigs. One had big glasshouses. Mount Pleasant had been carefully extended along its front by a copy of the projecting centre and gable. Flower gardens were still bright with chrysanthemums, and many houses were bowered in damson and pear trees. Most of the land around each house was grazing, with a patch of orchard near the house where washing blew on the lines in the sharp wind. Only one house was derelict, stucco gone, roof going, gate broken. Woodlands Road was just 9 ft wide, sheltered from wind by thick hedges and bushes. A small dumper truck carrying green stuff filled up the width.

I had a talk with Mrs J. Rutter of Primrose Cottage. She told me that her late husband had been born on the estate, and she herself had lived there sixty years, in three different cottages. Behind Primrose Cottage she had a good brick pony stable and cart shed, with hay loft above. Mr Rutter had been a painter and decorator and they had also grown strawberries for market. The cottage was named for the primroses which used to fill the field alongside in the flower-selling days. Red pears lay in the grass under her washing line, and she picked me a big bagful.

At Malvern View lived Mrs. I. Rutter, who had been fifty-four years in the house. She had come as a girl from Chaddesley Corbett vicarage farm, on the other side of the woods that stretch up to Dodford on the west. Her husband had owned this and the next-door property. Hundreds of dozens of baskets of strawberries they had sent to Birmingham market, and gooseberries, potatoes, peas, damsons, plums, and Bramley Seedling apples. Now she has a cow and two calves, and a lodger who works in Austin's at Longbridge, nine miles away. She showed me her hands misshapen with rheumatism and outdoor work. Small yellow damson leaves blew down round us. People didn't know what work was nowadays, she had always worked hard, but her husband had never got a week's wages in his life, he had owned his own land and sold his own produce. What did I think the derelict house and land had just sold for? £7,500, so they said.

More of the Dodford estate lies along the high road called Priory Road. Here is the mission church and the Priory site, and a cottage charmingly converted into a sub-post office and village shop. The shape, the chimneys, slates, roof sloping down at the back, all remain. Further afield, by Dodford Inn, there are more houses on Whinfield Road, which in its succession of large holes, ridges, lakes of mud with bricks sticking up in them, suggests what the estate roads were all like in the old days.

The estates are comfortable now, sharing the prosperity which has come since 1945 to villages throughout England, though the Land Company did not achieve it.

APPENDICES

APPENDIX 1

CHRONOLOGY OF THE LAND COMPANY

1845 April: Chartist National Delegates Meeting agreed the Land Plan. Subscriptions began during the year.

December: first conference devoted only to the Chartist Co-operative Land Plan.

1846 March: Heronsgate (O'Connorville) bought.

October: Lowbands bought. Company provisionally registered.

December: name changed to National Co-operative Land Company.

1847 January: Land Bank opened.

February: deposit paid on Mathon estate.

May: Heronsgate (O'Connorville) opened.

June: Snigs End and Minster Lovell (Charterville) bought.

August: Lowbands opened.

1848 January: Great Dodford bought.

May: Minster Lovell partly occupied.

House of Commons appointed Select Committee to enquire into the affairs of the company.

June–July: Select Committee sat.

June: Snigs End and Minster Lovell opened. 250 settlers now located. Another deposit paid on Mathon estate.

1849 February: Mathon abandoned and subscriptions returned.

July: Great Dodford opened.

1850 January: sixty-eight ejectment orders served on allottees at Minster Lovell.

1851 August: Act for winding up the company passed.

October: William Goodchap appointed official manager for the Court of Chancery, in charge of all the estates.

1855   August: Feargus O'Connor died.

1856   February: Vice-Chancellor declared sale of Minster Lovell allotments by O'Connor and mortgagees fraudulent.

1857   May: O'Connorville sold, and much of Snigs End sold.

1858   June: much of Lowbands sold.

APPENDIX 2

LIST OF ESTATES WITH SIZES, DATE AND COSTS, IN APPENDIX TO THE SELECT COMMITTEE, FIFTH REPORT, *1848*

Estates	*Number of acres*	*Contract made*	*Purchase completed*	*£ Purchase money*
Herringsgate, near Watford	103	March 1846	May 1846	2,344
Lowbands, near Gloucester	170	October 1846	December 1846	8,560
Minster Lovell, near Witney	297	June 1847	August 1847	10,878
Snig's End, near Gloucester	268	June 1847	November 1847	12,200
Dodford, near Bromsgrove	280	January 1848	May 1848	10,350
Mathon, near Worcester	500	July 1847	Not completed	15,350

APPENDIX 3

LISTS OF ALLOTTEES OR OCCUPIERS ON THE ESTATES

Heronsgate or O'Connorville: (1) *1846. Ballot names in the order of their plots*

2 acres

1 John Westmorland, London
2 John Lambourne, Reading
3 Michael Fitzsimmon, Manchester
4 William Mann, Northampton
5 Philip Ford, Wotton-under-Edge
6 George Hearson, Leeds
7 George Mansfield, Bradford-on-Avon
8 Richard Everson, Stockport
9 Charles Brown, Halifax
10 John Walwark, Ashton-under-Lyne
11 John Neale, Heywood
12 William House, Pershore
13 Henry Smith, Keighley
14 George Ramsbottom, Ashton-under-Lyne
15 William Mitchell, London
16 John Firth, Bradford
17 Ralph Kerfoot, Rouen

3 acres

18 James Short, Bilston
19 William Oddy, Bradford
20 George Richardson, London
21 Benjamin Knott, Halifax
22 Isaac Jowett, Bradford

4 acres

23 Thomas Meyrick, Worcester
24 Joseph Mills, Ashton-under-Lyne
25 David Watson, Edinburgh
26 Martin Griffiths, Worcester
27 James Cole, Bradford
28 Barbara Vaughan, Sunderland
29 Alfred Crowther, Ashton-under-Lyne
30 Thomas Smith, Wigan
31 James Greenwood, Heddon Bridge
32 Thomas Smith, London
33 Thomas Bond, Devizes
34 James Taylor, Manchester
35 Joseph Openshaw, Manchester
36 School and land attached

At second issue of the list, George Hearson of Leeds was replaced by Charles Smith of Halifax. By the date of location, 1 May 1847, Charles Tawes of New Radford replaced Charles Brown of Halifax, and Alfred Barker of Ashton-under-Lyne replaced Joseph Mills of the same place.

O'Connorville: (2) *Appendix to Fifth Report of Select Committee 1848*

2 acres

All names remain, except J. Hornby is listed as having paid £26 for one lot, and T. M. Wheeler as owning one lot, no price.

3 acres

All names remain. Mr King is listed as owning one lot for £60.

4 acres

All names remain, except Gamble replaces Greenwood for £90, and G. Wheeler is listed as having paid £80 for one lot.

School

Mr Graves the schoolmaster.

O'Connorville: (3) Occupiers of the plots at four dates: list on the 1846 engraving, census return of 1851, sale particulars of 1857, tithe roll of 1858

The list is compiled by G. Cornwall.

1	1846	John Westmorland		1857	Joseph Barwettsen
	1851	—		1858	Richard Hammond
	1857	Richard Port	7	1846	George Mansfield
	1858	Richard Port		1851	Robert Smith
2	1846	John Lambourne		1857	Robert Smith
	1851	John Lambourne		1858	John Howard
	1857	John Shaw	8	1846	Richard Eveson
	1858	Unoccupied		1851	Richard Eveson
3	1846	Michael Fitzsimmon		1857	Joseph Gates
	1851	Michael Fitzsimmon		1858	James Woods
	1857	Michael Fitzsimmon	9	1846	Charles Tawes
	1858	Unoccupied		1851	Thomas Heaton
4	1846	William Mann		1857	Thomas Heaton
	1851	Edward Whitmore		1858	Thomas Heaton
	1857	Edward Whitmore	10	1846	John Walwark
	1858	Mary Whitmore		1851	William Dimmock
5	1846	Philip Ford		1857	William Dimmock
	1851	Philip Ford		1858	William Dimmock
	1857	Philip Ford	11	1846	John Neale
	1858	Philip Ford		1851	Aris Hore
6	1846	Charles Smith		1857	William Hore
	1851	Joseph Burnett		1858	William Hore

12	1846	William House
	1851	William House
	1857	Richard Gratton
	1858	Richard Gratton
13	1846	Henry Smith
	1851	—
	1857	Thomas Bradford
	1858	Thomas Bradford
14	1846	George Ramsbottom
	1851	John Bradford
	1857	John Hewlett Bradford
	1858	John Hewlett Bradford
15	1846	William Mitchell
	1851	Elizabeth Newsome
	1857	Charles Newsome
	1858	Jane Langdon
16	1846	John Firth
	1851	Unoccupied
	1857	Thomas Ireland
	1858	Zachariah Brown
17	1846	Ralph Kerfoot
	1851	Henry Ivery
	1857	John J. H. Wolfe
	1858	John J. H. Wolfe
18	1846	James Short
	1851	George Pocock
	1857	Thomas King
	1858	Thomas King
19	1846	William Oddy
	1851	Edward Bukhock
	1857	Maria Marsh
	1858	William Howse
20	1846	George Richardson
	1851	William Betts
	1857	John Cartwell
	1858	John Cartwell
21	1846	Benjamin Knott
	1851	Elizabeth Blackborough
	1857	Stephen Blakeborough
	1858	Stephen Blakeborough

22	1846	Isaac Jowett
	1851	Thomas Meads
	1857	Thomas Meads
	1858	Thomas Meads
23	1846	Thomas Meyrick
	1851	Thomas Meyrick
	1857	Thomas Meyrick
	1858	Thomas Meyrick
24	1846	Alfred Barker
	1851	James Evans
	1857	William Stimpson
	1858	Thomas Crowther
25	1846	David Watson
	1851	Joseph Wheeler
	1857	George Wheeler
	1858	George Wheeler
26	1846	Martin Griffiths
	1851	Martin Griffiths
	1857	Martin Griffiths
	1858	Martin Griffiths
27	1846	James Cole
	1851	—
	1857	George Wheeler
	1858	George Wheeler
28	1846	Barbara Vaughan
	1851	—
	1857	John Cattell
	1858	John Cattell
29	1846	Alfred Crowther
	1851	Unoccupied
	1857	Philip Elliott
	1858	James Alcock
30	1846	Thomas Smith
	1851	James Purvis
	1857	Francis Bentley
	1858	Francis Bentley
31	1846	James Greenwood
	1851	Thomas Bailey
	1857	Thomas Bailey
	1858	Thomas Bailey

32 1846 Thomas Smith
    1851 John Sevster
    1857 John Gilbon
    1858 John Gilbon

33 1846 Thomas Bond
    1851 John Gamble
    1857 Joseph Barnett Sr
    1858 Joseph Barnett

34 1846 James Taylor
    1851 John Sturgeon
    1857 John Sturgeon
    1858 John Sturgeon

35 1846 Joseph Openshaw
    1851 Francis Hurlett
    1857 Joseph White the Elder
    1858 John Benson

The School

    1846 Mr Graves
    1851 James Lindon
    1857 Unoccupied
    1858 William Goodchap

Lowbands: (1) *1846 Ballot*

No acreage given, probably 2

1 James Young, Manchester
2 James Dennis, Salford
3 Sheriff Wyatt, Leicester
4 William Jennings, Bilston
5 Arthur Shaw, Nottingham

3 acres

1 James South, Blackburn
2 Cornelius Ashton, Manchester
3 John Dennis, New Bradford (*sic*)
4 Alexander Robertson, Aberdeen
5 James Driver, Northampton

4 acres

Winners

1 William Young Souter, Westminster
2 Saville Crowther, Mottram
3 Thomas Rawson, Manchester
4 Edmund Kershaw, Rochdale
5 William Charlesworth, Stalybridge
6 James Bearman, Bocking
7 William Addison, Manchester
8 Thomas Richardson, London
9 Henry Porter, London
10 George Webb, Reading
11 Thomas Aclam, Barnsley
12 James Halliwell, Hebden Bridge
13 James Wharnton, London
14 Christopher Doyle, O'Connorville
15 Isaac Weir, Manchester
16 John Renham, London
17 James Ferguson, Burnley
18 William Rogerson, Somerston
19 John Lee, Manchester
20 George Redfern, London

Second ballot listed as runners-up

John Hartley, Hebden Bridge
William Danley, Stockport
Richard Robinson, Clitheroe
George Smith, Halifax
William Johnston, Hindley
Thos Wm Dale, Macclesfield
John Cloud, Monmouth
George Forster, Manchester
William Sadler, Manchester
James Stott, Bradford

Lowbands: (2) *Select Committee Appendix, 1848*

2 acres

1	H. W. Bernard	11	John Gaskell
2	Geo Worrall	12	A. W. How
3	Henry Tanner	13	R. Butterworth
4	Geo Coupe	14	John Linney
5	William Piggs	15	Henry Lee
6	John Clark	16	Samuel Atherton
7	Edward Grey	17	Robert Massey
8	James Baker	18	John Holmes
9	James Goodward	19	Charles Payne
10	David Webster	20	Arthur Munson

3 acres

All names remain. William Pratt is listed as having gained one allotment by transfer.

Henry Parker, Mr Petit, Mr O'Connor, John Wallace, T. Clark, John Shuter, are listed as having gained an allotment by transfer.

4 acres

All names remain, except Thomas Rawson and Christopher Doyle. W. Reay and W. Bentley are listed as having gained an allotment by transfer.

School

Mr O'Brien, schoolmaster

Charterville: (1) *February 1848 Ballot*

2 acres

1	M. Stockley, Lamberhead Green
2	W. Hay, Stockport
3	H. Grimshaw, Ashton-under-Lyne
4	E. Tibbles, Cirencester
5	W. Smith, Newcastle-upon-Tyne
6	H. Gose, Manchester
7	O. Hornby, Manchester
8	S. Ashworth, Rochdale
9	J. Bennett, Stockton
10	D. Denton, Huddersfield
11	B. Sleddaw, Rochdale
12	T. Bankell, Radcliffe
13	J. Ashaman, Dudley
14	J. Clark, Norwich
15	R. Butterfield, Bradford
16	T. Gilbert, Coventry
17	A. Brierley, Leeds
18	R. Jones, Bilston
19	T. House, Norwich
20	E. Stallwood, Hammersmith
21	J. David, Pershore
22	H. Heskit ⎫ Leigh
23	J. Crampton ⎭

3 acres

1	J. Bowers, Birmingham
2	M. Dyson, Ashton
3	C. Arnold, Leicester
4	J. Holmes, Nottingham
5	C. Graham, Hull
6	J. Townson, Oldham

7 J. Hornsby, Stockport
8 W. Bottrill, Northants
9 T. Kirk, Hull
10 R. Tippler, Northants
11 J. Horne, Brighton
12 J. Z. Barber, Westminster

4 acres

1 B. Jackson, Oldham
2 W. Atkins, Peterborough
3 R. Goodwill, Leeds
4 T. Pickersgill, Westminster
5 J. Benson, Manchester
6 A. Dunford, City of London
7 S. Rathery, Dewsbury
8 R. Seed, Clitheroe
9 M. Cornwall, Bradford
10 W. Coombes, Newton Abbot
11 P. Lontel, Alva
12 P. O'Leary, Kidderminster
13 C. Hill, Rochester
14 J. Price, Pershore
15 W. Smith, Carlisle

16 J. Smart, Branham, Wilts
17 C. Barton, office list
18 J. Littlewood, Leeds
19 A. Lockwood, Wakefield
20 J. Beattie, Glasgow
21 J. Baker, Birmingham
22 J. Kendall, Bradford, Wilts
23 J. Plaice, Lambeth
24 E. Sikes, Huddersfield
25 T. Holland, Manchester
26 J. Ramsey, Glasgow
27 J. Stanton, office, Coggeshill
28 G. Johnson, Mottram
29 J. Bennett, Wotton-under-Edge
30 H. Lester, Reading
31 A. Willis, Rochester
32 J. Hoe, Nottingham
33 A. Rice, Cheltenham
34 E. Coolan, Navana, St Germain, France
35 J. M'William, Manchester
36 J. Shawcross, Manchester
37 J. Campbell, Manchester
38 J. Gathard, Lambeth

Charterville: (2) *Select Committee Appendix 1848*

Two acres	Transfer	Two acres	Transfer
H. E. Grimshaw	H. Heskett	Richard Jones	William
William Hoy	J. Crompton	A. Brierly	Holditch
Michael Stockley	J. Bennett	James Davies	
Thomas Bankell	Luke Tomlinson	Thomas House	
John Ashanan	John Clark	Duke Denton	
Richard Butterfield	Ann Miles	Brierly Lleddow	
Samuel Ashworth	Maria Merryman	Edmund Stallwood	
William Smith	Charles Tinham	T. Gilbert	
Othaniel Hornby	William Ashforth	E. Tibbles	

Four acres	Transfer	Four acrcs	Transfer	Three acres
Samuel Rothery		Moss Wolf		
Patrick O'Leary		A. Rice	W. Crabtree	Thomas Kirk
William Smith		Eli Sikes		Mark Dyson
Mrs John Hoe		R. Seed		J. Townson
Thomas Holland		J. Bennett		Charles Arnold
John Smart		A. Willis		J. Hornby
Abraham Lockwood		Eli Coolon		J. Holmes
George Johnson		J. Plaice	T. Turner	R. Tippler
Henry Lester	Mr Carter	W. W.		W. Bottrill
		Coombes		
John Gathard		J. M'William		J. Horne
Thomas Pickersgill		T. Loutel		J. Bowers
James Shawcross		A. Dunford		C. P. Graham
James Campbell		J. Stanton		Ann Price
John Benson		C. E. Hill		J. Z. Barber
James Price		C. Barton		
John Littlewood		J. S. Beattie		
Benjamin Jackson		W. Atkins		
Robert Goodwill		Hervey Gorse		
Robert Howard				
Peter Ashton				

Charterville: (3) *Goodchap's Schedule of Allottees 10 June 1852*

No of Allotment	Name	No of Allotment	Name
	Two acres		Three acres
8	Cooper John	2	Stone Samuel
10	Batts George	3	Matthews Thomas
11	Haydon Noah	4	Smith Chas
12	do. do.	5	Hayes John
20	Holloway Joseph	6	Nippard Chas
23	Wheeler Walter	7	Wilks Edward
		8	Wright Thomas
		9	Stone Samuel
		10	Aston William

No of Allotment	Name	No of Allotment	Name
	Four acres		Four acres
1	Robinson George	20	Kirkman Henry
3	Littlewood John	22	Willis Charles
9	Hinton John	23	Cross Wm
10	Lovesay Thomas	27	Bennett John
13	Bunting George	38	Langstone Samuel
16	Belstead Thomas	39	Aston John
18	Mason Thomas	School House	Hart Masfen

Total of rents   £256

PRO reference, C. 121–401.

Snigs End: (1) *Directors' List of June 1848 Ballot*

2 acres

1   Emma Andrews, Banbury
2   S. Whalley, Manchester
3   J. Holt, Manchester
4   J. Hudson, Leicester
5   J. Carter, Upton-on-Severn
6   C. Frith, Greenwich
7   W. Curtis, London
8   W. Peckitt, office list
9   C. Jay, Hull
10 R. Wilson, Walsoken
11 C. Firth, office list
12 J. Harmer, office list
13 J. Smith, Birmingham
14 S. Needham, Derby
15 T. Sutton, office list
16 J. Langley, Norwich
17 F. Staples ⎱ Family ticket,
    J. Staples ⎰ office list
18 J. Teague, Bilston
19 Mary Clarkson, Addingham
20 I. Goodhall, Market Lavington
21 W. Gray, Market Lavington
22 C. Buddecombe, Southampton
23 E. Edesbury, office list
24 W. Dart, Exeter
25 T. Hope, Ledbury
26 T. Ashman, Mells
27 R. Heppenstall, Hull
28 R. Bains, Newcastle-on-Tyne
29 J. West, office list
30 J. Robertson, Stalybridge
31 T. Halsale, Chorley
32 R. Daniels, office
33 D. O'Brien, Alva

3 acres

1   J. Kay   ⎱ Family ticket, Ash-
    T. Buckby ⎰ ton-under-Lyne
2   J. Watson, Dewsbury

3   J. Buswell, Banbury
4   A. Cleland, Glasgow
5   G. Close, Nottingham
6   T. Saville, Halifax
7   R. Winter, Hull
8   H. Oliver, Newport Pagnell
9   Matthew Brown, office list
10 Donal Robinson, Edinburgh
11 W. Gent, Wellingborough

4 acres

1   Doyle, O'Connorville
2   Baker, Birmingham
3   G. Wheeler, Reading
4   Cornwall, Bradford
5   Rawson, Manchester
6   Smith, London
7   Kindell, Bradford
8   W. Colston, Derby
9   J. Wakeman, Torquay
10 T. Newson, Dewsbury
11 D. Powell, Merthyr Tydfil
12 J. Brand, Sleaford
13 J. Rice, Bradford
14 T. Franklin, Limehouse
15 J. Kinross ⎱ Family ticket, Alva
    A. Kinross ⎰
16 J. Lawton, Retford
17 J. Simpson   ⎱ Family ticket,
    Esther Hunt ⎰ Manchester
18 R. Jarvis, office list
19 J. Smith, Rouen, France
20 E. Gee, Wigan
21 W. James, Merthyr Tydfil
22 J. Miller, Newton Abbot
23 J. Carew, Manchester
24 J. Ramsey, Glasgow
25 W. Jarrett, office list
26 T. Launchbury, Kidderminster

Snigs End: (2) *Select Committee Appendix 1848*

Two acres	Transfer	Two acres	Transfer
Thomas Ashman		James Harmer	Jane Boyer
Emma Adams		R. Heppenstall	
C. H. Buddecombe		Thomas Halsale	
Robert Baines		Constantine Jay	
John Carter		John Langley	
W. H. Curtis		Stephen Needham	
Mary Clarkson	H. Cullingham	Dennis O'Brien	
William Dart		William Peckett	
Richard Daniels		John Robertson	
Edward Edesbury		James Smith	Mr Russell
Charles Frith		Thomas Sutton	
Charles Firth	E. B. Jukes	George Staples	
Isaac Goodall		Henry Staples	
William Gray		John Teague	
James Holt		Samuel Whalley	
John Hudson		Robert Wilson	
Thomas Hope		John West	
— Franklin		Thomas Rawson	

Snigs End: (2) *Select Committee Appendix 1848* (continued)

Three acres	Four acres	Transfer	Four acres	Transfer
John Boswell	Mr Baker	C. G. Whittaker	John Rice	
M. W. Brown	James Brand		John Ramsey	
Alex Cleland	Mr Connal		Mr Smith	Crews
George Cox	W. Colston		Joseph Smith	Newton
William Gent	James Carew		J. L. Simpson	
Henry Oliver	Mr C. Doyle		Esther Hunt	
Donald Robinson	Edmund Gee	John Skilling	George Wheeler	
Robert Winter	T. Franklin		James Wakeman	John Croft
James Watson	Robert Jarvis		Thomas Barlow	
Thomas Saville	William Jarrett		Walter Kenworthy	
John Kay	Jarvis Kendall		Charles	
Thomas Buckby	John Kinross		Richardson	
	Andrew		William Lambert	
	Kinross		John Tattersall	
	John Lawton		Thomas Lambert	
Transfer	W. James			
	John Miller			
S. Brown	T. Launchbury			
	T. Newsome			
	Daniel Powell			
	Mr Rawson			

Great Dodford: (1) *1851 census returns, giving name, occupation and place of birth*

William Ash, farmer, Newton, Staffs
Stephen Baker, farmer, Kent
John Bucknole, gardener, Lyme Regis
Thomas Bungay, farmer, Wiltshire
William Burridge, grocer, Shaftesbury, Dorset
Peter Burton, agricultural labourer, Leigh, Lancs
James Cameron, hatter, Scotland
John Coggill, farmer, 4 acres, Newark
John Crane, farmer, 4 acres, Spratton, Northants
Nathaniel Dewhurst, farmer, 4 acres, York
James Finlay, stone mason, Northumberland
William Foster, gardener, Souldern, Oxon
Henry Green, gardener, Chesterton, Cambs
William Hodgkiss, East India Company pensioner, Cork
James Johnson, agricultural labourer, Peterborough
Ann Lawes, Salisbury
John Orrell, plumber and painter, Bermondsey
William Robinson, farmer, 2 acres, Malton, Yorks
Alexander Shaw, carpenter, Scotland
William Topp, pawnbroker, Middlesex
James Town, gardener, York
John Wallace, gardener, Hertfordshire
Hannah Ward, Yorkshire
Robert West, farmer, 4 acres, York
Ann Wood, Scotland

P. Searby, 'Great Dodford and the later history of the Chartist Land Scheme', in
  The Agricultural History Review, Vol 16, 1968, Part I.

(2) *Winding-Up Act, 1851, Schedule 2*

John Ward, £225 for 6 acres
Henry Blackledge, £141 15s for 4 acres
James Kelshaw, £390 for 5 acres
Robert Rudd, £141 15s for 4 acres
James Finlay, £30 for 3 acres
Wm Hackett sr, gentleman, £345 12s 6d for 9 acres
G. Hemming, confectioner, £280 for 8 acres
James Blair, of Dudley, tea-dealer and grocer, £215 5s for 6 acres and £120 for
  4 acres
James Topp, broker, £77 10s for 4 acres
James Birch, yeoman, £124 for 6 acres

Peter Summerton, stone mason, £157 for 4 acres
John Wilkes, farmer, £190 for 4 acres
Joseph Hill, stay maker, £120 for 6 acres
Wallace Russell, gentleman, £354 for 4 acres

AUTHOR'S ACKNOWLEDGMENTS

I would first like to thank everybody, unknown by name, who has been patient with me, a stranger asking questions, and interested enough in the process of history in their own locality to stand and talk about old times, old names and buildings, mills, quarries, romances.

Then, more particularly, I would like to thank the staff of the Public Record Office, both at Chancery Lane and Ashridge; the Clerk of the Records of the House of Lords; the county archivists, public librarians and local history librarians and their staffs of Gloucestershire, Oxfordshire and Hertfordshire; of Manchester, Leeds, Birmingham, Nottingham, Preston, and the City of Westminster (Marylebone); the principal and sub-librarian of the Royal Agricultural College at Cirencester, the editor of the *Wilts & Gloucestershire Standard* there, and the manager of the *Western Times* at Exeter.

In connection with O'Connorville, I am glad to acknowledge a great debt to Mr Godfrey Cornwall, who has been completely open-handed with his original material, to Mr A. H. Fordham and Mr A. S. Bird for much information, and to Messrs Vaisey & Turner of Tring, who let me see the only original coloured print of O'Connorville that I have traced. Among the estate residents I had the good fortune to find in one person a keen local historian, a natural artist and a professional cartographer, Miss Dorothy Haigh, who has drawn all the maps, plans and decorative pieces for this book.

For Snigs End and Lowbands I want to thank Mr and Mrs Travell of O'Connor Villa, Snigs End, Staunton, for telling me of their own connection with the Land Company and the estate, lending me documents, showing me their house, taking me round to other residents, and introducing me to Mr Charles Parsons of Staunton. Mr Parsons' expert knowledge as a local builder, and his two-generation knowledge of Snigs End, as well as his loan of documents, have provided most of my knowledge of the building work on these estates. I also want to thank Mr Lawrence of Messrs Bruton & Knowles, the estate agents of Gloucester, who let me see records containing details of Land Company sales; and the vicars of Corse and Redmarley d'Abitot, who showed me records and gave me a great deal of help and information.

For Charterville, I want to thank the Rev F. Harwood, vicar of Minster Lovell, who showed me records and gave much time to answering my queries and taking me round to meet residents; Messrs Lee, Chadwick & Co, solicitors, and Mr Sutcliffe of Messrs Habgood & Mammatt, estate agents, both of Witney, who let me interrupt their business and sit in their offices copying out records, and gave me every help in digging out local history; and Mr F. Brooks of Woodlands, Minster Lovell, who took trouble to provide for me the only plan of the estate I have been able to trace.

For Great Dodford, I must thank Mr Peter Searby of Cambridge University, who has been most generous with his own research and specialist knowledge of the estate.

I am grateful to the following for providing me with illustrations: Mr G. Cornwall, jacket, Plate I (above), Figs 6 and 12; Rowley, photographer, Rickmansworth, Plate I (below), II (a) and (b); David Miles, photographer, Cirencester, Plates III, IV, V and VI; Mrs R. Leadbeater, Plate VII; Plate VIII (a), Nottingham Public Library; Plate VIII (b), Michael Palmer, photographer, London W11; Figs 1 and 2, the Public Record Office; Figs 22 and 23, Messrs Habgood & Mammatt, Witney; Fig 28, Mr C. Parsons. Plans of estates are drawn from plans in Chancery records, or from those drawn for sales or title deeds.

Finally, and chiefly, I thank my husband, Charles Hadfield, who has supported my work from the beginning, taken time from his own canal books to help with my research, and provided the attitude and atmosphere which make it possible to write a historical study in a full-time domestic life.

ALICE MARY HADFIELD

NOTES

1 Donald Read & Eric Glasgow, *Feargus O'Connor: Irishman and Chartist*, 1961.
2 *Cork Southern Reporter*, 19 January 1833, quo Read & Glasgow, *O'Connor*, p 31.
3 The four verses are quoted in Read & Glasgow, *Feargus O'Connor*, p 96.
4 Select Committee on the National Land Company. *Parliamentary Papers* (Reports from Committees) Session 1847–8. Vol XIX. 2nd Report.
5 Ibid, 3rd Report.
6 Ibid, 1st Report.
7 *Northern Star*, 10 January 1846.
8 Select Committee, op cit, 1st Report.
9 Ibid, 1st Report.
10 *Northern Star*, 31 October 1846.
11 National Land Company's certificate (see illustration on p 31).
12 Select Committee, 2nd Report.
13 Ibid.
14 Ibid.
15 Ibid.
16 Hymn beginning 'O for a thousand tongues to sing', C. Wesley, 1738.
17 Public Record Office, B.T. 41/474, 5 and 6.
18 *Preston Guardian*, 16 January 1847.
19 *Gloucester Chronicle*, 23 January 1847.
20 *Preston Guardian*, 30 January 1847.
21 For the handbill, the illustration on p 38.
22 *Preston Guardian*, 30 January 1847.
23 See Chapter 8, p 89.
24 Select Committee, 2nd Report.
25 *Preston Guardian*, 30 October 1847.
26 Select Committee, 3rd Report.
27 *Manchester Examiner*, 23 November 1847; *Northern Star*, 30 October, 20 November 1847. There are slight variations.
28 *Preston Guardian*, 27 November 1847, 5 February 1848.
29 Ibid, 18 December 1847.
30 *Manchester Examiner*, 12 February 1848.

31 *Journal* of the House of Commons, Vol 103, Pt i.

32 *Preston Guardian*, 5, 19 February 1848.

33 *Berrow's Worcester Journal*, 5 July 1848.

34 Chinnery's affidavit supporting Roberts's affidavit before the Master in Chancery, *Northern Star*, 4 October 1851, and F. Boase, *Modern English Biography*, 1892, reprinted 1965.

35 Read & Glasgow, *Feargus O'Connor*, Chapter XV.

36 *Preston Guardian*, 19 August 1848.

37 *The Times*, 28 November 1855.

38 *The O'Connor Monument; respectfully dedicated to its supporters*, by Punch the Younger (Nottingham City Library).

39 *Vindication of the Dead* (Rylands Library, Manchester).

40 *Illustrated London News*, 4 September 1852.

41 G. Cornwall, 'Heronsgate and the Chartists', *Rickmansworth Historical Society Quarterly Magazine*, Vol II, No 1.

42 Select Committee, 1st Report.

43 *Northern Star*, 7 February 1852.

44 R. C. Gammage, *The History of the Chartist Movement*, 1854.

45 Cornwall, 'Heronsgate and the Chartists', op cit.

46 Select Committee, 3rd Report.

47 *Northern Star*, 27 February 1847.

48 *Gloucester Journal*, 12 December 1846, quoting the *Morning Advertiser*.

49 *Northern Star*, 20 February 1847.

50 Ibid, 20 February 1847.

51 Ernest Jones, quoted in Cornwall, 'Heronsgate and the Chartists', op cit.

52 'The Charter and the Land', quoted ibid.

53 Select Committee, 4th Report.

54 *Chartist Songs and Fugitive Pieces*.

55 Select Committee, 3rd Report.

56 Ibid.

57 Ibid.

58 *Northern Star*, 24 June 1848.

59 Ibid, 6 May 1848.

60 *The Labourer*, Vol I.

61 *Northern Star*, 16 September 1848.

62 *Illustrated London News*, 4 September 1852.

63 *Berrow's Worcester Journal*, 9 September 1852.

64 *The Uxbridge Record*, No 6, November 1965.

65 S. & B. Webb, *History of Trade Unionism*, p 164; Gammage, *Chartist Movement*, op cit, pp 79, 180; G. J. Holyoake, *Sixty Years of an Agitator's Life*, i, 105.

66 Sale notice: Messrs Hoggart & Norton, 62 Old Broad Street, London, auctioneers; Messrs Sewell & Newmarch, Cirencester, solicitors.

67 *Gloucestershire Countryside*, Vol 4, No 11, April–June 1943.
68 *Berrow's Worcester Journal*, 19 August 1847.
69 Select Committee, 4th Report.
70 *Berrow's Worcester Journal*, 4 November 1852.
71 Select Committee, 1st Report.
72 For all my information about Charterville legal matters, see Chancery Records C. 101/401.
73 Select Committee, 3rd Report.
74 Ibid.
75 Ibid.
76 *Northern Star*, 1 July 1848.
77 Ibid.
78 Ibid, 24 March 1849.
79 *Berrow's Worcester Journal*, 28 June 1849.
80 Ibid, 6 December 1849.
81 Minutes of Evidence, House of Commons, Vol 38, Group 21, 1851.
82 MS *History of Minster Lovell* (in possession of the vicar).
83 Select Committee, 1st Report.
84 *Preston Guardian*, 26 February 1848.
85 C. D. Sturge Collection I.Q. 333 (Birmingham Reference Library).
86 *Northern Star*, 24 June 1848.
87 P. Searby, 'Great Dodford and the later history of the Chartist Land Scheme', *The Agricultural History Review*, Vol 16, 1968, Part I.
88 Ibid.
89 *Northern Star*, 7 February 1852.
90 Searby, 'Great Dodford', op cit.
91 Sturge collection, op cit.
92 30 April 1885.

SOURCES

The *Northern Star*, from 1843.

The *Labourer*, a short-lived monthly magazine ed by O'Connor and Ernest Jones, 1848.

Jones, Ernest, *Diary*, in Local History Library, Manchester Central Library.

Select Committee on the National Land Company: *Parliamentary Papers* (Reports from Committees) Session 1847–8, Vol XIX.

Minutes of Evidence before the Winding-Up Act of 1851; Local and Personal Acts 14 & 15 Vict 1851, Cap cxxxix.

Public Record Office material:

- (a) C. 101/401
     C. 121/401
     C. 36/574
- (b) B.T. 41/474, 5 and 6
     B.T. 41/136
- (c) H.O. 45. O.S. 2665
- (d) Maps in the Public Record Office of O'Connorville estate, 1853, (C. 54/14661 no 6), Snigs End, 1853, (C. 54/14661 no 7), and Lowbands, 1853 (C. 54/14661 no 5).

25 O'Connor letters, in the British Library of Political & Economic Science, University of London.

Material in the County Record Offices of Gloucestershire and Oxfordshire, the Local History libraries at Gloucester, Manchester and Leeds, the Local History Council of Hertfordshire.

Local newspapers, including: *Gloucester Chronicle, Berrow's Worcester Journal, Oxford Journal, Western Times, Manchester Examiner, Man-*

chester Times and Lancashire and Cheshire Examiner, Manchester Guardian, Preston Guardian.

Vindication of the Dead, 15 May 1859, pamphlet in Rylands Library, Manchester.

Holyoake, G. J. *Sixty Years of an Agitator's Life*, 1892.

Gammage, R. G. *History of the Chartist Movement*, 1894.

Webb, S. and B. *History of Trade Unionism*, 1894, revised 1920.

Sturge, C. D. *Collection*, in Birmingham City Library.

Ashby, A. W. *Allotments and Small Holdings in Oxfordshire*, Part II, 1917.

Hovell, M. *The Chartist Movement*, 1925.

Rostow, W. W. *British Economy of the Nineteenth Century*, 1948.

Schoyen, A. R. *The Chartist Challenge*, 1958.

Armytage, W. H. G. 'The Chartist Land Colonies 1846–48' in *Agricultural History*, Vol 32, No 2, April 1958.

Read, D. and Glasgow, E. *Feargus O'Connor*, 1961.

MacAskill, J. 'The Chartist Land Plan', in *Chartist Studies*, ed Asa Briggs, 1965.

Mather, F. C. *Chartism*, 1967.

Searby, P. *The Chartists*, 1967.

Searby, P. 'Great Dodford and the later history of the Chartist Land Scheme', in *Agricultural History Review*, Vol 16, 1968, Part I.

See also the sources referred to in *Chartist Studies* and *Feargus O'Connor*.

INDEX

Numbers in italic type denote illustrations